Technology Enhanced Learning

Opportunities for Change

Technology Enhanced Learning

Opportunities for Change

Edited by

Paul S. Goodman
Carnegie Mellon University

LAWRENCE ERLBAUM ASSOCIATES, PUBLISHERS

2002   Mahwah, New Jersey   London

Lawrence Erlbaum Associates, Inc., Publishers
10 Industrial Avenue
Mahwah, NJ 07430

Cover design by Kathryn Houghtaling Lacey

Library of Congress Cataloging-in-Publication Data

Technology enhanced learning : opportunities for change /
  edited by Paul S. Goodman
      p. cm.
  Includes bibliographical references and index.
ISBN 0-8058-3665-9 (cloth : alk. paper)
ISBN 0-8058-3666-7 (pbk. : alk. paper)
1. Education, Higher—Effect of technological innovations on.
    2. Educational technology. 3. Information technology. 4. Distance
  education. 5. Computer-assisted instruction.   I. Goodman, Paul S.
LB1028.3 .T39685 2002
378.1´734—dc21   2001033063
                                                          CIP

Books published by Lawrence Erlbaum Associates are printed on acid-free
paper, and their bindings are chosen for strength and durability.

Printed in the United States of America
10 9 8 7 6 5 4 3 2

To *Richard M. Cyert*—

a leader in higher education who thought strategically,
saw opportunities that others did not,
and persisted until his visions were implemented.

Contents

Part II: Applications

9   Cognitive Tutors: From the Research Classroom   235
to All Classrooms
Albert T. Corbett, Kenneth Koedinger, and William S. Hadley

10 The Development of the Studio Classroom   265
Jack M. Wilson

11 Concluding Thoughts   289
Paul S. Goodman

Contributors by Chapter

1   Dr. Raj Reddy
University Professor
Carnegie Mellon University
Computer Science Department
Wean Hall 5327
Pittsburgh, PA 15213
rr@cmu.edu

Dr. Paul S. Goodman
Director, Institute for Strategic Development
Carnegie Mellon University
Graduate School of Industrial Administration
Posner Hall 236A
Pittsburgh, PA 15213
pg14@andrew.cmu.edu

2   Dr. Richard C. Larson
Director
Center for Advanced Educational Services
Massachusetts Institute of Technology
Cambridge, MA 02139
rclarson@mit.edu

Dr. Glenn P. Strehle
Center for Advanced Educational Services
Massachusetts Institute of Technology
Cambridge, MA 02139
strehle@MIT.EDU

3 ## Dr. Herbert A. Simon
University Professor
Carnegie Mellon University
c/o Paul S. Goodman
GSIA
Pittsburgh, PA 15213
pg14@andrew.cmu.edu

4 ## Dr. José-Marie Griffiths
Chief Information Officer
University of Michigan
Office of the Provost and Executive VP for Academic Affairs
5080 Fleming Administration Bldg.
Ann Arbor, MI 48109-1340
jmgriff@umich.edu

Dr. Alan McCord
Associate University Chief Information Officer
University of Michigan
5074 Fleming Administration Bldg.
503 Thompson Street
Ann Arbor, MI 48109-1340
amccord@umich.edu

5 ## Ms. Sara Lou Whildin
Campus Head Librarian
Penn State University
Delaware County Campus
25 Yearsley Mill Road
Media, PA 19603
slw@psulias.psu.edu

Ms. Susan Ware
Reference and Instruction Librarian
Penn State University
Delaware County Campus
25 Yearsley Mill Road
Media, PA 19603
saw@psulias.psu.edu

Ms. Gloriana St. Clair
University Librarian
Carnegie Mellon University
Hunt Library
Pittsburgh, PA 15213
gstclair@andrew.cmu.edu

6   **Dr. Paul S. Goodman**
Director, Institute for Strategic Development
Carnegie Mellon University
Graduate School of Industrial Administration
Posner Hall 236A
Pittsburgh, PA 15213
pg14@andrew.cmu.edu

7   **Ing. Carlos Cruz Limón**
President ,Virtual University
Instituto Tecnologico y de Estudios Superiores de Monterrey
Av. E. Garza Sada #2501 CP 64849
Monterrey, N.L., Mexico
ccruz@campus.ruv.itesm.mx

8   **Dr. Sanjay Srivastava**
Professor of Economics and Finance
Carnegie Mellon University
Graduate School of Industrial Administration
Pittsburgh, PA 15213
srivastava@cmu.edu

9 Dr. Albert T. Corbett
Senior Research Scientist
Human-Computer Interaction Institute
Carnegie Mellon University
NSH 3605
Pittsburgh, PA 15213
corbett@cmu.edu

Dr. Kenneth R. Koedinger
Senior Research Scientist
Human-Computer Interaction Institute
Carnegie Mellon University
NSH 3531
Pittsburgh, PA 15213
koedinger@cmu.edu

Dr. William S. Hadley
Vice President, Educational Services
Carnegie Learning Inc.
372 North Craig Street
Pittsburgh, PA 15213
bhadley@carnegielearning.com

10 Dr. Jack M. Wilson
Co-Director, Severino Center for Technological Entrepreneurship
Rensselaer Polytechnic Institute
110 Eighth Street
Troy, NY 12180
wilsoj@rpi.edu

11 Dr. Paul S. Goodman
Director, Institute for Strategic Development
Carnegie Mellon University
Graduate School of Industrial Administration
Posner Hall 236A
Pittsburgh, PA 15213
pg14@andrew.cmu.edu

Preface

Over the past seven years, I have had the privilege of representing Carnegie Mellon University in the formulation of strategic international alliances. Whereas there has been a diverse set of constituencies (e.g., government, industry), a major focus has been on alliances with other institutions of higher education.

What is striking is that whether you are in the U.S., Mexico, Colombia, Chile, South Africa, India, and elsewhere, presidents and administrators of universities are facing a common challenge. The information technology revolution is having and will have profound impacts on the educational process. An underlying theme is how to react to or adapt to technology to fit the mission and goals of the institution. The challenge gets displayed in questions such as: How do I get resources to respond to the constantly changing technology scene? If I had the funds, what are optimal infrastructure designs? How do I strategically think about the role of technology in providing greater access or enhancement for learning? Why should my professors change their approach to learning? What is the evidence that technology driven education improves learning?

For me, what is striking is that many of these questions are introduced in conversations with administrators of large public institutions, a small private college, an old prestigious institution, or a newcomer to higher education, and so on. That is, there is a common set of questions across a diverse group of institutions in very diverse countries.

These experiences are the motivation for the book and shape its design. Our design strategy has three dimensions. First, the target audience is presidents, deans, department heads, and designers of new learning environments in tertiary institutions. Although our focus is on higher education, most of the issues are relevant for other educational levels (i.e., pre and post college).

A second design decision is to focus on a set of critical issues. These range from developing strategic positions in response to dynamic changes in information technology environments, to understanding the role of learning and technology, to creating effective organizational change.

For each issue we want to help the reader frame the problem and consider some viable approaches to each issue. We realize the higher education audience is very diverse within and between countries. There are not any simple answers. In the chapter on the role of digital libraries in education, for example, the basic questions everyone must address are well articulated. The ability to frame and decompose this complicated area is a contribution. The solutions for a large, well-financed public university will not be the same as for a new private university. But both institutions must deal with the dilemmas articulated in this chapter on digital libraries.

The third design decision is to introduce a section on applications. I want to move from conceptual discussions to real examples of new technology and learning. I selected applications based on whether they had persisted over time, evolved, and demonstrated some level of effectiveness. The applications are diverse, but in no way are meant to be comprehensive. My intent is to immerse you in an application and then for you to abstract some more basic principles. These principles should complement the issues from the earlier section.

In any book, you need to focus the reader's attention. We have done this around a set of issues and applications. My intention is that these two sections should interact and inform the reader in similar and different ways. The end result should be to stimulate your problem solving skills and choices around technology and learning in higher education.

There is no intention to be comprehensive. The book is not an advocacy for technology. Rather it poses for educators questions about how they should respond to this changing part of their environment. The only prescription is that you will have to change or adapt, not how you should specifically adapt. However, underlying this conversation are important societal issues. Technology can provide greater access to education, but in many countries, resource constraints limit the availability of technology and, hence, the access to education. The consequence is some have access to education and economic opportunities while others do not. We have not explicitly addressed this issue. That would have been a different focus and a different book. However, one would be remiss not to note some of the more macro societal implications. They are implicit in the book.

This book and its value are built around some excellent researchers and contributors to higher education. Some are leaders in fields such as computer science, psychology, and educational technology. Still others have invested their professional lives in designing new learning environments. They all have achieved excellence in their fields and, hopefully, will stimulate you to think differently about the relationship among technology, learning, and education.

ACKNOWLEDGMENTS

The production of a book involves many people. Bernie Leppold managed the whole process of contacting the contributors, formatting the book and references, and so on. Cathy Senderling served as the editor. Many people such as Denise Rousseau, Susan Ambrose, and Bob McKersie provided comments on the chapters, as did the anonymous reviewers selected by Lawrence Erlbaum Associates.

In closing, I would like to acknowledge The Ford Foundation, its offices in Mexico, Chile, and Brazil and, in particular, Norman Collins and Pablo Farias for supporting this book.

Part I

Issues

*T*his section explores a set of critical issues in thinking about the role of technology, learning, and education in tertiary institutions. Each chapter explores a critical issue. Chapter 1 sets the stage by outlining basic trends in computing, telecommunications, software, and their implications for education. Topics such as changes in computing power, new generations of computing, optical networking, wireless telecommunications, Internet2, as well as new developments in software are explored. Then, some of the critical implications of these trends for the birth and death of universities, learning, and the role of human, organizational, and technological infrastructures for new learning environments are outlined.

Chapter 2 builds from these trends in technology to focus on strategic questions for universities. The analysis begins with an exploration of technology-enabled education in the past, present, and future. Next, the authors focus on a variety of forces changing the nature of tertiary education. These include the new private sector competitors, the decline of local monopolies, Internet2, the changing economics of education, and the drive for lifelong learning. All these forces require new forms of strategic decisions by universities to survive and enhance their positions.

Chapter 3 argues that learning, not technology, should be the driver of any educational innovation. Our basic focus here is on learning and what we know about how people learn. The next element is the learning task—what should the individual be able to do as a result of their experiences and what knowledge and skills must they acquire? A basic thesis is that new technological learning environments must be congruent with how individuals learn and the nature of the learning task.

Chapter 4 examines strategic decisions about designing the technological infrastructure. The audience for this chapter are people responsible for designing and implementing infrastructure, allocating resources for this infrastructure, or users. A hierarchical model of infrastructure, beginning with the basic physical infrastructure and including components such as facilities and operations, middleware, core applications, and specialized applications, is presented from both technological and social–political perspectives. The focus of analysis is to frame choices about design, planning, funding, and outsourcing.

Chapter 5 explores the role of the digital library as an integral part of the educational environment. A series of dilemmas is explored, including difficulties in defining user needs in digital libraries, lack of clarity in the role of digital libraries and the teaching–learning process, competing priorities for collection development and preservation, economics of information, copyright and fair use problems, monetary costs, and cultural implications of digital libraries. The identification and delineation of these dilemmas provides decision makers with a good guide for the design, funding, and implementation of digital libraries.

Finally, chapter 6 argues that the fundamental issue underlying all these topics is the capability of creating effective organizational change among the human, organizational, and technological components. There is a long history in the educational and noneducational sectors about ineffective implementation of technology-related change. Resistance to change from students, professors, administrators, and others all speak to ineffective organizational change. The focus in this analysis is on three fundamental change processes—planning, implementation and institutionalization, and factors that improve the probability of success in these processes and the entire change process. Extensive use of guides for effective changes and examples are also provided.

Chapter 1

Technology Trends and Implications for Learning in Tertiary Institutions

Raj Reddy
Paul S. Goodman
Carnegie Mellon University

*U*sing technology to enable learning through the creation and communication of information is a time-honored tradition. More than 5,000 years ago, the invention of writing spurred the first information revolution, making it possible for one generation to accumulate information and communicate with the generations that followed it. When printing was invented about 500 years ago, the second information revolution began, marked by mass distribution of the printed word. Just 50 years ago, the invention of computers ushered in the third information revolution, making it possible to transform raw data into structured information, to transform that information into knowledge, and to transform knowledge into action using intelligent software agents and robots.

Whereas the use of computers to enhance learning dates back to the 1960s, these early efforts have not yet had a widespread systemic impact on education. In this chapter, we examine two questions: What are some current trends in computing and related technologies, and how might these trends influence the education system? This chapter begins with an exploration of technology trends in computing, telecommunications, and software. These classes of technology are highly interrelated in their impact on learning and education. Then we examine some of the implications of these trends for learning environments and educational institutions.

COMPUTING TRENDS

The third information revolution has already transformed the way we live, learn, work, and play, and these changes will likely continue. There are several important trends in computing. First is a dramatic growth in capacity that continues without signs of stopping, coupled with dropping prices. Second, computers continue to shrink in size; today, some prototypes are about the size of a couple of coins. At the same time, computing capabilities continue to become more integrated into everyday life, leading to situations of *pervasive* or even *invisible* computing in which access to technology is nearly constant as one moves from place to place.

More Power at Less Cost

The most amazing aspect of the technological revolution is its exponential growth. Over the past 30 years, the computing performance available at a given price has doubled every 18 months, leading to a hundred-fold improvement every 10 years. This means that 18 months from now, we will have produced (and consumed) as much computing power as was created during the past 50 years combined. These exponential increases have occurred in conjunction with a dramatic drop in price: While a *supercomputer* cost about $10 million in 1990, a machine with the same capabilities can be bought for less than $100,000 today.

Figure 1.1 illustrates the exponential growth of computing capacity. The Y-axis measures millions of instructions per second (mips) as a function of time, starting from 1994, when this figure was first made. The band shows the expected range of performance in any given year. The lower bound is the performance to be expected if the performance doubled every 24 months, while the upper bound assumes that performance doubles every 15 months. In the year 2000, then, we can expect personal computers to process 800 to 1,600 mips. In the year 2010, we should see systems with the capacity to process more than 50,000 mips, and by 2020, we should see processors that can handle one trillion operations per second—all for the price of a PC today.

The expansion in secondary computer memory (disks and their equivalent) will be even more dramatic. While processor and memory technologies have been doubling every 18 months or so since the 1950s, disk densities have been doubling about every 12 months, leading to a thousand-fold improvement every 10 years. Four gigabytes of disk memory (which can be bought today for about $50) will store up to 10,000 books, each averaging 500 pages—more than anyone can read in a lifetime. By the year 2010, we should be able to buy four *terabytes* for about the same price, enough for each of us to

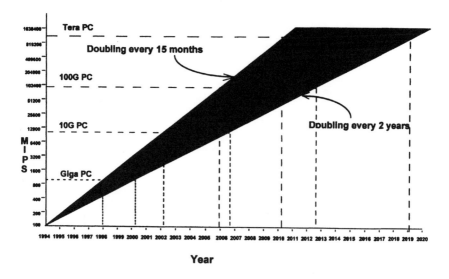

FIG. 1.1. Exponential growth trends in computer performance.

store a personal library of several million books and a lifetime collection of music and movies, all on a home computer.

If you wish, you would be able to capture every word you speak, from birth to your last breath, in a few terabytes. Everything you do and all you experience can be stored in full-color, three-dimensional high-definition video in under a petabyte. And if current trends continue, the necessary storage capacity to accomplish all of this will cost $100 or less by the year 2025.

Figures 1.2 through 1.4 show a different visualization of exponential growth coupled with rapidly dropping prices. In a span of four years the power of entry-level PCs will have gone from 200 mips to 1,600 mips (Fig. 1.2), the memory capacity will have grown from 200 megabytes to more than a gigabyte (Fig. 1.3), and the cost (Fig. 1.4) will have tumbled from $1,500 to just $500.

Figure 1.5 shows projections on the number of components per chip as a function of time. Assuming the same exponential trajectory by Year 2000, we should have a billion components per chip. This density is expected to grow to between 10 and 100 billion components per chip by the year 2010. The two key factors driving this growth are the average minimum feature size and the size of the chip. The feature size is expected to go from about 250 nanometers at present through under 100 nanometers by 2010. The size of the chip is expected to grow from about 20mm square to close to 100mm square by 2020.

Power

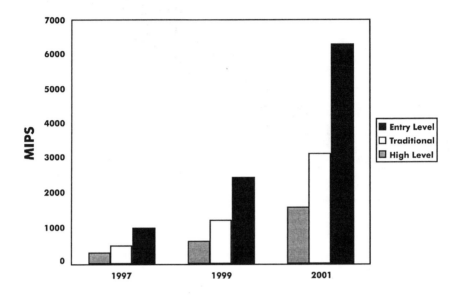

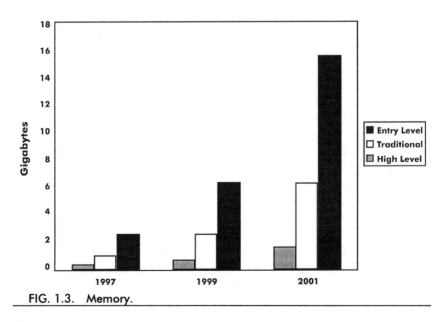

FIG. 1.3. Memory.

Price

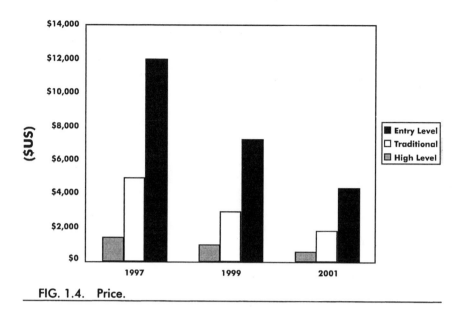

FIG. 1.4. Price.

Forms of Computing

As time goes on, the same computing power becomes available in smaller and smaller packages. Although it is not available commercially at this time, researchers have created a personal computer the size of two inch-square coins. Every feature of today's desktop computer is in that tiny space. Conceivably, this computer could be carried in one's pocket or worn on their body. This trend toward smaller, more portable computers is expected to continue for at least another decade or longer because of the expectation that computing power will continue to double every 18 to 36 months.

The issue, then, is if you have computers that are a thousand times more powerful and a thousand times smaller than the current PCs, will this change how we use computers? At one level, the implications will be minimal. At a different level, it will be significant. If the power is critical, this functionality will be the same whether it is a cubic foot or a cubic millimeter. On the other hand, having a mobile learning environment in your pocket gives you some degree of flexibility so that you could conceivable learn while you are on the move. Wearable computers are an example of how size plus other features can facilitate how we learn. Combining wireless technology (discussed in a later section) with size provides an alternative platform

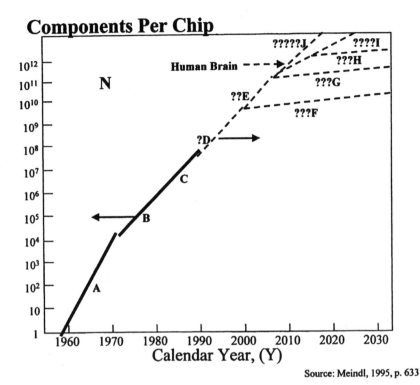

Components Per Chip

Source: Meindl, 1995, p. 633

FIG. 1.5.   Components per chip. Data from "Low power microelectronics: Retrospect and prospect," by J. C. Meindl, 1995, *Proceedings of the IEEE, 83.* Copyright © 1995 IEEE by the Institute of Electrical and Electronic Engineers. Adapted with permission.

for work. We do not have to be in a specific office or location. We have increases in mobility, flexibility, and convenience.

I am an architecture student working at a building site. Using the wearable computer, I can access information that would inform my design work. Or I am an engineering student working at a factory and need to review information on new scheduling algorithms. This technology enables me to access information where and when I need it.

A basic idea in tracing these trends is to match the changes in technology with the form of the learning task. The combination of computing power, size, and wireless capabilities matched the requirements in the learning tasks for the architecture and engineering students. In these cases, people need information at a specific time and in a specific case. In other scenarios, place or time may not be important. The key idea is to think first about the task, and then relate the computing functionalities to the task. This is a basic theme in chapter 3—"Cooperation Between Educational Technology and Learning Theory to Advance Higher Education."

New Generations of Computing

Although computers continue to shrink, people are working on the next generation of computing. Different people have different ideas about what form this next step will take. These ideas include ubiquitous computing, pervasive computing, and invisible computing.

Ubiquitous computing has primarily concentrated on collaborations in which geographically dispersed participants use technology—such as computerized writing surfaces—to share their ideas with one another in real time. In *pervasive* computing, users have access to computing power wherever they are, implying global access to personal information regardless of one's location. This is already seen to some extent, for example, when a person traveling from Pittsburgh to San Francisco need only access a computer to connect to their e-mail account through the Internet, or to download lecture notes and slides stored on a server thousands of miles away. It is possible, now, simply to go to a new location with a web-based projection system, type in an Internet address, and access the information needed for the presentation.

Taking these concepts a step further, the basic premise of *invisible* computing is that as equipment gets smaller and smaller, the access to computation and information will be embedded in a universal infrastructure similar to the electrical system. Whereas you may not see a physical keyboard or screen when you walk into your room, the computers on your body will talk to computers in the wall, and they will figure out what kind of information you are likely to need or access or should be informed about immediately. If you need a screen, the painting on the wall might become one. If you need a keyboard, your palm-sized computer might turn into one. If you needed a lot of computational power, the high speed network will give you access to computer servers and memory servers and disk servers and other kinds of capabilities for which you would end up paying.

Many of the concepts summarized here will be realized in the next 10 years or so. That doesn't mean the existing desktop computers will disappear—they will remain, because people will continue to use them for two or three decades in addition to the other, newer technologies. Note that other important research initiatives such as optical computing, DNA computing, and quantum computing are in very conceptual stages. Although we should pay attention to developments in these areas, their impacts on learning environments are very unlikely in the foreseeable future.

TELECOMMUNICATIONS TRENDS

Both of the major trends in telecommunications—optical networking and wireless communication—will have profound impacts on society. What remains to be seen is how quickly we can connect individual homes, rooms, and offices with the new technology, and at what cost.

Optical Networking

In optical networking, sometimes referred to as optical communication, information is shipped on a fiber-optic wire at one billion to one trillion bits per second. In this area, the trend is toward expanding *bandwith*, or the amount of data that can be sent over a wire. Through wavelength division multiplexing, for example, information is transmitted at a particular frequency that has been broken into small wavelengths, each one of them transmitting several gigabits of information. In the laboratory, people have been able to send more than a trillion bits of information on a single wire—up to 50 times more than all the telephone calls that happen in this country on a single day.

Unfortunately, although huge—almost unlimited—bandwidth can be achieved, you can only take advantage of it if there is a fiber coming to your room or office or home or learning environment, and that is expensive. This is known as the *last mile* problem. Several companies have already achieved a nationwide fiber-optic system, such as the one operated by Qwest Communications. Installing cable in a metropolis is somewhat more problematic, because you have to dig up the streets and run the risk of cutting into power lines and other incidents. Still, the new telecommunications technology is beginning to spread. In Pittsburgh, it has been announced that fiber soon will be available near homes and businesses, perhaps within two or three miles. To get the last leg of the connection, if you are the only one that wants it, the cost is around $100,000. But if 100 people in the same neighborhood joined together, the cost would be only $1,000 each. Even then, it will still cost $10 to $15 per month just to use the fiber, not including the infrastructure, computers and other needed equipment and connections. After taking those things into account, the unlimited bandwidth will cost about $100 a month.

Despite the current problems, this trend towards unlimited bandwidth is going to continue, because it's a natural direction and the existing copper infrastructure is aging and will need to be replaced over the next 20 years or so. Otherwise, the number of repairs the phone company has to do in a month or a year will increase greatly, and the repairs will cost more than replacing the lines. At that time, it will make sense to replace the old infrastructure with a new fiber-optic one. The total cost of replacing the nation's copper infrastructure is estimated at $160 billion. Because that is a large amount of money, some people are worried about the return on the investment. By the time the old infrastructure needs to be replaced, however, unlimited bandwidth should be available at an acceptable cost. Whether the penetration will be the same as cable or network television penetration is still anyone's guess.

Wireless Telecommunications

The other trend in technology is toward wireless communication. Because of the last mile problem, many are wondering whether it would be less costly to send information by wireless means. Right now, the cost of wireless transmission and wireless transceivers is significantly higher than wired transmission for high bandwidths, but that may not be the case 5 to 10 years from now.

One issue with wireless communication is speed. For example, wireless Andrew, Carnegie Mellon University's new wireless network, is based on the wireless ethernet, which is running at 10 to 11 megabits. Although this is relatively good for individual users, the current technology is a short medium. If 100 people are broadcasting at the same time, everybody is using one-hundredth of that 10-megabit bandwidth, which is not very different from the local area networks we used to live with, like ethernet. This is just a wireless ethernet; basically, you have to accept whatever speed you get based on the number of other users.

Although one can get used to this limitation for certain activities, there is not enough bandwith to use the system for tasks such as receiving a video lecture at home. One alternative is to cache your lecture ahead of time, so it does not matter how much bandwidth you have access to, and download the entire lecture onto your on-site computer and view it when you need it. This is turning out to be a good solution because the cost of computer memory is dropping so significantly. In 10 years, when a terabyte of memory is expected to sell for $10, you can store 300 hours of educational material in full color video, or 30,000 hours of the same educational material purely as audio and slides. You can have every course conceivable on your desktop.

If we think ahead to the future of telecommunications and computing, it is likely that we will never have a purely wireless environment. Instead, it will be a hybrid environment. That is, if you are in a room, you will have a connection via fiber optics, giving you 10 megabits of capability. But if you need to access information outside your office or home, you will be able to do it at respectable speeds. It will be a thousand times slower than the speeds available over fiber optics, but it will be a hundred times faster than what you have today. You will choose the environment that best suits what you need to do—if all you are trying to do is access your e-mail, you will not notice any difference whether you are using wireless or wired. But if you are trying to watch a high-definition TV movie, you will not do it in the wireless world.

Internet2

Internet2 is a broad name used for a number of different experiments that are being done in the research community. The federal government passed the *Next Generation Internet* law, which recommended studying what the world would be like if we had 100 times the current speed or 1,000 times the current speed. Internet2 is the generic name for a network 100 times the speed, and the Internet3 or Supernet is 1,000 times the speed.

Although speed clearly is an essential focus of these efforts, there are other issues concerning security and dependability. It is difficult to read the newspaper without spotting examples of accounts that deal with hackers compromising our networks, and there can also be problems with legal traffic. For example, in 1999, we had two or three spectacular crashes, such as the online Victoria's Secret fashion show, where huge numbers of people were trying to access images from a single site, causing the system and network to crash. This happens because the current system is not scaleable—it is fragile. The Melissa and Love Letters attacks are other examples of newer disruptions to the Internet. A lot of discussion and activity is currently under way regarding how to build a dependable and secure Internet, and doing so will require a significant redesign of pieces of the Internet. These activities would be initially demonstrated in the research environment and then slowly migrate into wider use.

SOFTWARE TRENDS

When considering the future of software, we need to ask how the development of new applications may help or hinder the learning enterprise. Specifically, we should be concerned with three aspects of learning—lectures, laboratories, and libraries. The issue with lectures, assuming that human beings are giving them, is primarily one of content creation. Software for that is relatively straightforward and will be feasible. But the other two aspects—laboratories and libraries—are a different kettle of fish. Maximizing the potential of software to change how labs and libraries operate may take longer, and cost much more, at least in the short term.

Electronic Laboratories

Laboratories are essentially simulation environments where one can create various experiments and learning experiences. Although this has been done for years in subjects like chemistry and biology, what does it mean to create a simulated laboratory to teach a subject such as geography or English? The answer is still vague, because this is unexplored territory. We can imagine building a digital earth that would let you fly like a butterfly and experience a particular geographic environment at different levels of detail. You could be 100 miles away and then dive down closer and closer, even to the microscopic level. Nobody in the past has had this type of simulated environment, but a future generation could have it.

Creating something that detailed is likely to be a hugely expensive proposition. In today's world it would cost $1 million to $10 million for each little experiment, something like building a video game, and it won't be widespread. However, if we can eventually build software that enables professors to think about the kinds of simulations they would like to see and then produce them at a much lower cost, it could have a dramatic impact. What will happen, of course, is that a lot of professors will produce average simulations, and occasionally someone will come along and write a best-seller, a classic that everybody will use. Ultimately, that is the process of evolution we need to see.

Digital Libraries

The third key of learning is digital libraries, which are characterized by huge amounts of information including paintings, music, books, lectures, and so on. Here, the main questions are how to create that information content, where to store it, and how can you quickly find a particular book, magazine, article, or other piece of data when you need it? Digitizing all the information that exists in the world is a major undertaking. Scanning the more than 100 million books that have been written in many different languages and putting them in a searchable form is an incredible task that is going to take decades, even with continuing improvements in scanning technology and scanning costs.

The question of finding the right information is perhaps even more important, and it requires a new organizing principle of information for the digital age. It is easy to provide a manual search mechanism when few attributes are required. In a conventional library, the Dewey Decimal System enables you to search for a book by the author, topic, or title, and then know exactly where to go to find it. The problem that people are running into with digitized information is that the amount of information is growing exponentially. The number of web sites has grown from 5,000 to 50 million over the last 10 years or so, and the information they contain is very dynamic. At the same time, search engines are becoming more powerful and people are creating more sophisticated, semantically based retrieval mechanisms. All of that will, in fact, improve the quality of search and finding information.

However, there is a different dimension, that of video and audio information, which cannot be routinely indexed and searched at present. Let us say you wanted to listen to a 10-second sequence of notes in a musical composition; this would be next to impossible because it is not easy to specify, it is not easy to find. Human beings do not even have the right vocabulary. The first step is to take this analog information, whether it is an image on a page or a sequence of musical notes and convert it to symbolic information that can be searched more easily. This is called the *signal to symbol* transformation problem. A related research area is exploring the use of iconic indexing, where rather than searching the captions of pictures for Bill Clinton's name, you just give it a picture of Bill Clinton and search for that. Basically, you can prespecify iconic representation—faces of people, a certain kind of airplane, or a certain kind of animal—and the search engine would find these images in the digital database.

The problem with all the search mechanisms for two- and three-dimensional data is that the cost of matching up the files is prohibitive even if you have infinitely fast super computers. Sorting through millions of images and reporting back within a few milliseconds (I am assuming you do not want to wait a whole day for the information) requires a lot of computation. Also, while we have made progress in search engines dealing with nontextual information, there is still a lot of work to be done in performing multiattribute searches. However, based on my earlier comments about competency, power, costs, and increasing bandwidth, I am very optimistic about the technological capabilities of digital libraries. Note that chapter 5 discusses the continuing economic, legal, and organizational obstacles.

Intelligent Agents

Software continues to help machines grow in their capacity to learn and to teach. It took decades for programmers to build a computer system that could play chess better than the world champion, a process that required a number of new technological breakthroughs that did not initially exist. Ultimately, they reached their goal, so we now have a system that has beaten the world champion. By the same token, you can ask whether it is possible to create an intelligent tutoring system that is better than the best teacher in a given subject. I believe the answer is yes.

The main difference between nonintelligent tutoring systems and intelligent tutoring systems is that the latter often take on functions that a human tutor or a professor would provide a student. For example, the reading tutor knows about the domain of reading education, and when a child makes a mistake it is able to follow different strategies, depending on the kind of mistake and the place the mistake occurs and how important it is. The math tutor goes one step further. It keeps track of the reasoning processes of the student solving an algebra problem and provides advice along the way to help the student solve the problem. And while this is exactly the right long-term model, it is also a time consuming, expensive model. It is also not fully understood by a large number of people.

One very interesting challenge will be understanding what exceptional means in a particular subject. The role of a teacher contains so many dimensions—communicating, grading, mentoring, motivating, and so on—that we need to fully understand before we can build intelligent agents to perform these components.

SUMMARY

Major developments are taking place in computing, telecommunication, and software that will shape learning and the institutions that provide learning. While we have treated these trends separately, it is their intersection that provides excitement. For example, there is currently much interest in the future of collaborative learning, a form of learning that will evolve into learning communities that are distributed in space and time. Rich collaborative learning communities will depend on significant synergistic developments in computing, telecommunications, and software.

The drivers of new learning environments and future developments will not be simply computing power or bandwidth. It will be the combination of computer power, greater bandwidth, lower costs, and software that facilitates storing, indexing, and accessing multiple forms of data that will permit this development of new forms of learning opportunities. Different combinations of technology will be tied to different learning tasks. Also, it is important to note that this picture of technological trends is meant to be illustrative, not comprehensive. Many issues emerging on the research frontier will shape learning and the institutions that provide it, but we have not explored these issues here.

IMPLICATIONS

The second organizing question for this chapter is: What are the implications of these technological trends for learning and education? This question, of course, frames the rest of the book. Each of the following chapters explores, in more detail, the implications of these trends for strategic decision making, learning, infrastructure, change, and digital libraries. Each also uses some specific applications of technology-enhanced learning to uncover critical issues in implementing these technology trends in the context of higher education. The goal of these chapters is to frame and highlight critical points for discussion in universities; they are not intended to provide a comprehensive map of all issues related to technology and learning.

Our discussion of implications will identify some cross-cutting themes. While we will not mirror the chapters, we will raise some issues and questions that may appear across chapters. Perhaps more importantly, we will take some positions to stimulate discussion.

The Population and its Diversity

Although this book focuses on tertiary educational institutions, the technological advances we have discussed are independent of educational institutions. Focusing on tertiary institutions is a somewhat arbitrary means of drawing on our experience to analyze the potential effects of these advances. However, even the selection of postsecondary institutions introduces tremendous diversity. More than 10,000 institutions of higher learning exist in the United States alone, ranging from small community colleges to liberal arts colleges to large public research universities. Within these different institutions, there are differences in goals and missions. Because of this variety of viewpoints, it is important to acknowledge that our comments about the implications of various technology trends must take into account the type of institutions being discussed (e.g., small community college vs. private research university), their goals, and their historic and market context.

Another key question related to diversity is whether to view these trends and their implications from the perspective of the United States or other developed countries, or approach the topic from a more global point of view? Cross-national differences in economic, political, and cultural dimensions are important in understanding the impacts of technology and the speed with which those impacts take hold. We believe that the technological changes that Americans are experiencing and benefitting from today will be available to countries such as India and China in less than five years; it may take slightly longer for the trends to spread to other countries. However, our arguments are based on functionality, not equivalence. The 100 or so inhabitants of a small rural village in India likely share four or five television sets among them. In the United States, the ratio of people to television sets is nearly one-to-one. So while India may not have universal access to television, computers, or other technology, there might instead be classroom-type environments with multipurpose equipment (e.g., a machine that functions both as a personal computer and a videocassette recorder) and both satellite and wireless communication of information from anywhere, downloaded overnight so the children could study it the next day. This functionality would be available at a nominal cost, roughly the cost of a television set today.

Surviving the Revolution— the Birth and Death of Universities

Universities are one of the oldest forms of formal organizations. They have persisted over long periods of human history with many of their functions relatively unchanged. An important question, though, is whether the information revolution we are currently experiencing will affect their survival rates. Whereas acknowledging the diversity of the population we are discussing, our expectation is that many of these institutions will not survive, at least in their current form. A number of forces are driving this scenario, led by the changing market for educational providers as well as by technology itself.

First, as outlined in chapter 2, the providers of education are changing. Whereas universities have historically held a monopoly on higher education, a new set of education providers is already evolving and will continue to grow in strength and number. As new entrants into the education market, these providers will be more nimble and capable of innovation than the older institutions. As the newcomers expand their market segments, some universities and other tertiary institutions will be unable to compete, and thus will not survive. Second, technology by itself will provide new options for learning. Students will be able to access information, classes, and courses from many sources in a distributed way. Geographical proximity— which in the past affected college selection to some degree—will no longer be an important predictor, as these new educational opportunities can bridge both space and time.

We believe that postsecondary institutions have always experienced a natural cycle of birth and death, but that current and future technological changes will increase their failure rate. An interesting question, however, has to do with the survivors. What will be some of the common features among this group of institutions? Given the strong organizational inertia that characterizes tertiary institutions (see chap. 6), why will some persevere where others fail? At least in the short run, prestige and reputation will be important contributors to survival; reputation effects have important time lags. At another level, those that survive will be much more attuned to the changes in the technology and market demographics. They will have both better sensing mechanisms and better mechanisms for experimenting. Chapter 2 provides a rich discussion of the strategic issues that all surviving institutions must confront.

Finally, another important feature among the survivors will be a fundamental change in educational philosophy and practice. It is unlikely that one can introduce fundamental changes in the function of an organization without also changing its structure. For example, the standard calculus sequence will no longer be three semesters of courses presented in the traditional delivery mode. Instead, classroom learning as we know it today will play a much smaller role, and subjects like calculus will be learned in new ways (which are likely to be based on the principles of learning set forth in chap. 3).

There will be movement away from institutions with physical boundaries, students and classrooms that are defined by these boundaries, and a credentialing function tied to experiences within the boundaries. The credentialing function will continue, but the students and courses are likely to be distributed in space and time. One's education will come from multiple institutional settings and the legitimating of that learning will come from a common source. This will be a very different university from the one we occupy today.

Technology and Learning

Another important issue is whether technology or learning is driving the design of new learning environments. Chapter 3 presents a model of how people learn and argues that technology should support these learning principles. In effect, the author argues that learning is the driver, not technology. However, we can think of examples in the worlds of education and work—as well as our personal lives—in which technology is the driver. For example, current telecommunication capabilities lead to many distance learning lectures and web-based courses. These forms of education, enabled by technology, are proliferating. The issue is whether these educational mechanisms really enhance learning. Does anyone stop to ask whether these delivery forms of education are really making a difference?

Similarly, we have noted that developments in software will permit the production of complex stimulated environments. These *edu-tainment* environments will not be limited to the physical sciences but will be spread across diverse intellectual areas. An important challenge in creating these complex, simulated environments across multiple disciplines is determining whether and how they enhance the learning process. Without addressing these questions, the excitement about building new *reality environments* may become an end in itself. Students may value the novelty and feel of these new virtual laboratories, but we must examine whether they learn differently using these tools or simply prefer them to reading textbooks or researching a topic in a traditional laboratory.

As with laboratories, libraries are also becoming more distributed and global. If current trends continue, we are soon likely to see digital libraries containing books from around the world. People would simply access the library's website to get the information they need on any topic. Ultimately, even language differences will not be a barrier; if I search for articles on a particular subject and a paper comes up in Japanese, for example, I will be able to access a rough translation. The dilemma is how we will use this vast amount of information in any effective way. Humans are only able to focus on limited amounts of information. The pace of human life seems to be accelerating in a way to preclude thoughtful use of this information.

This issue of whether technology or learning is the driver of the design of new learning environments is a fundamental issue. Both the understanding of and resolution of this question will have significant impacts on the tertiary institutions, their professors, students, and other constituencies.

Human, Organizational, and Technological Infrastructures

Education occurs in an institutional setting of some kind. The common features are human beings, such as students and professors, and an organizational structure. One nice feature of technology is that you can buy it, adapt it, and (usually) make it operational without it putting up much resistance. In contrast, humans and organizations are not as accepting of change. The critical issue is how to design, align, and implement changes across human, organizational, and technological infrastructures. Serious discussion and work regarding the use of technology to change education processes must acknowledge the roles of human and organizational infrastructures and the shifts that must take place in those infrastructures in order for technological advances to be applied in a meaningful way. A useful aspect of chapter 4, which is about technological infrastructures, is that it presents a broader view of the meaning of infrastructures. In addition, chapter 6 looks at change in tertiary institutions as a function of these three infrastructures.

CONCLUSIONS

This chapter's basic thesis is that major technological developments are already underway. We have provided a brief picture of the emerging developments in computing, telecommunications, and software. These forces, coupled with changes in market and demographic trends, pose a real challenge to the functions and processes of higher education institutions. As previously illustrated, focusing only on the evolving technological infrastructure is clearly a mistake. A body of research in the industrial sector shows that improvements in levels of technology per se do not necessarily improve an organization's functioning.

As a body, our tertiary institutions seem to exhibit tremendous organizational inertia. The dilemma is how to reconcile the presence of significant changes in the environment and an organizational unawareness or unresponsiveness to that environment. We believe that this dilemma poses some interesting opportunities for institutions, and only those that respond creatively will survive the revolution. We will see that the survivors are both responsive to and willing to experiment with new learning environments, new roles for students and professors, and new configurations of institutions. Failures and successes in these experiments will be common. Organizations that do not initiate these changes will not survive.

This is a time of transformation. The external trends are real; they cannot be ignored. At the same time, there is no ideal type of transformation, either in process or form. The diversity of tertiary institutions throughout the world will condition the transformations that take place. Also, although we have focused on tertiary institutions, many of the trends and issues raised can be generalized to other settings.

REFERENCE

Meindl, J.C. (1995). Low power microelectronics: retrospect and prospect. *Proceedings of the IEEE, 83.* New York: The Institute of Electrical and Electronic Engineers. 619–635.

Chapter 2

Edu-Tech: What's a President to Do?

Richard C. Larson
Glenn P. Strehle
Massachusetts Institute of Technology

News Item 1. (April 2, 1999[1]). *Columbia Establishes Company to Develop Digital Media and Online Learning Center Offering Courses, Quality Information Resources. Ann Kirschner, Former NFL VP, To Head "Morningside Ventures."* "Interactive, online, multimedia programs will be among the most important educational developments in the 21st century...."—Columbia University President George Rupp

News Item 2. (June 23, 1999[2]). *UNEXT.COM LAUNCHES CARDEAN TO PROVIDE WORLD-CLASS BUSINESS EDUCATION VIA THE INTERNET.* "UNext.com, a privately held Internet education company, has formed an academic alliance with four highly respected universities to develop a world-class business education curriculum delivered over the Internet. The participating universities are Columbia University, the University of Chicago, Stanford University, and the London School of Economics and Political Science."

News Item 3. (MIT, November 8, 1999[3]). *MIT and University of Cambridge announce historic education and research partnership.* "This agreement creates a bridge of the minds across the Atlantic between

[1] http://www.columbia.edu/cu/pr/19513.htm
[2] http://www.unext.com/WhoWeAre/CardeanRelease.asp
[3] http://web.mit.edu/newsoffice/nr/1999/cambridge.html

21

Cambridge, England and Cambridge, Massachusetts.... MIT programs for distance education with Cambridge will be based in part on experience gained in MIT's distance learning alliance with the National University of Singapore and the Nanyang Technical University."—MIT President Charles Vest

<u>News item 4.</u> (March 10, 2000[4]). The Cornell University Board of Trustees has approved a recommendation to create e-Cornell, a legally separate but Cornell-controlled for-profit company to create and market distance learning programs. Distance learning will be a fundamental part of higher education in the 21st century, and this resolution enables Cornell to take a leadership role in the process. The benefits of e-Cornell will accrue to Cornell students on-campus and to prospective students, alumni, and others who will be able to access the wealth of Cornell's educational resources through distance learning programs."—Cornell President Hunter Rawlings

*W*e could have continued these news releases *ad infinitum*. But the point is this: The *Academy*, long cherished as a bastion of scholarly learning sheltered from the hectic pace of daily lives, is now becoming engulfed in a sea of swirling currents, driven by new technologies, new markets, new competitors, and new financial models. The academy, where transformation was once measured in time units of generations of tenured faculty, is now undergoing change at an unprecedented rate. Slow motion is being pressed by Internet speed. What is a university or college president to do? That is the question behind this essay. Our particular focus is education and technology, what we call technology-enabled education, including both on-campus and distance education. The confluence of economic trends and enabling technologies places the academy in a precarious position, with an unprecedented set of opportunities and an equally enormous set of risks. Our goal is not to suggest right or wrong answers; there appear to be none. Rather, we attempt to lay out the issues, place the current situation in context, illustrate by example, and speculate on the future. Our bias is positive—we view the current era as one of magnificent opportunity for colleges and universities and for our most precious assets—our students.

Four trends are coming together to make the current era unique in higher education:

---

[4]http://www.news.cornell.edu/releases/March00/trustees.ecornell.2.html

1. New technologies have made possible innovative learning environments for our students that may lead to enhanced and more efficient learning at less expense.
2. Tuition costs for both public and private colleges and universities have grown at 3.3 times the Consumer Price Index (CPI) since 1980, making the costs of attending colleges prohibitively high for many middle-class Americans and causing them to search for alternatives.
3. The Internet has reduced the marginal costs of *educational content distribution* to near zero, but with relatively high startup costs for developing such content.
4. Increased access to postsecondary education and lifelong learning provide a new paradigm for most nations going forward into an increasingly knowledge-based world economy.

EDU-TECH—WHAT IS IT AND WHAT IS IT NOT?

The first major trend creating the current confluence is technology and its impact on education. *Technology-enabled education* (TEE) is education that is enhanced and improved as a result of technology. The technology does not drive the education; students' learning needs do that. However, TEE allows educational environments and opportunities that were not possible before the technology was in place.

One type of TEE is a simulated, computer-based virtual reality environment in which the learner must accomplish a goal, often within a given time frame. This approach has been made popular and respected by Roger Shank of Northwestern University's Institute for the Learning Sciences,[5] who calls it *experiential, nonlinear, goal-oriented learning.* This approach has become especially popular in industry—for example, new recruits to General Electric's financial services operations must take and pass one of these virtual reality simulated tests; in this case they must design and implement a new line of GE business that turns a profit in 24 months. If there is no simulated profit, there is no actual job at GE! Designing and creating one of these simulated learning environments is not inexpensive, with price tags usually more than $1 million. At MIT we have used this pedagogy to develop CD-ROM applications to help students learn foreign languages: You're trapped in a foreign city. A contract is out on your life. Only your native-speaking friends know how you can escape. But they have been poisoned, and their memories are deteriorating at 10% per hour. Devise a

---

[5]http://www.ils.nwu.edu/index.html

strategy for visiting and interviewing your friends (in their native language) that allows you to survive!

Another example of TEE is the studio-based learning implemented at Rennselaer Polytechnic Institute (RPI) under the direction of Professor Jack Wilson (Wilson, 1999). In the early 1990's, Wilson and his colleagues at RPI decided to look at large lecture-based introductory courses in science and engineering. They found that attendance at these lectures averaged about 70% nationally, and even the students who did attend were not always 100% attentive. Moreover, these courses were expensive, with six contact hours per week, in lectures, recitations and laboratories. So, with an eye toward cost control and pedagogical reform, they designed studio courses having four hours of contact—but more effective contact—per week. According to Wilson (1999, p. 47), "The studio courses are ... designed to bring interactivity often found in small enrollment interactive courses to meet the needs of large enrollment courses. Lecture, recitation, and laboratory are combined into one facility, the studio, where the faculty conducts hands-on interactive learning sessions." As a result of RPI's large-scale implementation of the learning studio in freshman and sophomore courses, student attendance is up to over 95%, outside evaluations have been positive, and RPI has been showered with prestigious awards for its substantial positive reform in education.[6] (See chap. 10)

New Words, Familiar Ideas

TEE carries with it a new vocabulary related to teaching and learning. Some traditional words and concepts are being pushed aside or at least being supplemented by others:

<u>Old</u>	<u>New</u>
Student	Learner
Teacher	Mentor or Coach or Co-learner
Teaching	Learning
Passive learner	Active learning
Teaching material	Accomplishing a goal
Linear	Nonlinear
Synchronous	Asynchronous
Classroom teaching	Distance learning

---

[6]These are among the awards that RPI has received: 1995 Theodore Hesburgh Award for Innovation in Undergraduate Education from TIAA/CREF; Boeing Outstanding Educator of the Year Award (1995); Pew Charitable Trust Prize (1996); 1997 Excellence in Education Award from Bell Atlantic. See Jack Wilson's home page for more details: http://cde.rpi.edu/wilson.html.

The first three words on this list place the emphasis on the person learning, not the person doing the teaching. The focus is customer-oriented rather than producer-oriented. The mode is learner pull rather than teacher push. The next two paired entries can be considered in terms of a student passively sitting in a large lecture versus a learner designing and building something to demonstrate knowledge of theory or principals. The trend, based on education research, is toward active, goal-oriented learning. *Linear learning* can be thought of in terms of a student opening a book on page 1 and reading straight through, page by page, over the course of a semester. *Nonlinear learning* occurs when the learner seeks supporting materials—text, images, videos, etc.—in a sequence that she determines, based on her learning style, prerequisite knowledge and current educational needs. In a nonlinear learning environment no two learners traverse the learning space in the same way or cover exactly the same content.

The last two pairs of words have techie sounds and often create controversy when discussed among faculty colleagues. *Synchronous learning* takes place when the teacher and student are in the same place at the same time, such as in a classroom. If teacher and student are not in the same place but communicating with each other at the same time (perhaps via telephone or interactive television), then we still have synchronous learning. Learning becomes *asynchronous* when the teacher and learner are not communicating with each other at the same time. Asynchronous learning is not new. Early examples date to 30,000-year-old cave drawings, etchings and pictures that still teach us, many millennia after the teacher has passed on.[7] A more academic example is the Egyptian library of Alexandria, dating to 330 BC, to which scholars and students traveled to learn asynchronously from the masters. The Alexandrian Library had a copy of every existing scroll known to the library's administrators, with a collection estimated at up to 700,000 papyrus scrolls.[8]

Distance learning, either synchronous or asynchronous, occurs when teacher and student are not located at the same place. Distance learning is not new, and it may be older than you think. Although correspondence schools have existed since at least the early 20th century, distance learning really took hold in 1450 A.D., when Johannes Gutenberg invented the printing press. Once the printed book became ubiquitous, first hundreds then thousands, and soon millions of readers benefitted from the thoughts and writings of great authors. And yes, there were critics. Monks, who spent hours meticulously transcribing texts, complained that the printing-press

---

[7] http://www.culture.fr/culture/arcnat/chauvet/en/gvpda-d.htm The Chauvet—Pont—d'Arc Cave

[8] *New York Times*, Nov. 6, 1999. p. A4.

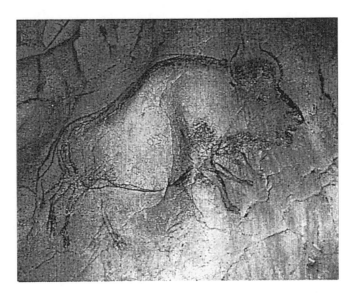

FIG. 2.1.   Cave drawing that is 30,000 years old (the Chauvet–Pont–d'Arc Cave).

editions were of poorer quality and did not last as long as their originals. Apparently they were right, but that still did not save their jobs.[9] And there were those steeped in centuries-old oral tradition who feared that the printed book with its accompanying and newly popular *silent reading* would cause the demise of face-to-face live story telling. What actually transpired was much more complex, as each mode of communication eventually supported and enhanced the other (Chartier, 1989).

Distance Learning ≠ Technology-Enabled Education

Although technology-enabled education is often equated to distance learning, we believe that distance learning is a subset of technology-enabled education (TEE). Distance learning has an unfavorable image in many circles. It brings up memories of decades-old, low-quality correspondence schools (Match Book U, as it were) and *sunrise classrooms* that were once shown early in the morning on network TV stations. In contrast, most distance learning today is a carryover of the in-class teaching that we are familiar with in our brick-and-mortar universities. Distance learning courses deliv-

---

[9]Johannes Trithemius, *In Praise of Scribes* (1494), quoted in O'Donnell, "The Pragmatics of the New: Trithemius, McLuhan, Cassiodorus," archived @ http://ccat.sas.upenn.edu/jod/sanmarino.html.

ered over the Internet often use text-based slides and lecture notes to support the assigned reading of printed textbooks and online course packs. Such asynchronous delivery is particularly used by institutions that offer a large number of courses and are seeking to replace their correspondence courses with Internet access. More advanced uses of technology, such as synchronous delivery using video conferencing, have made it possible to nearly duplicate the live classroom, minimizing faculty preparation. That is, most distance learning delivered synchronously using video today is in the classic lecture style which students view the talking heads in a passive-listening mode. But much more is possible.

Figure 2.2 contains an etching of a steam-driven railroad train of 1837, the *De Witt Clinton*.[10] The steam engine had just been engineered for powering railroad trains. But look at the cars on the train: they are stagecoaches with the horses removed and new rail-compatible wheels placed on them! Talking head lectures in a distance learning, technology-enabled environment are analogous to these stagecoaches—one takes that which is familiar or comfortable and transposes it virtually unchanged into a totally new, technology-enabled environment. The real potential of the new environment is rarely tapped. As analogies, consider: early movies, with emphasis on filming traditional stage dramas or plays; or first transoceanic flights, flown on amphibious Pan American Airways Clipper ships, with captain,

FIG. 2.2.   Stage coaches attached to steam engine (Mohawk and Hudson's *De Witt Clinton*, 1837). Copyright © 2000 by the President and Fellows of Harvard College.

---

[10]A replica of the *De Witt Clinton*, manufactured by the West Point Foundry in New York City and operated by the Mohawk and Hudson Railroad, can be found in the Ford Museum, Dearborn, Michigan.

cocaptain and galley; or even the computer you currently use, with its QWERTY keyboard, designed in an era of manual typewriters, and laid out (in 1874) to minimize the frequency of jammed keys.[11] We are in the early stages of both distance learning and technology-enabled education. We must be careful not to evaluate the results of technology-enabled distance learning until we learn how to replace the stagecoaches.

The academy has not been known for using innovative technologies in the delivery of education. For instance, the blackboard remains education's dominant delivery technology. One might ask tongue in cheek: What is the difference between cave drawings and a blackboard? Answer: Invention of the eraser! Many of us now also use the overhead projector, an invention originally driven more by bowlers who needed to see their scores projected, than by teachers. Other more recent technologies used in teaching were also invented for other purposes: television, computers, and videoconference systems (marketed first for corporate meetings). But that is changing—we are now seeing inventions, both in hardware and software that are driven solely by the education marketplace.

Distance Learning Today and Tomorrow

Today, distance learning can include any learning environment available to both on-campus and off-campus students. It can be Jack Wilson's learning studios or one of Roger Shank's experiential simulations. But too much of distance learning today attempts to glue the pedagogy of the past onto newly available technology platforms. If video or audio is involved, this usually means broadcast-style lecturing that students receive in passive-listening mode. If the web is involved without lecturing, students may receive the material as a *Sunday color supplement*, a type of rotogravure containing syllabus, linearly listed reading assignments and color images. In a sense these approaches are analogous to selling buggy whips to drivers of those new-fangled horseless carriages.

Newly arrived students from the Nintendo generation often drive an institution's first investments into TEE. These students are accustomed to using personal computers and the Web to obtain information. It is frequently the students who are asking for course websites, online lecture notes and other technology enhancements to on-campus courses. A recent survey of colleges and universities indicates that the use of technology for on-campus courses is a higher priority than the development of courses for online deliv-

---

[11]http://inventors.about.com/education/sciphys/inventors/gi/dynamic/offsite.htm?site= http://popularmechanics.com/popmech/spec/9608SFACM.html

ery across the Internet (Green, 1999). As student demands and competitive pressures increase the need for TEE on-campus, institutions need to provide some guidance and standards to assure the rapid and effective development of such materials. Luckily for institutions wanting to move towards distance learning, much of the investment in TEE can be transferred into the distance-learning world.

To address the need for standardized technology, the Instructional Management System (IMS) group has been meeting to develop agreement on the technical standards for delivering distance learning.[12] Such standards have been slow to be developed and are needed across a wider spectrum of the distance learning process. The primary work of the IMS group revolves around the production of technical specifications for IMS—compliant environments and materials. The first version of the IMS technical specifications and an integrative prototype, released in March 1998, is organized around the development of specifications in four areas:

Meta-data

Packaging and run-time services

Profiles

Enterprise integration

The IMS technical specifications will provide general guidelines and requirements for developers to create interoperable content and management systems.

The growth of distance learning has been held back by the lack of quality educational content and the lack of standardized easy-to-use technology. This results from a lack of standards for describing and developing distance learning courses, the uneven quality of courses being offered, and the rapid growth and diversity of equipment and software in the classroom, the conference room and on the desktop. To meet the learning needs and time constraints of students, courses may need to become much shorter and meet more limited learning objectives than our traditional courses of 15 or more weeks with 45 or more hours of class lectures. Even the concept of *course* may have to be examined and replaced by new alternatives in the just-in-time, at-my-place world of distance learning.

Within a few years many of the current problems will be largely behind us. The English-speaking world does not need hundreds of individual distance learning offerings for each of the most popular introductory undergraduate courses. It may only need a few of each. If this is the case, the opportunities for

---

[12]http://www.imsproject.ord

winner-take-all course development and delivery will encourage both traditional educators and for-profit companies to develop courses of high quality.

Potential learners will have easy access to information about the educational opportunities at colleges and universities through the growing numbers of higher-education Web portals—websites that provide links to a broad
array of educational resources and services. If either the quality of our teaching or our course offerings is not competitive with our peers, we will need to
improve in order to compete. One message of e-commerce is that easing a
person's access to information and ease of purchase can quickly change the
competitive environment. We believe this will also happen in higher education. Faculty and their deans can expect students to make them aware of
other institutions that are perceived as offering better programs and courses,
at least as measured by the information on their websites.

With almost every course potentially available to every distance learner,
many may survive, but only the best will prosper. Institutions are likely to be
faced with increasing demands for transfer credit for courses taken at a distance. Although institutions may choose to limit such credit to their own
courses, the competition to recruit capable students may make it difficult to
do so. The financial model for distance learning results in low marginal costs
for additional students coupled with a need for large student enrollments to
justify large course development costs. As a result, there will be large incremental revenues, net of expenses, for each additional student enrolled.

Individualized Learning Through Technology

Technology holds the promise of bringing learning to students in individualized ways with the ability to frequently assess and respond to their learning
needs. A major problem with earlier technologies, such as videotapes, was
the inability to individualize the delivery to students or give them frequent
opportunities to personally interact with their teachers or with other students. Learning is recognized as a social experience, best for most students if
not delivered in isolation from teachers or other students. To alleviate this
problem, some distance learning courses use a blended combination of
off-campus delivery and on-campus tutoring and classes. In two of our MIT
graduate degree programs, we use synchronous two-way videoconferencing
to include remote learners in the classroom and tutoring portions of
courses, supplemented by asynchronous text-based Internet support.[13] In
this way, we have created for our remote learners much of the experience
that students would expect from an entirely on-campus program.

---

[13]Systems Design and Management, MIT Singapore Alliance.

We have spoken to many educators on our campus and elsewhere about the ways that students use technology to enhance their learning. One important observation is that online access to full lecture materials provides an opportunity to review this material in its original form several times, leading to greater comprehension. Instructors have told us that it is often the average student or the student near the bottom of the class who, if motivated, can gain the most from access to such lecture materials. Slower learners, or those with minimal course prerequisites, now can access the lectures and lecture materials and not have to rely solely on their class notes and textbooks. Additionally, nonnative speakers can review material that may have been difficult to understand the first time simply because of their language comprehension.

Distance learning often substitutes for, rather than duplicates, the on-campus learning experience. It may not be the best way for all students to learn, but it can be a good method for many of them. A relative of one of the authors recently reported very positive learning experiences using correspondence courses from one of our state universities. She particularly mentioned the care with which the faculty commented on her written papers. Because she lives in a remote area, her options are distance learning or no learning. For most of us, learning entirely from a textbook is quite difficult, so having a professor's guidance in asynchronous text form is what much of distance learning is about these days. With continual interaction and feedback, the student is mentored through the learning process, not just given an exam at the end.

The Internet is now bringing information to students from universities around the world. It will not replace traditional classroom instruction, but understanding the alternative learning environments that are available can change society's expectations for the university experience. Students can now make comparisons on the Internet with similar on-campus or distance learning courses being provided by other educational institutions. This should encourage creativity in teaching, rather than reduce it, and should certainly encourage more course preparation by faculty.

Over the longer term, the increased learning taking place at a distance can increase, rather than reduce, the demand for on-campus learning. Through distance learning, we can increase the proportion of the population that have successfully completed the basic courses that are a prerequisite for more advanced courses. The opportunity to engage with fellow students and faculty through on-campus learning in the more advanced topics should have both personal and professional appeal.

People still want to go to live concerts, theater, and sporting events even though technology brings these programs to them at a distance in both synchronous and asynchronous forms. The availability of such programs through technology has increased our understanding and causes attendance at the live event to be a more meaningful experience. We believe distance learning will have the same impact on our campuses. We will increasingly hear about the imaginative use of visual materials for distance learning, such as charts, graphs, simulations, animations, and short video clips. It will be an environment of experimentation and change. New pedagogies will result in improved learning outcomes. With quick access to information on the Web, information about these improved learning outcomes will be quickly transmitted to both educators and their students.

THE PRIVATE SECTOR

The total preschool, education, and training market in the United States is estimated to be $700 billion per year.[14] Of particular interest is the postsecondary education market, which totaled $233 billion in the 1996 to 97 academic year.[15] Globally, the urgent need for alternatives to traditional brick-and-mortar institutions is pressing. According to Sir John Daniel, Vice-Chancellor of the Open University in England:

> In most of the world, higher education is mired in a crisis that mixes three issues: access, cost, and flexibility. Unless we resolve this crisis, billions of people in the coming generations will be denied the intellectual liberation of the academic mode of thinking ... Right now, one large, new campus would need to open every week, somewhere in the developing world, just to maintain present participation rates. Half of the world's population is now under 20.... Our traditional concept of the campus university will deny higher education to nearly all these young people. (Daniel, 1997, pp. 10–11)

Without an educated workforce, there is no nation in the world that can effectively expand its economy and meet the long-term needs of its people.

The private sector sees segments of the education market—both in the United States and overseas—as low-hanging fruits. Much of the private-sector interest is driven by costs, particularly the rising cost of a college education. The listed tuition costs for both private and public U.S. colleges and universities have increased 3.3 times more than the CPI since 1980 (U.S. Bureau of Census, 1998), while rising 48% more than the costs of health care during this period. The private sector sees huge opportunities here for

---

[14]*New York Times*, Nov. 4, 1999. p. A1, A21.

[15]http://www.census.gov/statab/www/part2.html#education; education 1996 last revised Nov. 10, 1999

improvements and lower cost, as higher education has undergone no fundamental restructuring, in contrast with the banking, retail, health care and other service sectors during the same period of time. The players are becoming more numerous and famous, including (among others) former Massachusetts Governor William F. Weld , former junk-bond king Michael Milken, one-time presidential candidate Lamar Alexander, Microsoft cofounder Paul Allen, and media mogul Ted Turner. Education is a service industry estimated to account for 10% of the entire gross domestic product (GDP), but—in 1999—less than 0.2% of market capitalization in the stock market. Health care, by comparison, is about 14% of the GDP and about the same percentage of valuation in the stock market (Moe, 1999). If education were to reach its 10% rightful place in stock market valuation, we are looking at a 50-fold increase in market valuation of education providers in the years ahead. The factor of 50 is most likely an overestimate due to the public and charitable nature of many current education providers, including K-12 public schools and public and private universities. But even in those markets, the private sector is acquiring a sometimes substantial share.

For-profit firms have been moving into educational markets at increasing speed. We can divide these companies into three categories. The first includes those traditional suppliers providing goods and services that institutions either cannot provide themselves or prefer, usually for cost reasons, not to perform in-house. These include the builders, manufacturers, and suppliers of facilities, equipment, and other supplies; financial and legal services; student housing and dining; and textbook publishing. Recent efforts to outsource more campus functions have added to the list. The second category includes those (usually new) companies providing education-specific equipment, software, and services to educational institutions. An example would be a firm that licenses a Web platform for hosting a university's courses; three such firms are discussed in the next section. The third category includes higher-education management companies, higher-education Web portal companies, *virtual universities*, and others that are providing TEE services directly to students.

Traditional universities and colleges are already relying on for-profit equipment and software suppliers for TEE support. In the future, we expect them to become increasingly dependent on such help in developing and delivering courses for both on-campus use and distance learning.

Some New Entrants

There are growing numbers of for-profit nontraditional educational providers. The largest private university in the United States today is the University of Phoenix, owned by the Apollo Group (NASDAQ symbol: APOL). On August 31, 1999, the University of Phoenix had 66,800 students registered in degree programs, including 10,000 distant learners. All Apollo Group institutions had 86,800 degree-seeking students. The student registration numbers at the University of Phoenix are growing at 21% per year.[16] The annual growth rate of its online virtual campus is 59.4%. At one point, the positive earnings of the Apollo Group exceeded analysts' expectations 14 quarters in a row. If one had invested $10,000 in the company at its initial public offering in December 1994, that investment would be worth approximately $119,000 just five years later.

To be a faculty member at the University of Phoenix, one needs a day job in the area in which one is to teach. In dealing with faculty, the standard protocol is that the Apollo Group contracts with faculty to write courses. A certain set of faculty members has the right to participate in a stock option program at the company's discretion. All faculty have the ability to purchase stock through an employee payroll stock-purchase plan. The faculty members are compensated for writing or reviewing courses, but there is no revenue sharing with faculty whose courses turn out to have large market appeal. In sharp contrast with most nonprofit colleges and universities, the intellectual property for a course is owned by the university and is performed by faculty as a work for hire.[17]

Many other for-profit companies are making inroads into the education markets. Among them,

Sylvan Learning Systems, Inc. (NASDAQ: SLVN). Sylvan has an established market focusing on private supplemental education for K-12 learners, with over 700 Sylvan Learning Centers (mostly franchises) throughout the United States.

Caliber Learning Network (NASDAQ: CLBR). Formed in October 1996, Caliber is a joint venture between Sylvan Learning Systems, Inc. and MCI WorldCom. Caliber serves both the corporate training world and nonprofit colleges and universities, having contractual agreements with the University of Pennsylvania's Wharton School, the Johns Hopkins School of Medicine, the Marshall School of Business of the University of Southern California, and Dickinson College and Teachers College of Columbia University. The latter agreements aim to distribute university-created content out to the world and to bring professional expertise and other college's courses into the brick-and-mortar campus. (Just after this book was going to press, on June 15, 2001, Caliber filed for Chapter 11 bankruptcy protection. This serves as a vivid illustration of the quickly changing landscapes in e-learning.)

---

[16]http://www.apollogrp.edu/ln-index.htm

[17]Private correspondence with Apollo Group, Inc., 3/16/00, 3/29/00.

WebCT (privately held company). WebCT is a leading provider of Web-based tools and platforms for colleges and universities. According to corporate literature, as of September, 1999, WebCT had more than 3.6 million student users in 97,000 courses at over 800 colleges and universities in more than 40 countries.[18] Students spend an average of 243 minutes each, per course, per month, using this Internet-based application to access course content, take quizzes, submit homework, and interact with instructors. By offering a rich suite of course tools, WebCT enables instructors to create and customize their courses quickly and easily. The alternative for a college or university is to create all the Web-based platforms and support in a home-grown manner, on campus. This can be expensive and time-consuming. So, here we see an application domain in which virtually every college and university is confronting the decision whether to contract out.

Blackboard.com (privately held company). This firm competes directly with WebCT, providing Web-based platforms and online course creation services. Clients number more than 1,600 institutions in every state and more than 70 countries.[19]

eCollege.com (NASDAQ: ECLG). This firm competes with the two above, providing services for creating web-based courses and entire online campuses.[20]

Walden University (privately held company). Walden offers graduate degrees, including PhDs, totally online. Walden, accredited by North Central Association of Colleges and Schools,[21] is one of a growing number of totally virtual colleges.

Prospects for Ed Tech Firms

It seems unlikely that all for-profit education companies can survive and prosper in the years ahead. The high marketing costs and the need to continually upgrade software will make it difficult for most to be profitable. It seems likely that we will witness large-scale consolidations among those organizations serving higher education institutions.

We have been developing a database listing more than 600 companies serving the higher education market, and the numbers seem to be growing at a rate of about one new company a day. The great majority of them were formed to serve the TEE needs of colleges and universities, rather than de-

---

[18]http://www.webct.com/company

[19]http://blackboard.com

[20]http://www.ecollege.com

[21]http://www.waldenu.edu

liver courses directly to students. More than a hundred of those we looked at have focused on the need for these institutions to develop, deliver, and manage TEE courses both on campus and at a distance. Their offerings of software platforms, software tools and software solutions are highly competitive with one another, often combining tools for specific functions with other software to create a single software platform that can provide a standardized way for a specific institution and its faculty to prepare content, deliver, it and manage the process. These companies need to constantly upgrade their offerings to survive the competition and serve the unique needs of institutions.

Many of the vendors who operate in this burgeoning TEE marketplace tell us it is often easier to sell to the corporate training market than to colleges and universities, which are noted for long purchasing cycles and decentralized decision-making. It appears that many of these vendors sign a small number of institutions relatively easily and then need to develop extensive marketing plans to compete for additional customers. The leaders say they each have hundreds of institutions using their software products, although on many campuses this may involve only a few faculty members and only a few courses.

Microsoft and other large suppliers offer more advanced tools with each new version of their application software. These standard tools are likely to begin providing more of the functionality that is now only provided by customized platforms and solutions offered by smaller companies. In a few years, the demand for customized products may decrease, while the demand for consulting services that can help faculty and administrators to use the standard tools effectively in delivering TEE to students will increase. In particular, as the number of courses fully utilizing technology on our campuses moves from a small number to many, the faculty will demand more assistance, which will further increase the market for consulting services. We note as an example that the developers of computers for special purposes have often found it impossible over the long term to compete with the suppliers of general-purpose computers.

Web Portals Fill the Marketing Gap

A growing number of higher-education Web portals bring for-profit companies into direct contact with students. These websites provide potential students with information from a large number of institutions, categorized by specific programs and courses. The portals face a multiple marketing challenge. To be successful, they must market their services to educational institutions that provide the courses, then market to individual faculty so courses can be developed, and finally market to potential distance learning students. A few universities have formed for-profit companies to market their distance education courses, which may have some cost advantages if they offer a broad range of high-quality courses at a competitive price.

If we apply the principles of e-commerce to e-learning, we will recognize the importance of having a strong brand name. Colleges and universities with strong academic reputations should have an advantage in selling their courses to the distance learning market. This advantage will be limited, however, if these institutions apply to their distance learning offerings the same restrictive admission standards as applied to their on-campus education programs. This is likely to be an important issue among faculty and administrators planning distance learning programs and also among the educational institutions and the for-profit companies managing the Web portals to their courses. It seems likely that institutions will continue to divide their offerings into credit and noncredit programs and courses and will seek the same quality of students in for-credit distance learning courses and degree programs that they have on campus.

THE INTERNET: IS IT CHANGING EVERYTHING?

Until the spring of 2000, the Internet continued to spawn companies with huge market valuations but virtually no profits. One e-commerce greeting card company was sold for over $800 million though it had never earned a dime of profit. Another company, having annual revenues of slightly more than $1 million, placed special computers around the Internet to supercharge subscribing Internet sites (providing guaranteed fast downloads); it garnered a market valuation greater than that of Sears Roebuck.

These seemingly high market valuations were telling us that investors were betting that, in many areas of business, the Internet will change everything. In some cases, this bet has been made in education, too. The Internet brings the marginal cost of distributing educational content down to nearly zero. Many of the firms reviewed in the previous section can offer their products and services only because of the Internet. The Internet is also recognized as an important new environment for learning. Neil L. Rudenstein, recent President of Harvard University, says it "has distinctive powers to complement, reinforce, and enhance some of our most effective traditional approaches to university teaching and learning" (Rudenstein, 1997, p. A.48).

At MIT, we are using the broader bandwidth Internet2 to deliver five new professional masters degree programs to students on our Cambridge-based campus and to students 12 time zones away in Singapore.[22] But beyond formalized distance learning, the Singapore MIT Alliance (SMA) involves collaborative faculty research, student exchanges, and a wide variety of activities that result in a type of global campus spanning the Pacific. Plans for a similar, perhaps more expansive, partnership have been announced by MIT and the University of Cambridge in the United Kingdom. These types of global partnerships, resulting in shared campuses across the globe, are representative of what we have called "MIT Learning Networks" (Larson, 1999, p. 59).

Another innovative MIT project provides an internet-based video tutor for students taking core subjects, such as freshman physics (Newtonian mechanics) and linear algebra.[23] The video tutor is available online 24 hours per day to offer a wide variety of media in a learner-pulling environment, including many hours of short video clips with the lecturing professor working through illustrative homework problems and discussing difficult conceptual topics. The environment simulates a face-to-face office-hours conversation that the learner may have with his professor.

MIT's near-term business model for its multimillion dollar investments in video tutors is to offer these password-protected Internet sites to other colleges and universities on a site license fee basis. We imagine that other colleges and universities have similar plans for their high-production-value educational content.

As we proceed below through various strategic issues related to higher education today, we will see that the Internet drives or facilitates much of the movement away from business as usual.

THE END OF LOCAL MONOPOLIES

Students located on a physical campus used to represent a captive audience for the educational offerings of that college or university. This is no longer necessarily the case as evidenced by this example: A few years ago, MIT Professor Tom Eagar was required to fill out some forms stipulating that he could teach as a Purdue-certified instructor. After becoming certified, he gave his popular course on welding to both on-campus MIT students and distant learners—practicing engineers watching Eagar on videotape at General Motors in Detroit. These GM engineers took the Eagar course for grades and credit as a Purdue University course. Over two to three years,

---

[22]The Singapore MIT Alliance ("SMA" Program), http://web.mit.edu/sma/index.htm.

[23]The physics video tutor is called, "PIVoT," Physics Interactive Video Tutor. See http://curricula2.mit.edu/pivot

the Detroit engineers took other courses by videotape from Purdue, RPI, Columbia University, and the University of Arizona. All of their course credits went toward a masters degree from RPI, Purdue, or Columbia. Still today, GM engineers can apply to the programs at Purdue, Columbia or RPI, then select courses from a diverse menu of offerings from the four listed universities to earn their degrees.

Another example: The oldest continuously operating satellite distance learning university in the United States is the National Technological University (NTU), dating to the preInternet early 1970s. NTU produces few courses itself. Rather, most courses originate at brick-and-mortar universities and are beamed up to the NTU satellite and then out to NTU graduate students at satellite receiving sites in corporations and other locations around the United States and Canada. NTU, an accredited university, graduates about 165 masters students each year, with the average student having taken courses from seven brick-and-mortar universities via the NTU redistribution arrangement.[24]

These inter-school arrangements are hardly rare. For decades MIT, Harvard, and Wellesley College have offered cross-registration courtesies to their students. MIT students could cross-register for Harvard courses and vice versa. This arrangement has been used sparingly over the years and undoubtedly was motivated by mutual respect among the institutions and—importantly—by geographic proximity.

With the advent of the Internet, however, the geographical constraint is no longer relevant. First by satellite transmission and videotape, and now by the Internet, cross-registration is easily done. It is now a possibility for virtually any university using the Internet and related technologies of distance learning. As the *Economist* proclaimed several years ago, "distance is dead." "The death of distance as a determinant of the cost of communications will probably be the single most important economic force shaping society in the first half of the next century" (Cairncross, 1995). Today, students at the National University of Singapore and at Nanyang Technological Institute are taking MIT courses live via Internet2, earning graduate degrees in Singapore. This use of the live Internet stretches over 12 time zones!

To see the future potential for electronic cross registration, just visit the World Lecture Hall, http://www.utexas.edu/world/lecture/, where many hundreds of Internet-based courses are listed in alphabetical order from accounting to zoology. We do not know how many of these courses are available for electronic cross-registration between and among colleges and universities, but we anticipate that the number will grow dramatically in the years ahead.

---

[24]From National Technological University, private correspondence.

All this e-mixing-and-matching leads to numerous new business opportunities. Our favorite, only partially offered tongue-in-cheek, is Virtual Ivy U (VIU). With a modest investment of, say, $400 million, an entrepreneur could buy 500 acres in some nice sunny warm spot, perhaps in Costa Rica. She could then design and build a beautiful campus with dormitories, world-class athletic facilities, housing for mentoring adults, and other amenities. Most important, the new campus could be connected to the world by fiber optic cable to Internet2, the Internet's high bandwidth offspring. Teacher-Mentors would be invited to stay for a few months to a few years. These will be professors on sabbatical from traditional universities, retired CEOs, poets, musicians, and other interesting, supportive folks. Then VIU will open, posting an announcement in the national press:

Virtual Ivy U Open for Applicants for the Class of 2010.

- Must have high school record comparable to that of those admitted to Harvard, Princeton, MIT or Stanford.
- No faculty at VIU, but Teacher-to-Learner ratio is 1:5.
- Students take courses from Harvard, Princeton, MIT, Stanford and other leading universities via Internet2. They learn from Best in Class.
- Tuition: $30,000/year

The logic behind VIU is this: 18-year-olds attend a college or university campus to accomplish two things in four years. First, they must learn how to learn and often to learn specific educational content that prepares them for a career. Second, they must navigate treacherous waters to make the transition from adolescents living in supportive family environments to independent adults. At VIU, content is learned via the Internet from the best teachers anywhere. Professionals who deliberately choose to spend part of their adult lives mentoring support the transition to adulthood. The local monopoly on content is over, as all content learned at VIU is from off-campus. All campus-based students become distance learners!

EDUCATION AND THE FUTURE EARNINGS OF STUDENTS

The market for learning is often driven by expectations of rising earnings. The earnings difference between those with and those without a college degree is widening. In 1997, males with a bachelor's degree earned 76.8% more than high-school-only graduates, whereas in 1980 the earnings differential was only 59.6%. For women, the earnings differential was 78.2% in

1997 and only 43.2% in 1980. Women in 1997 were 47% of the workforce as compared to 44% in 1980.[25]

Men tend to have a greater opportunity than women to take early-career jobs that pay well, a fact that was recently cited as a possible cause for the declining proportion of male college students. As reported in *The Chronicle of Higher Education*, less than 45% of today's college students are men, down from about 55% in 1970.[26] *The Chronicle* also reported that women make up 58% of adult students. Some young men may be opting for the appeal of early career earnings while sacrificing potentially much larger life-long incomes derived from a college education. One obvious conclusion of current trends is that those preparing to deliver distance learning courses should expect large enrollments from women.

THE TUITION BIND AND DISCOUNT PRICING

College tuition levels, rising at over three times the CPI for more than15 years, may have met a wall of price resistance in certain market segments. A major challenge for institutions dependent upon tuition has been the difficulty of increasing net tuition revenue at the same growth rate as the retail tuition rate. Discounts are routinely offered in various forms, such as student aid, loans, and work-study. For 213 private institutions, a study found that

> Net tuition revenue as a percent of the tuition sticker price for the top liberal arts institutions and universities has declined since 1990, bottoming out in 1996 and recovering a bit in 1997 to 70% and 73% respectively. The remaining 177 institutions are still experiencing a decline in net revenues, nearing 60% of tuition sticker prices (Brenaman, 1999, pp. 23–24).

These results occurred during a remarkable economic period of low unemployment and low inflation. What should we expect in years when such favorable economic conditions for students and their parents no longer exist?

Discounted tuition is now becoming an applied science. The academy has borrowed a successful pricing technique from the private sector—*yield management* or *revenue management*. And with the Internet, its use appears to be growing. Born in the deregulated airline environment of the 1980s, revenue management attempts to segment the market and to price each segment in such a way that all capacity of a service is utilized, producing revenue at the maximum possible level. In airline parlance, each empty seat

---

[25]http://www.census.gov/population/ /socdemo/education/tablea-03.txt

[26]*The Chronicle of Higher Education*, Nov. 18, 1999, http://chronicle.com/daily/99/11/99111803n.htm.

near takeoff time is a revenue opportunity. If the plane takes off with an empty seat, the revenue opportunity has been lost forever. Although reluctant to admit it, many colleges and universities do the same thing.[27] As reported above, average tuition payments nationally average between one half to three fourths of published (retail) tuition.

The use of revenue management techniques by colleges and universities is likely to grow in the years ahead, as parents become ever more cost conscious. According to the popular press, there is some evidence already that parents who are Ivy League alumni are happy sending their children to less difficult and less expensive state colleges and universities. Their attitude: we have made it, but we see no reason why our kids have to work so hard or why we should pay so much!

Revenue management sees its final evolutionary state in the form of auctions. On the Internet, a popular site is priceline.com, where one can bid on airline tickets, cars, hotel rooms, and a host of other big-ticket items.[28] But there is a new player: eCollegebid.[29] With this online service, the parents of a college-bound child can enter the child's characteristics and the maximum tuition price they are willing to pay. The colleges participating in the eCollegebid consortium that are willing to accept the offered parental bid reply in the affirmative within two weeks after the bid is submitted. As of this writing, no college had joined the eCollegebid consortium. But even if this particular venture fails, its very existence may be evidence of things to come. And, at all but perhaps the most elite institutions, tuition growth at over three times the CPI is very likely a thing of the past.

THE REVOLUTION IN THE U.S. SERVICE SECTOR: CAN IT HAPPEN IN HIGHER EDUCATION?

Consolidation, Invention, Reinvention

Most service—sector industries in the United States have experienced considerable consolidation and reinvention in recent years. The reinvigorated sectors include health care, banking, retailing, and information processing services.[30]

---

[27]Revenue management as applied to college admissions is now an accepted area of scholarly research. For example, see Elinam and Dodin, 1995.

[28]http://tickets.priceline.com

[29]http://eCollege bid.org

[30]An excellent synopsis of reinvention of U.S. services industries can be found in *Intelligent Enterprise*, James Brian Quinn, The Free Press, New York, 1992.

In the case of *consolidation*, a key factor has been a desire to reduce costs. Cost reductions were accomplished by spreading information systems and other central fixed organizational costs across a larger revenue base, by increasing purchasing power with vendors, and by reducing staff through the amalgamation of redundant products, offices, and functions. Cost reductions have been driven by increased price competition in a low-inflationary environment and, in the case of health care, adverse government policies relating to financial support and cost recovery.

Invention of a service is driven by market opportunity. Federal Express and Amazon.com are two textbook examples. *Reinvention* is often required to maintain and grow market share as well as to reduce costs. Retailers becoming e-tailers is a recent example of reinvention. But coming late to the party may limit ultimate market share; Barnesandnoble.com is struggling to catch up to the upstart, Amazon.com, which exists solely as an online venture. Are there lessons here for higher education?

We believe that the Internet (and its related technologies) will drive the consolidation, invention, and reinvention of many institutions of higher education. The press releases offered at the opening of the paper give credence to this viewpoint. However, it is likely that the process will be neither easy nor straightforward. Take the problem of brick-and-mortar investment, known as *physical plant*. Similar to hospitals, educational institutions have a major investment in physical plant that may make it difficult to consolidate with others. The major restructuring of hospitals has, to date, been largely operational and financial. The number of hospitals has declined by just 11% since 1980 while the daily census of patients has declined by 35% (U.S. Bureau of Census, 1998).[31] Universities are likely to face similar barriers to physically consolidating their operations.

While health care is often cited as a harbinger of possible change in higher education, major consolidations have occurred in other service industries, such as banking. Since 1980, the number of commercial banks in the U.S. has declined by 37% and similar decreases have occurred in the number of savings institutions. The number of commercial bank offices, including branches, has increased, however, by 30% as the fewer independent organizations continued to expand their outlets (U.S. Bureau of Census, 1998).[32]

The location of colleges is far from optimal. Our colleges and universities, like many hospitals, banks, and other service organizations, are still located in geographic areas that often reflect the limitations of 19th century transportation and communications, rather than the advances of the 21st century. The

---

[31]Table No. 200 Hospitals-Summary Characteristics: 1980 to 1996. Source: American Hospital Association, Chicago, IL. Hospital Statistics, Annual.

[32]Table No. 804. Banking Offices, by Type of Bank: 1980 to 1997.

implications of TEE, with its large up-front costs, low marginal costs, and reduced dependence on physical distance for delivery, are not hard to imagine. A university in another time zone could become a competitor in the local market or a collaborator—via a type of electronic consolidation.

But consolidations have not yet taken place in higher education. There has even been a continued small increase almost every year in the number of campuses providing at least four years of education (U.S. Bureau of Census, 1998).[33] Peter Drucker (Boston Globe, 1999, May, p. 23) has argued that, "Universities won't survive. The future is outside the traditional classroom." Prof. David Collis of Yale University stated in 1998 that, "The primary observation is that colleges and universities must recognize and accept that it will be more difficult to compete in the higher education business in the future. While acceptance will not by itself solve any problems, plans that realistically reflect the future have a better chance of succeeding than those that merely project the past." (Collis, 1998, p. 57) More recently, Collis stated that his earlier comments were overly cautious, and the changes he suggested will happen much sooner than he ever believed possible (Collis, 1999).

TEE offers the opportunity for colleges and universities to join together to achieve many cost and educational benefits of joint programs and collaboration. Whereas telemedicine is not yet pervasive enough to wipe out the effects of physical location of brick-and-mortar hospitals, telelearning via the Internet may be able to do just that for brick-and-mortar universities. The resulting collaborations may yield savings while preserving the many benefits of retaining our campuses. The incentives are likely to increase for partnerships among educational institutions and for alliances with for-profit suppliers of services. As Collis (1999, p. 20) recently stated, "The need for universities to enter alliances also highlights a second strategic necessity that I believe has become even more important than last year—speed." University presidents should be looking at entering such relationships and then "be ready to seize opportunities as they arise."

The Importance of Institutional Mission

The consolidations taking place in many industries to save money do not necessarily reduce companies' ability to carry out their mission. As colleges and universities sort out their choices in the era of TEE, they may well look to their institutional mission to help in these decisions.

---

[33]Table No. 306. Higher Education—Summary: 1970 to 1996.

In *Managing the Non-profit Organization*, Drucker (1990, p. 45) tells us of the importance of mission. "We hear a great deal these days about leadership, and it's high time we did. But, actually, mission comes first. Nonprofit institutions exist for the sake of their mission. They exist to make a difference in society and in the life of the individual ... And yet, mission needs to be thought through, needs to be changed."

If technology can be a transforming force for higher education, we should assume that some institutions would use it to achieve a comparative advantage, particularly to improve their ranking in the competitive market for students, faculty, and financial resources. The public institutions may have some advantage as state governments see technology as a way to increase the educational opportunities for their citizens while also replacing their future campus expansions in bricks and blackboards with bits and screens. We already find the largest distance learning programs in the U.S. primarily at public institutions, although some private institutions have been leaders in innovative forms of content development and delivery.

THE GROWING NEED FOR LIFELONG LEARNING

In September 1999, a group of public university presidents and chancellors signed an extraordinary report: *Returning to Our Roots: A Learning Society* (Kellogg Commission, 1999, p. ix).[34] The report begins:

> We write as twenty-four presidents and chancellors of public state universities and land-grant institutions to make the case that our institutions must play an essential role in making lifelong learning a reality in the United States.... For the first time, we now have the technological means to make (lifelong learning) a reality. We are convinced that public research universities must be leaders in a new era of not simply increased demand for education, but rather of a change so fundamental and far-reaching that the establishment of a true 'learning society' lies within our grasp.

The report, teeming with examples of a new vision, goes on to make recommendations in three areas: (1) Making lifelong learning part of the core public mission; (2) Creating new kinds of learning environments; (3) Providing public support for lifelong learning.

Other countries have recognized the importance of lifelong learning. For instance, from MIT's distance learning partners in Singapore we hear:

---

[34]Signed by the Presidents of 21 universities. Available at http://www.nasulgc.org/Kellogg?learn.pdf.

Education and training are central to how nations will fare in this future. Strong nations and strong communities will distinguish themselves from the rest by how well their people learn and adapt to change. Learning will not end in the school or even in the university. Much of the knowledge learned by the young will be obsolete some years after they complete their formal education. In some professions, like information technology, obsolescence occurs even faster. The task of education must therefore be to provide the young with the core knowledge and core skills, and the habits of learning, that enable them to learn continuously throughout their lives. We have to equip them for a future that we cannot really predict.[35]

Lifelong learning is becoming a necessity, as the careers of professionals typically span six or seven job types with perhaps as many different employers. Those in technology-related jobs must renew their mental hard drive every few years. Sun Microsystems' Scott McNealy claims that, unless renewed, the value of the content of an engineer's brain decays in value at a rate of 25% per year.[36] Christopher Galvin, president of Motorola, declared that the company no longer wanted engineers with four-year degrees, but preferred those with "40-year degrees" (Wilson, 1999, p. 45). Even the concept of an engineer remaining an engineer may be obsolete. The typical engineer only does engineering for the first six or seven years of her life, then typically moves on to management or other functions. Imagine if you have a college degree preparing you for only the first seven years of a 45-year career! How do you study for the other 38 years? The answer appears to be in lifelong learning.

This is the stance taken by MIT President Charles Vest, when he announced that MIT would provide lifelong learning content to a new venture, PBS The Business Channel:

> Today's workforce faces unprecedented challenges in keeping current in the latest developments in science and technology.... An education that stops at age 22 or even age 26 is an obsolete education ... professionals must continue their education throughout their careers ... we cannot expect continuing education to be provided only within the ivied walls of brick-and-mortar universities. We must now use the computer and telecommunication

---

[35]http://www1.moe.edu.sg/Speeches/020697.htm; Speech by Prime Minister Goh Chok Tong at the opening of the 7th International Conference on Thinking, June 2, 1997, "Shaping our Future: Thinking Schools, Learning Nation."

[36]From Sun Microsystems, private correspondence (3/20/00), Scott McNealy's full quote: "An employee in a technology business faces a 20–25% per year skills obsolescence and must retrain regularly to stay skills current."

technologies, invented in part at our research universities, to deliver excellent learning experiences at the professional's place of work.[37]

The arrangement with PBS The Business Channel is yet another example of a nonprofit university partnering with a for-profit content marketer and redistributor. The for-profits seem often to have unique skills and scalability to reach markets not traditionally served by the brick-and-mortar university.

Depending on whom you ask, one finds that the market for lifelong learning is $50 to $200 billion annually. Much of this is training in contrast to education, the former focusing on skills particularly relevant to a current employer, the latter concerned with ways of framing, formulating, and solving problems. But whatever the true dollar number for lifelong education, the potential market is enormous. The private sector wants this market and is aggressively going after it, while many of us in academia still are contemplating our next move.

Starting from a small base, the number of students in distance learning programs delivered by colleges and universities is growing rapidly. Whereas in 1998 there were 710,000 U.S. students in distance-learning programs, 4.8% of the nation's 14.6 million higher-education students, International Data Corporation forecasts that the number will rise to 2.23 million, out of 15.1 million students overall, by 2002 (Business Week, 1999). This prediction assumes that the number of distance learning students is independent of those higher education students on our campuses. We believe there is some overlap and that the number of distance learning students includes many that are taking just one distance course.

Market Segmentation and the Mature Learner

Distance learning is an all-inclusive term that needs to be broken down into constituent parts or market segments, the level at which strategic decisions should be made. For instance, a university's decision makers may decide not to compete with its premier on-campus undergraduate program via distance learning, but to offer post-graduate studies at a distance in order to leverage its positional advantage. As growth in distance learning continues, we can expect the programs available to meet the increasingly specialized needs of each market category of students. The precollege and college-age markets will, of course, be important and should be further segmented. Mar-

---

[37]*MIT Tech Talk*, V. 41, #4, Sept. 28, 1996. http://web.mit.edu/newsoffice/tt/1996/sep18/42738.html

kets for mature learners can target adults, alumni, businesses, professionals, military-government workers, and the senior population, just to list some of those frequently identified. A university struggling with the idea of getting into distance learning might well be advised to identify which market segment(s) it feels most qualified to serve.

Given a national paradigm shift to lifelong learning, we believe that postgraduate education is poorly served now by our colleges and universities and yet represents the most rapidly growing market segment. Beyond college age, postgraduate learners are usually employed or have other obligations and cannot regularly attend day courses on a typical college campus. They want reasonable-cost access at a time and place of their choosing. But they also want their learning to be a collegial rather than isolated experience, including interaction with their teachers and fellow students. Upon successful completion of their studies, they want a certificate of achievement, often in the form of college credit. This credential can later be used to gain access to more advanced courses.

One option seems obvious: *our alumni.* A typical brick-and-mortar university has 10 to 15 times the number of living alumni as active on-campus students. To demonstrate the potential impact of this market on an institution, imagine that each living alumnus took the equivalent of just one course per year during his or her active professional life after graduation. One course per year is about 10% of the course load of a full time on-campus student. But with approximately 10 times the number of active alumni as on-campus students, such market penetration just into the alumni pool could have the effect of **doubling** the number of course registrations. There should be no controversy on campus about breaking into this new market—at one time in their lives all alumni had the credentials to get into our hallowed halls as freshmen. We credentialed them. They are family. Yet, by and large, we ignore them in terms of their lifelong educational needs. In the future, we see a paradigm in which the university-of-choice at age 18 is the default educational service provider for life. By *default*, we mean it is our business to lose. If we do not perform, the customer—our alumnus—will brand switch to another lifetime educational service provider.

Marketing to alumni should be relatively straightforward, as most institutions maintain current lists of addresses and affiliations. Marketing to other postgraduate learners can be much more difficult and usually requires entry through the employer of the potential learner. To help this process, many large corporations now have a senior officer responsible for learning, rather than just training. A recent article in the MIT *Sloan Management Review* called "What is a Chief Knowledge Officer?" is helpful in understanding their role in corporations (Earl & Scott, 1999, pp. 29–38).

A New Business to Support Lifelong Learning

How do we finance lifelong learning? We can use an analogy. The provision of preventative as well as reactive health care for the physical body gave rise to the HMO: Health Maintenance Organization. But lifelong care for the contents of the brain is just as important as the overall body's physical health. So let us propose creation of the EMO, Educational Maintenance Organization.[38] Patterned after the HMO, the EMO would provide a lifetime of educational care, both on an emergency and preventative basis. Monthly payments to an EMO could be made from a tax-advantaged, actuarially computed, employer-subsidized account. As with an HMO, there would be modest copayments and certain annual caps.

An example of emergency EMO care: Your boss is sending you to Singapore to negotiate a contract with a client. You have never before negotiated a contract. You need emergency training in the art and science of negotiation, perhaps served to you in your business class seat on your flight to Singapore. An example of preventative EMO care: An annual one-week on-campus visit to your alma mater to be updated on advancements in the technical field in which you work.

By capturing a huge number of member learners, an EMO could use that leverage to negotiate favorable prices for all sorts of educational products and services. A university negotiating with the EMO might be willing to substantially discount its educational offerings in exchange for a guaranteed annual minimum numbers of learners (in both scheduled, preventative learning and emergency learning).

Do Distance Learning Students Learn?

We often hear critics ask whether distance learning students actually learn. One of our colleagues has even labeled distance learning an oxymoron. Another, who is otherwise known as a distinguished applied scientist, states emphatically, "There is no substitute for face-to-face teaching and learning." Our stance is that the effectiveness of face-to-face teaching and learning should be viewed as a research question.

Let us look at some facts. According to statistics from the National Technological University (NTU), the average grade point average of NTU students (distance learners) is 0.3 grade points above campus-based students taking the same courses (based on a 4-point scale).[39] Silicon Valley distance

---

[38]We also discuss EMO's in Penfield and Larson, 1996.

[39]Private correspondence with the CEO of NTU Corporation, November 1999.

learners taking engineering courses via television from Stanford University have traditionally scored about 2 points higher than students who are based on the Stanford campus (based on a 100-point scale).[40] Early results from the Singaporean students taking courses over Internet2 from MIT show no statistically significant difference in grades from their MIT campus-based counterparts.

There is one Internet site, http://teleeducation.nb.ca/nosignificant-difference/, that reports on 355 studies dating from 1928 citing "no statistically significant difference" between the performance of distance learners (using the technology of the day) and campus-based students. The site has recently added research results that point to some newly found significant differences, virtually all in favor of the technology-enabled learner. There are those who question the rigor of the underlying educational research (Merisotis & Phipps, 1999, pp. 13–17; Institute for Higher Education Policy, 1999) and—no doubt—some of the methodology might not stand up to scientific scrutiny. But even given that weakness, the overwhelming preponderance of evidence demonstrates proof of concept: distance learning students do learn, and some learn better than their campus—based counterparts.

If you want to join the debate, visit http://distancelearn.about.com/education/adulted/distancelearn/blpoint.htm, read the contributions of two debaters, James Perley, "Back to the Future of Education: Real Teaching, Real Learning" (Technology Source, September/October 1999), and Mary Harrsch, "Back to the Future or Back to the Past?" (Technology Source, September/October 1999), and then contribute your opinion in an online chat room.

Institutional Responses to Distance Learning

Our essay suggests that distance learning is an appropriate option for university or college presidents to consider in their strategic planning. Distance learning offers the potential for long-term financial rewards and short-term recognition as an innovator. In addition to all the considerations cited above, what are the largest remaining risk factors? In our opinion, it is not technology, cost, or acquiring market penetration—all important issues that are not easy to solve. In actuality, the most difficult challenge is achieving faculty buy-in and general change of the culture of the institution. (See chap. 6.)

There is a general reluctance of the members of the academy to change. Reasons are always stated for not doing things. The rapid growth of distance

---

[40]Private correspondence with Dr. Andy DiPaolo, Stanford University, 1998.

learning and technology-enhanced education has caused considerable controversy in this regard. Some faculty are quick to compare the educational quality of small classes taught by leading scholars with the impersonal nature of many distance learning courses. We have yet to hear them cite the huge lecture hall format used on many campuses for core courses as the comparison with distance learning. To combat the expected faculty resistance, leading by example is not an unreasonable model for institutional change in the domain of distance learning and TEE. Early successes by early adopters may create market demand among the faculty.

To move beyond the early adopters, we need to identify those factors that retard scalability and sustainability of TEE and distance learning in an institution of higher education. Let us start with faculty time. Institutions recognizing that faculty time is their most precious resource will be leaders in supporting faculty who want to use technology for education. These services will be provided both within our institutions and also by the rapidly growing for-profit education service industry. The faculty members who are the best candidates for developing courses for distance learning are usually those who have already used technology to enhance their on-campus courses. They have worked late at night and on weekends to do this, and their online materials developed for on-campus use can often be adapted for distance learning. But here is the cultural change: faculty members are used to teaching in handcraft mode. They do everything themselves, sometimes with a teaching assistant. This method of design and production does not scale across a campus, nor does it acquire significant market share off campus due to the noncompetitive quality of the end result. Faculty time must be leveraged with the aid of highly skilled professional assistants, including instructional designers, production coordinators, and Web designers.

This gets us to the interplay between the economics of distance learning and institutional culture. To become a serious player in this marketplace, an institution cannot do distance learning at the margin. Substantial up-front investment is required. The development of distance learning course content can cost between a few thousand or a few million dollars, a difference of as much as one thousand times. The Open University of the United Kingdom allocates an average of $1.5 million U.S. and 18 months in production to create one of its courses, which is usually given to thousands of students. Although course quality and the cost of course preparation may be only loosely correlated, a student who has participated in a well-prepared distance learning course developed at major expense may be unwilling to invest his time and money in a rather simple course that only cost a few thousand dollars to develop. Such inexpensive courses dominate distance learning today, frequently using online slides or notes to lead one through a textbook. This is not likely to be the case in the future. Note that the exception will be courses that are also heavily supported by the personalized skills of a teacher who can transcend time and distance, possibly core courses that are required toward the student's degree.

Faculty culture gets back into the picture here in at least two ways. First, the faculty member loses control of the final product that the students experience. Second, faculty compensation will be altered. Those who are good at distance learning will be financially rewarded by their institutions (else they would go off campus to do essentially the same thing for a for-profit provider). Increased differentials in faculty compensation will almost guarantee jealousy on the part of faculty members who are not as good at distance learning or whose academic subject areas are not in demand by distance learners. Managing this process promises to be a challenge to even the most experienced administrators.

For the college or university that has chosen to invest heavily in TEE and distance learning, we recommend that the administration view the process as one of extensive institutional change. There are myriad factors in addition to the few we have cited above that must be managed carefully to maximize the likelihood of success. We highly recommend the recent book by A. W. Bates (2000) to guide this implementation process.

The Financial Outlook

Will technology-enabled education and its close cousin, distance learning, be a financial drain on our future or will they eventually enhance our financial situation? This is a question that every college president must be asking. The recent past provides some optimism about the future. As we have discussed, Jack Wilson at Rensselaer Polytechnic Institute has been able to introduce award-winning TEE in learning studios at no net increase in costs, but simply adding technology to business as usual usually increases costs. Due to public pressures and the competition for good students, it has not been practical to pass along in the form of higher tuition the rising costs associated with standard on-campus use of technology for education.

As for distance learning, the high cost for initial course development and delivery, combined with the possibility of relatively modest enrollments per course, make it unlikely a net source of funds for most of those involved. The exception is those institutions that have decided to reach for a significant market share. Distance learning and technology-enabled education require substantial up-front investments. Any viable business model must recognize that an institution cannot successfully dabble in this area at the margins, with incremental investments.

We know that some portion of distance learning students in undergraduate programs will require financial support from public sources, particularly federal loan programs. Such federal programs are only now beginning to assist distance learners. This will result in considerable emphasis on for-credit courses in undergraduate programs, even if some of the students are not seeking either credit or advancement toward a degree. It is assumed that a large portion of distance learning students will be mature learners supported by their employers. While they may not need course credit to be reimbursed, some form of certificate of achievement will often be necessary. Distance learning administrators also need to be sensitive to those professional learners who seek annual educational units or credits to maintain their certification.

The long-term financial success of distance learning will depend upon relatively large enrollments per course and asynchronous delivery to permit the full amortization of course development costs and still produce profits after expenses from tuition. The financing of such development costs will, on many campuses, be a major issue in the years ahead. It will be essential for these institutions to develop accounting methods that use the accrual accounting of Generally Accepted Accounting Principles (GAAP), rather than simple cash-flow accounting, to understand the situation in each academic unit. For private institutions, the FAS No. 117—Financial Statements of Not-For-Profit Institutions, and the Audit Guide may need to be applied more fully to smaller academic and administrative units.

Because rapid growth increases the need for cash, distance learning is likely to be a net drain on the cash flow of most institutions for some time. However, distance learning may also be a positive factor in the educational programs of innovative colleges and universities. This is an entirely new way of delivering education, of collaborating among scholars, and of managing the educational programs of our institutions. Each institution should view it as an opportunity to deal with some of their important educational problems. For example, smaller colleges or those with specialized courses may often find themselves short of qualified faculty or without enough students to justify a course. Off-campus programs may lack sufficient contact with faculty on campus, and on-campus students may want access to materials or scholars at other locations. Alumni and friends may want access to the best of your on-campus courses. Your faculty and students may seek opportunities to collaborate with colleagues at other locations. All of these situations provide an opportunity for creative distance learning solutions. Technology-enabled education and distance learning are in their infancy, and we can only begin to define some of the useful applications to the needs of our institutions.

MAKING DECISIONS: NEW STRATEGIC DIRECTIONS

The assets of a nation are no longer in its subterranean natural resources such as petroleum, iron ore, gold, silver, and diamonds. The assets of a nation in the 21st century are primarily between the ears of its citizens.[41] This reality is the driving force behind the explosive worldwide growth in demand for education.

An irony facing many college and university presidents is that demand for higher education has never been greater, but neither has the competition and the pressure for change. Edu-tech offers numerous opportunities for both growth and decline. A temptation is to sit tight and hope all of the push toward TEE will go away. After all, television was supposed to drastically change education, but in the end had much less influence than expected. Perhaps the Internet, the desktop computer, multimedia, hypermedia, technology-enabled pedagogy, and private-sector competition are all passing fads, too. We do not think so. We recommend that colleges and universities initiate deliberate strategic planning, each institution assessing its individual situation and creating a comprehensive plan for the coming decades.

Although we believe that the most appropriate strategies for each institution will vary by institution, there are some general issues that all may wish to consider. Here, we offer some generalized proposals, recognizing that they most likely will not apply in all situations. We hope that these suggestions may be relevant in structuring the thinking of a college or university president in these interesting times.

1. *Strategic Alliances.* Hundreds of for-profits are now seeking to grab the attention of elite colleges and universities. Their song: Sign with us and get these rewards! Many sought-after educational institutions have endowments of hundreds of millions and sometimes billions of dollars. In contrast, some of the dot-com suitors can only guarantee payments for several month's payroll, if that. Why would a financially

---

[41]YUKOS Oil, Russia's second largest oil company, recently announced a program that dramatically reinforces the refocusing of a nation from minerals and hydrocarbons to knowledge industries. Under the project title of Generation.ru, the national initiative funded by Yukos is intended to train a total of 10 million young Russians in Internet technologies by the year 2005. According to YUKOS chairman Mikhail Khodorkovsky, "Production of competitive intellectual and information products and not oil should become Russia's main industry." (Press release, YUKOS Oil, 3/22/00)

secure college or university bet its future in distance learning with a marginally funded dot-com startup? Yes, the pressure is on to do something, and to do it more quickly than universities and colleges are accustomed to. But do not bet the ranch on a hugely risky venture. Our own belief is that, should an educational institution want to align itself with a for-profit redistributor of distance education offerings, its best option is often to form a consortium with like-minded sister institutions and create its own for-profit spin-off. Why should a months-old dot-com reap the benefits of an institution's significant brand-equity, built up over decades and perhaps centuries?

2. *Learning Continues After Graduation.* An educational institution's active alumni constitute a primary hidden market for its instructional offerings. As we have argued, with reasonable assumptions, an institution can double its course enrollments if meaningful lifetime educational services are offered to its alumni. The college or university that an adolescent enters at age 18 can become the default educator for life of that individual. If a university president is looking for revenue growth opportunities as well as for increased allegiance with its alumni base, then providing lifelong learning to alumni seems to be a low-hanging fruit.

3. *Institutional Resistance to Change.* One measure of the fluidity of an institution is the average time it takes to get a 50% turnover in personnel. That figure provides a rough estimate of the time required to erase institutional memories and enable the organization to welcome significant change. For a high-tech firm, this duration may be only six months; for a university with its tenure system, it is closer to 20 years! The potential changes that will be brought about by edu-tech are monumental and will be resisted by many. So-called faculty culture is part of this. Faculty members grow accustomed to the way things are and have always been, and do not often react favorably to significant change in their environment or increased demands on their time. The first coauthor of this essay, himself a tenured faculty member, even pleads guilty to this charge. A college or university president has the challenge of introducing programs and processes to move the faculty culture in directions more compatible with change in teaching and learning. Having a college or university support faculty-initiated innovations can be a helpful first step in this process, with the success of early adopters creating faculty market demand for further innovations.[42]

---

[42]This is one step that MIT has taken recently, with upwards of $5,000,000/year available to faculty for experiments in TEE via an open RFP process.

4. *Who Owns What?* Edu-tech promises nightmares for college and university administrators in the domain of intellectual property (IP). Textbooks have traditionally been the purview of faculty members, who have been free to write the books and sign royalty-granting contracts with publishers. The Web is creating challenges to that model. Often a Web-creation by a faculty member is aided greatly by other campus-employed professionals, such as graphic designers, Web developers, photographers, animators, and video production specialists. In these circumstances, the realization of a faculty member's intellectual vision is in a multimedia form that requires major investment by the university. Some universities now contend that IP is shared or perhaps even 100% owned by them. But boundaries are fuzzy and exact definitions appear to be sorely lacking. We are not aware of any college or university that has established a clear, crisp, concise, and unambiguous IP policy for Web-based educational creations. As a result, campuses have all sorts of Web learning modules being made with many differing interpretations regarding who owns what. Unless this situation is resolved soon in a deliberate fashion by those who are directly involved—faculty and their administrations—the eventual resolution will derive from new case law as a result of contentious lawsuits. This seems to be a terrible way to fashion policy on IP. The issue may be too large and difficult for one institution to lead the way and set a precedent. Perhaps it is time for leadership from many higher-education institutions to utilize one of their many interinstitutional alliances and to attempt to craft edu-tech IP policies that could be accepted by all.

5. *Conduct Research Onto Learning.* A research university has two core competencies: research and education. Rarely do the two coincide in the form of research on education. One way to change the faculty culture in an exciting and culture-compatible manner is to introduce the notion of doing scholarly research on education and learning in one's own domain of excellence, be it physics, Shakespeare, economics, microelectronics, or operations research. How do students best learn Newtonian mechanics? How do they get excited and engaged in Shakespeare? How do we design learning environments in mathematics to achieve deeper and longer lasting learning? Faculty members pursuing this approach become active designers of educational experiments that can be carefully evaluated and reported in a growing scholarly literature. The fact that students' activities can be better tracked in Web-based learning environments offers important opportunities for data mining, allowing for new analyses of students' learning activities, learning styles, and knowledge acquisition.

Recent programs at Stanford, RPI, Vanderbilt, and MIT have indicated some success at this approach.

6. *Prepare for New Competitors.* The private sector wants to profit from the large courses that in some sense are commodities in our institutions of higher education. These include the core courses taken by all freshmen and many sophomores. Imagine that by the year 2010 each of these subjects will be available in multiple versions from for-profit companies or other universities. There may or may not be live tutors available, either locally or via the Internet. Course providers will charge a tuition that is a fraction of usual brick-and-mortar tuition. To make matters worse, each such course will have had at least $2 million to $5 million invested in its design and creation. Picture the next equivalent to the young Paul A. Samuelson, who creates with Pixar-quality producers the next version of Economics 101, but this time web-based with all the features we have discussed and more. It could become a true category killer, just as Samuelson's original textbook has been for decades. We at the nonprofit institutions face the huge risk that the private sector will eat our lunch in these large courses, courses that generally subsidize the remaining parts of the curriculum due to their large enrollments and cost-favorable student-teacher ratios. One plausible response to this threat is to join the competition: License the Internet versions of these courses but add value to the student's experience by providing local mentoring and active learning opportunities. In that way, the combination of high-production-value, professionally produced learning materials with carefully crafted local mentoring and learning creates an enriched learning environment that cannot be duplicated.

7. *Students Will Benefit From Change.* The new technologies offer potentially enormous improvements in pedagogical models. Students with differing cultural backgrounds, learning styles, and prerequisite knowledge will eventually benefit from edu-tech. Ultimately, each student's learning environment may be specially tailored to his or her own situation, an exemplary application of mass customization. Old-fashioned campus-based course packs will become a thing of the past, as materials available online will be far superior and offer vastly more content. Students will study in an immense nonlinear space of knowledge, offered from around the world over digital networks, not preselected and prepackaged by a local professor. With or without deliberate interinstitutional collaboration, it will exist in this way with our students. Local controls over content will thereby deteriorate, creating yet another challenge to maintaining the brand equity of one's institution.

8. *Prepare for New Financial Models.* Since the 1970s, nearly all major service sectors in the U.S. have undergone substantial and fundamental change. This has not yet happened in the higher-education sector. We believe that it will. The pressures on tuition will increase as major for-profit providers enter the higher education marketplace and as brick-and-mortar universities and colleges start to compete with one another via distance learning. Commodity-based higher education for large-enrollment core courses will likely become better and cheaper. Retaining a viable market for high-priced on-campus education will be a challenge for every college and university president, first for the so-called non-elites and eventually—we believe—for all. The perceived value-added from the on-campus experience will most likely lie in the market niche that a college or university selects as its focus going forward. Creating a workable financial model under these assumptions will be a huge challenge, suggesting both defensive and offensive strategies and opportunities. The core of the defense could be choosing and defending a particular market niche. The essence of the offensive strategy could be the exporting of some part of that niche expertise via the Internet and related technologies. But one does not want the exporting to cannibalize one's core on-campus market. It will be a challenging and exciting time, one requiring the skills and deftness of a high wire balancing act.

REFERENCES

Bates, A. W. (2000). *Managing technological change: Strategies for colleges and university leaders.* San Francisco: Jossey-Bass.

Bray, H. (1999, April 11). Article 3, *Boston Globe Magazine* (p. 23).

Brenaman, D., Lapovsky, L., & Meyers, D. (1998). Private college pricing: Are current policies sustainable? In M. E. Devlin & J. W. Meyerson (Eds.), *Forum Futures 1999.* Report summary of 1998 symposium presentations. Published by Forum for the Future of Higher Education, Yale University: Cambridge, MA.

Cairncross, F. (1995). A survey of telecommunications: The death of distance. *The Economist.* September 30. In O. Morton (Ed.), *Exploiting the information age.* London: Profile Books.

Cairncross, F. (1997). *The death of distance.* Cambridge, MA: Harvard University Press.

Chartier, R. (Ed.). (1989). *The culture of print, the power and the uses of print in early modern Europe* (pp. 7–8, 126–132, 219–220). NJ: Princeton University Press.

Collis, D. (1998, September). When industries change: Scenarios for higher education. In M. E. Devlin & J. W. Meyerson (Eds.), *Forum futures 1999.* Washington, DC: Forum Publishing, 1999. Originally presented at the Forum for the Future of Higher Education, Aspen, CO, September, 1998.

Collis, D. (1999, September). When industries change revisited: New scenarios for higher education. Presented at the Forum for the Future of Higher Education Conference, Aspen, CO. Available: Forum for the Future of Higher Education, 238 Main Street, Suite 201, Cambridge, MA, 02142.

Daniel, J. S. (1997, July–August).Why universities need technology strategies. *Change, 29*(4), 10–17. Article adapted from the author's speech to the *American Association of Higher Education.* National Conference, March, 1997.

Drucker, P. F. (1990). *Managing the non-profit organization.* New York: HarperCollins.

Earl, M. J., & Scott, I. A. (1999, Winter). What is a chief knowledge officer. *Sloan Management Review, 40*(2), 29–38.

Elimam, A. A., & Dodin, B. M. (1995). *Yield management in higher education.* Presentation at the Institute for Operations Research and Management Science, New Orleans. San Francisco State University, College of Business, San Francisco, CA.

The Institute for Higher Education Policy. (1999, April). *What's the difference? A review of contemporary research on the effectiveness of distance learning in higher education.* Sponsored by the American Federation of Teachers and the National Education Association.

Green, K. C. (1999). *The campus computing project.* The 1999 Campus Computing Survey, P.O. Box 261242, Encino, CA. Available: http://www.campuscomputing.net/

Kellogg Commission on the Future of State and Land-Grant Universities. (1999, September). *Returning to our roots: A learning society.* Washington, DC: National Association of State Universities and Land-Grant Colleges.

Larson, R. C. (1999). MIT learning networks: An example of technology-enabled education. In M. E. Devlin. & J. W. Meyerson (Eds.), *Forum futures 1998.* Washington DC: Forum Publishing, 1999, 59–74. Originally presented at the Stanford Forum on Higher Education, Aspen, CO, September, 1997.

Merisotis, J. P., & Phipps, R. A. (1999). What's the difference? Outcomes of distance vs. traditional classroom-based learning. *Change,* May/June,.13–17.

Moe, M. T. (1999 April). *The book of knowledge.* Merrill Lynch Report, p. 7. San Francisco: Merrill Lynch & Co.

Penfield, P. & Larson, R. C. (1996). 2014: An education odyssey. *OR/MS Today, 23*(5), 50–52.

Quinn, J. B. (1992). *Intelligent enterprise.* New York: The Free Press.

Rudenstein, N. L. (1997, February 21). The internet and education: A close fit. *The Chronicle of Higher Education,* A48.

U.S. Bureau of the Census. (1998). *Statistical abstract of the United States* (118th ed.). Washington, DC: U.S. Department of Commerce.

Weber, J. (1999). School is never out-Continuing education is evolving at net speed. *Business Week,* October 4, pp. 164–168.

Wilson, J. (1999). Continuous learning: The killer application of technology. In M. E. Devlin & J. W. Meyerson (Eds.), *Forum Futures 1998* (pp. 45–48). Yale University, New Haven, CT: Forum. Available: http://www.nacubo.org

Wyatt, E. (1999). Investors see room for profit in the demand for education. *The New York Times,* November 4, pp. A1 and A27.

Chapter 3

Cooperation Between Educational Technology and Learning Theory to Advance Higher Education

Herbert A. Simon
Carnegie Mellon University

*I*n this book are reports from people who are at the forefront of developing new information technologies for education and have read their visions of the future. The particular viewpoint from which I should like to address these topics is that of the individual learner—the college student. I come to my particular vision of the future—as fallible and conjectural as any attempt to scrutinize the future must be—from a background of 50 years of university teaching, simultaneous with 40 years of research on human thinking and using computer programs to simulate human thinking and learning processes and a like number of years of experience in applying new knowledge about people's thought processes to university education.

I am afraid that all of that experience has not yet taught me the answers to all, or even most, of the basic questions of how to conduct university education. However, I think that as educators we do have some answers today that we did not have just a few years ago, and I think that we now know how to ask some of the hard questions that should be answered before trying to design and install systems incorporating high technology in the classroom. Therefore, my remarks may focus more on the questions you should ask about proposed innovations in education, than on the specific answers that can be given. In the coming years, many new technologies will be proposed to you for use in your university, and you will have the task of raising difficult questions in order to decide when and how these technologies can contribute to the mission of the university.

SOME BASIC PRINCIPLES OF DESIGN

Let me begin with two basic principles that, I believe, must govern the design of any scheme for improving education at the university level, and especially the design of schemes that will make use of electronic technologies—or any technologies, for that matter (Simon, 1998).

Focus on the Learner

Learning takes place in the head of the student, and depends entirely on the activities of the student. This principle is obvious, but it has some important consequences, not all of which are always observed in experiments with new educational methods. The activities of teachers, and the impact of textbooks or lectures or electronic displays influence education only to the extent that they affect the behaviors of the students. Designing effective methods requires predicting, with some accuracy, how students will respond to them.

This principle applies to existing technologies as well as new ones. Educators must not begin this design work by assuming, without evidence and comparison of alternatives, that lectures provide effective learning experiences for students, or reading textbooks, or watching computer displays, or working in laboratories, affect learning. It all depends on how students react to these experiences and what they actually do while they are experiencing them. And their reactions depend on the precise content of the experiences and how they are presented.

Analyze the Learning Task

The analysis of student behaviors must begin with analysis of the learning task: What should students be able to do as a result of their learning experiences; and what knowledge and skills must they acquire in order to achieve these abilities? Educators now have available a tested technology, based upon experimental findings and computer simulation of human thinking and problem solving, for discovering the structure of tasks and the structure of the knowledge and skills people must have in order to perform them. I will presently make a few comments about this new technology for educational design, but you will see some samples and products of its application in the other chapters.

Design of technology must follow, not precede, the task analysis. It is wholly inefficient and ineffective to begin with a favorite technology—whether it be television films, computer displays of virtual reality, World Wide Webs, or any other—and then seek out possible applications to educational tasks. That is like buying twelve dozen hammers, then searching for nails to pound. Instead, we must first discover which nails need pounding, and then what hammers can drive them home effectively. Technology must be the servant, not the master.

Finally, we must resist the temptation to use technology just because it is available. We human beings are fascinated with new technology—nowadays especially with the new educational technology. And those responsible for inventing and developing the technology are even more fascinated with it than the rest of us are. We must resist the temptation to climb Mount Everest just because it is there.

Sometimes the printed book and the blackboard may be more effective aids to learning than the latest computer display (as someone who has been deeply involved with electronic technology for almost half a century, I hesitate to say this, but it is true). Which will work better is not to be assumed, but must be demonstrated. As academicians, as the proponents of reason in human affairs, we cannot settle for less.

The principles I have just proposed apply to any educational design activity—

- Learning depends wholly on what the student does; only indirectly on what the teacher or the university does.
- Analysis of student behaviors begins with the analysis of the learning task.
- We must not use technology just because it is available. We must use it when, and only when, we can see how it will enable us to do the educational job better.

BASIC PRINCIPLES FOR USING INFORMATION TECHNOLOGY

These are some design principles that are especially important in our information age (Druckman & Bjork, 1994).

Attention is the Scarce Factor

In today's world, information is no longer the scarce factor in human learning and application of knowledge. The scarce factor is human time to attend to all of that information which is pouring in on us from newspapers and magazines—even books—television, telephone and fax, the Internet and e-mail. There are only a certain number of hours each day, say about eight, that we can devote to acquiring information and processing it. The information revolution has not increased the available time by one hour—not even by one minute. Therefore, the design question, for any information system, whether for business or education, is not to produce or distribute more information; it is to select the information that is going to fill those eight hours—and therefore to displace, and leave unattended, the information that does not fit within this time limit.

There has been much talk about information superhighways, but little talk about traffic jams and the lack of parking spaces. Those persons who have been trying to use the World Wide Web for any of a wide variety of purposes are already experiencing the glut of information it can produce, and the tendencies for less important information to crowd out more important information. I do not say that we should begin to burn our books—most of us have a revulsion to that idea—but I do say that we must learn how to choose (and to design our information systems to help us to choose) which books we and our students will pick up and study.

Artificial Intelligence Must Help us to Filter Information

We must enlist the help of computer science to design artificial intelligence systems—so-called expert systems—that will share the load of selecting out intelligently the small fraction of information potentially available to us to which we should pay attention (Anderson, Corbett, Koedinger, & Pelletier, 1995). Creating such systems is perhaps one of the most important tasks that researchers in artificial intelligence can address during the next decade. For example, the Web will be useful only to the extent that intelligent search engines—far more selective than the key-word searches that are now available—filter out all information except that tiny fraction that is most relevant to our queries. The same principle applies to the enormous data bases that modern scientific instruments and researches are providing for scientists: enormous star catalogues, complete genome maps for organisms, and the like. The fact that these databases exist does not make them available; they are practically available only to the extent that they are supplied with intelligent search engines that can target the most relevant information and hide the rest from us.

We Must Sample Knowledge: Not Cover It

In designing courses and curricula for our students, teachers must apply ruthlessly the principles of sampling. Mastery of the world's knowledge—or even a single department of knowledge—is no longer a viable educational objective. Nor was it ever a desirable objective. Our task is to enable our students to deal not only with today's knowledge but also with the knowledge of the future, which we cannot predict but which will be increasingly at the heart of their professional work during their lifetimes.

Educators today have the slogan of *just-in-time learning*, which refers to selecting certain elements for learning when needed. But such learning is only possible for someone who already has basic skills of problem solving and of learning. Education, and especially university education, must focus on developing in our students the skills of problem solving, understanding in depth and independent learning. Subject-matter content is only relevant as it provides a small core of learning and examples for developing and practicing these skills.

As teachers cannot predict with any accuracy the directions in which knowledge will grow, it matters only a little which examples are selected for the curriculum. Of course I will make some distinctions between what is basic and likely to endure, and what is ephemeral. Newton's Three Laws of Motion are unlikely to disappear from the physics curriculum or Mendel's Laws from the first course on genetics. But at best, our forecasts of what is important will be guesswork, and much of what will be basic does not yet exist. (Did we anticipate for students of even ten years ago the full impact of the computer revolution?) In any case, we must not let the false god of coverage divert our students into superficial learning and away from the acquisition of basic problem solving, understanding, and learning skills.

IDENTIFYING AND ORGANIZING INFORMATION FOR LEARNING

Previously, I have argued that when designing new systems for learning educators must generally focus on the learner and analyze the learning task itself. I have also listed several principles to follow when using information technology as a tool. This section provides further guidance on how to identify and organize the information that students are to learn.

Design Around the Processes of Information Absorption

In designing technology for students, whether it be textbooks or the latest methods of presenting tasks electronically, educators must apply what is known about the ways in which people absorb information, the rates at which they can absorb it and the amounts, and the forms of presentation that facilitate or interfere with the absorption of information. Absorbing does not mean memorizing information, but acquiring it with understanding and in forms that make it easy to use and rapidly accessible whenever it is relevant. An expert in any domain must have a large database, but like the electronic databases being built today, it must be richly indexed with access routes, so that the relevance of information will be detected by the patterns the expert notices in the situations that he or she encounters, and when relevance is noticed, a path will be found to the information associated with the cue.

Expert Performance Demands Selective Search and Recognition (Intuition)

The two main tools possessed by experts that permit them to find problem solutions and to find them quickly are (1) highly selective search of the problem space, guided by recognition of familiar patterns in the situations encountered along the way, combined with (2) direct recognition of patterns that signal situations already well known from past experience. These pattern recognition processes give the expert the feeling of solving problems intuitively. *Intuition* is simply recognition that is based on knowledge acquired through a combination of training and on-the-job experience.

Our understanding today about how experts do their work, and how they differ from novices in their domains, is that they are able to recognize tens of thousands, or even hundreds of thousands, of familiar patterns that turn up from time to time in the situations they deal with every day. When they encounter such a pattern, they recognize it, and the recognition in turn reminds them of information associated with it. The information either suggests a direction for further search or a solution to the problem. For example, an expert medical diagnostician sees symptoms in a patient, or in the results of tests performed on the patient. The symptoms are the patterns that remind the physician of the corresponding disease and give access to all the knowledge they possess about how to treat it.

I will mention one well-known experiment that demonstrates the expert's power of recognition. Place before a chess grandmaster a chessboard from an unknown game and let them observe it for only five second and then remove the pieces. If you now ask the grandmaster to replace the 25 or so pieces on the board, he or she will do so almost perfectly—with at most one or two errors. If you now put the same board before an amateur for five seconds, they will be able to recall only six or seven pieces. Now place the same pieces on the board at random. Again, the amateur will be able to replace six or seven pieces—and the grandmaster, only about one more, seven or eight! There is nothing special about the expert's eyes; there is a great deal that is special about the images of familiar chunks of information that he already has stored in memory.

Knowledge is Stored in Productions: An Indexed Encyclopedia

Because of the central role of recognition in expert performance, the skills of the expert can often be described in terms of IF-THEN rules: If such and such conditions are present, then take the following actions. This means that instruction, to be effective, must teach both the action part of the rules and the condition part. An examination of typical textbooks in mathematics and the sciences shows that while the actions associated with certain skills are usually taught systematically, the conditions under which these actions are relevant are not mentioned at all, or at most, given only brief and unsystematic attention.

For example, in elementary algebra instruction, students are taught that they may add and subtract the same number from both sides of an equation, or divide both sides by the same number. They are much less often taught explicitly what to look for in the situation to recognize when they should add, subtract, multiply or divide. In the same way, in physics or chemistry, the laws of the subject tell us what conditions any physical or chemical situation must meet; the laws (and often the textbooks) do not tell us how to recognize what to do in order to bring a system from its current condition into a desired state.

All too frequently, the teacher writes a long proof on the blackboard. The student (at least a good student) checks each step of the proof as it is written down, and agrees that it is correct. But at the end of the proof, the student complains to the teacher: "I have checked each step, and it is correct, but how did you know at each point just what step to take next?" This will happen whenever we ignore the condition side of the IF-THEN rules and teach only the action side. This problem, and its solution, was recognized by the analysis of common learning tasks and by attempts to build computer systems that could learn to perform these tasks.

Worked-out Examples Teach Crucial Problem-Solving Skills

A method that has been found to be powerful in helping students acquire problem solving techniques that address both the condition and the action parts of rules is learning from worked-out examples. A worked-out example

(Singley & Anderson, 1989) (for instance, a step by step solution of a chemistry problem) shows how an initial situation is gradually transformed into a final situation that solves the problem. Typically, at each step, one or more features of the situation that differentiate it from the final situation are removed, so each new situation more closely resembles the final situation. When students learn to study worked-out examples, they acquire the skill of comparing successive steps in the solution, of noticing what change has been brought about at each step, and then comparing that difference with the final solution to see how the situation has moved closer to the end. With this skill, students become able to learn new problem-solving procedures with little or no explicit instruction, and to learn them not by memorization of a rote formula but by acquiring cues that enable them to recognize, at each step, what to do next and what is accomplished by doing it.

Learning from examples has been shown experimentally to be an extremely powerful and efficient learning method. This approach is now at the core of sophisticated computer tutoring systems, as well as paper and pencil systems that have been constructed after careful analysis of the structure of the task. Note that while technology may perform a very important role in carrying out the task analysis, and even in delivering the product in the form of a tutoring program, the design is not driven by the technology but by the painstaking analysis of human learning processes and of the requirements of a particular task.

PRESENTING KNOWLEDGE

Much of the new instructional technology is concerned with presenting visual and oral material to students electronically. The fact that information is carried by light waves instead of sound waves does not automatically make it more effective for learning. Almost everything depends on whether it causes the student to be more active or more passive, and reflects the serial nature of human attention.

Passive Versus Active Mental Activity

The lecture has been with us for nearly a thousand years. Yet it is a procedure that permits the student to be wholly passive—even to daydream about things unrelated to the content of the lecture. In the early years of the university, the lecture was essential, for in an age when there were no printed books, it gave students the opportunity to prepare their own textbooks by taking notes. However, that is no longer a credible excuse for lecturing, either face-to-face or by television.

In each case, teachers must ask what thought processes the lecture is arousing in the listeners and how it arouses them. This question must be raised as vigorously with the new technology as with the old. If computer screens simply provide us with a stream of information, verbal or pictorial, students can receive it just as passively as they can listen to lectures. The new technology will improve education only to the extent that it induces continuous mental activity in the student by presenting tasks that require thoughtful responses.

Serial Nature of Human Attention

If student passivity is a barrier to learning that our educational designers must continually struggle against, the serial, one-at-a-time nature of human attention is a basic biological constraint that they must respect. Educators hear about the billions of neurons in the human brain, all emitting signals in parallel at an enormous rate. They are told that thinking is therefore a highly parallel process, with many thoughts proceeding at once. But, this is a figment of the imagination that does not correspond to the reality of human thought. It is true that the brain has billions of neurons, and even more synapses between them. It is true that there is almost continuous activity throughout many parts of the brain. But it is not true that human beings can pay attention to more than a few things at a time: probably only to one at a time.

A few years ago, the rather unkind joke was made about a distinguished North American that he could not chew gum and walk at the same time. That is probably an exaggeration, but the next time you are driving an automobile, please notice (with extreme care) how well you can carry on a conversation while driving. When traffic is very light, the conversation may go well; as traffic increases, however, you will find that the conversation, and especially the driver's part in it, will begin to lag—I hope it will lag, else you are likely to have a serious accident! To the extent that you do converse while driving, you are probably not carrying on both activities simultaneously but time-sharing—alternating a few times per second between the two. It has already been noticed in the statistics of auto accidents in the United States that those who use car phones suffer a much higher accident rate than those who do not.

I have already explained how people arrive at intuitions. They do not require very rapid parallel search of the whole memory. What they require, and what makes them possible, is a well-indexed memory that provides direct paths from recognizable cues to information that is relevant to the situation in which the cues are seen. The experimental evidence is clear that human beings, when carrying on thoughts that call for either recognition or attention (and almost all thought does), process information in a serial rather than parallel way. The bottleneck lies in what psychologists call short-term memory. If you look up a phone number in the directory and cross the room to dial the number, you will probably succeed, for the capacity of your short-term memory is about seven digits (more accurately, about seven familiar *chunks* of any kind). But do not try to keep two unfamiliar phone numbers in mind at the same time; you will fail.

There is no point in presenting information to people at a rate faster than they can process it. For example, in lectures I often do not use any overhead displays, because I do not think that listeners can both listen and read at the same time. I am selfish. I wish to control your attention. In the classroom, I usually use the blackboard rather than an overhead projector, for as the moving hand writes, the students' attention follows.

Using Pictures and Diagrams

Modern computer technology offers the possibility of presenting information in pictorial or diagrammatic form. We are all familiar with the old saying that "a picture is worth a thousand words." I think that saying is quite true, if the picture is thoughtfully designed. All of the things I have said about passivity and seriality apply just as well to pictures as they do to words. I will just mention a few things educators have learned about the use of pictures and diagrams.

A common mistake teachers make is to suppose that pictures or diagrams that convey their message clearly to them (the teachers) also will convey it to students. That is a fallacy, for hidden in the simple diagram is usually a great deal of encoded information about the topic. The diagram can be understood only if that information can be detected and decoded. For example, the instructor in an economics course displays a simple supply and demand diagram. A descending line shows the quantity of goods that buyers will purchase at increasing prices; an ascending line shows the quantity of goods that sellers will offer at these prices. The point of intersection marks the price and quantity when the market is at equilibrium. Every student can see this point: It is perceptually salient in the diagram. But can the student explain why this is the point of equilibrium and what will happen if the price is higher than this equilibrium price, or lower? This requires knowledge that is only acquired gradually. So, although teachers may use the diagram to assist learning, it is only fully understood after the learning has taken place—it does not produce the learning instantly or effortlessly.

Notice that in presenting this example, I did not provide you with a visual diagram. Instead, I counted on your visualizing the situation in your mind' eye—the device for forming mental images that almost all of us carry around in our heads. Einstein's first paper on special relativity, published in 1905, depended heavily on a visualization, which he encouraged his readers to carry out ["Consider a moving rod, and a light ray ..."], from which he derived directly the equations that lead to the Lorentz Transformation—the key to his theory. Einstein did not bother to print a diagram in his paper—he relied on the mind's eyes of his readers.

Is More Better?

In Einstein's problem, a moving rod and a moving light ray were key elements. Would it help the learner to have a computer display of these movements? Possibly, but possibly not. Consider this example: I constructed such a display for my students, complete with clocks that showed the times at every point. Rather than helping the students, it thoroughly confused them—the display was realistic, but perhaps it was the wrong display.

I then gave the students paper and pencil and the text of Einstein's paper, and asked them to try to understand it, making drawings whenever they thought it would help. They did make drawings—but never of anything moving. They drew the rod at the moment when a beam of light was emitted at its left end, and they drew a second picture of the rod, parallel to the first, at the moment the light reached its right end and was reflected. Instead of the movement, they drew the situations before and after the key events, and were able to read the equations almost directly from their drawing. In this case, the old-fashioned method proved better than the technology-driven approach.

The great modern architect, Mies van der Rohe, said that less is better. Educators might well emulate him in our use of technology. The best diagram for teaching is not necessarily the most elaborate or realistic (*virtual reality*—although I am sure there is a place for that also in teaching). For many, if not most, purposes, the diagram will be static rather than moving. Even so, reading it will require knowledge as well as perceptual skill.

TEACHING THE TEACHERS

Before they take positions in elementary or secondary schools, prospective teachers must receive training in the art or science—whichever you wish to call it—of teaching. It is assumed that some things can be taught about the principles of learning and the practices of teaching, and that people who aspire to teach should learn these things at the outset. I have been struck by the fact that there is no similar requirement, at least in North American universities, for university professors. It is true that many of them gain experience as teaching assistants while earning their doctoral degrees, but this is too often viewed more as a way of financing their graduate work and lowering university instructional costs than as a serious learning exercise. These students seldom receive a serious, systematic exposure to what is known scientifically and practically about learning and teaching, provided by someone who is an expert in these topics. As a result, we might say that universities are institutions for training professionals, but they are staffed by amateurs.

A hundred years ago, the same could have been said about medical doctors. During that hundred years, though, the science of biology and the related knowledge about medicine advanced enormously, and now doctors must be thoroughly trained in the knowledge and practices that stand on that scientific base. Do we have similar knowledge today about learning and teaching processes that would justify a similar revolution in the training of university teachers?

I have not attempted to present here a systematic answer to that question, but through various hints and examples, I have tried to show that our understanding of these matters has, indeed, come a long way, and has now reached a point where there is much to teach and much to learn. At my home university, we are beginning—but only beginning—to take seriously the education of our faculty as teachers (we have long since taken considerable care of their education as researchers). We have a long-established Teaching Center that offers a wide variety of services (for example, videotaping class sessions and discussing the sessions with the teachers) for teachers both young and old. There is a major focus on training teaching assistants and new faculty and also working with established faculty who feel that they have problems with their teaching or simply would like to learn things to help them teach better.

At the university we also have a Center for Innovative Learning, whose mission is to develop and experiment with new methods of teaching. This center is involved in a collaborative way with the professors who teach core courses in subjects such as physics and statistics to understand what the students are and are not learning. The goal is to find new environments that will enhance learning based on knowledge of human learning and problem solving. Modern educational technology is an essential part of the center's approach, but its program is also based squarely on the new knowledge of human learning and problem-solving processes discussed in this chapter.

These are only beginnings, yet I believe they illustrate activities that are still rather rare in universities but will become more and more common over the coming years.[1]

THE ECONOMICS OF THE UNIVERSITY

One of the questions in the minds of many—if not most—university presidents is: What will this all cost? At what price modern technology in the university? I would be remiss if I did not address that question before I close.

Cost of the New Technology

One very specific question that is relevant to our topic of educational technology is how we can create and employ that technology without raising university costs. It is clear that this will not happen if we proceed on a do-it-yourself basis, with every university designing and building its own software. There has to develop (and is just beginning to develop) a nationwide and worldwide market in educational technology so that development and manufacturing costs can be shared by large numbers of users, as they are today in the case of textbooks. Universities might well consider the kinds of collective activity that would facilitate and accelerate the growth of such markets. Also, as such markets develop, I hope that there will be associated with them more effective institutions and processes for evaluating the effectiveness of the products (a kind of Consumer's Union for educational technology?) than now exists for textbooks.

Costs of Delivering Education

Looking at costs more generally, at top-level North American universities today, it costs the students nearly 10 times as much tuition to sit in lectures as it would cost them to spend an equivalent amount of time at the cinema. I will not comment on the relative merit of these two uses of time, but the fact is striking and sobering. Within a period of a few years, the cinema, because of the savings offered by permanence and reproducibility, nearly eliminated

---

[1] I have been talking entirely about the university's teaching mission, but of course the university also has the goal of contributing new knowledge through research and the training of new researchers. There is a story I could tell about the impact that the information revolution is already having on the conduct of research, and the even greater impact it is going to have in the future. I cannot address this topic here, but I want at least to mark it for your attention.

vaudeville from theaters of the United States. Yet, it had no similar effect, nor did television, on university teaching—almost no effect at all.

How do we explain the rapid diffusion of technology in the one case, and almost no diffusion in the other? Cost cannot be the answer, because it would operate in exactly the opposite direction. Is there some mysterious educational miasma that is transmitted from the professor who is actually in the classroom, which cannot travel across wires or through the ether or be captured on film? If there is, it would be well worth identifying by research, but I have a suspicion that such a miasma does not exist.

I am not trying to bring widespread unemployment to university professors, who, goodness knows, are not paid with utmost generosity, at least as compared with business executives, football heroes, and movie stars. But when an activity begins to absorb a large amount of society's resources, as higher education does today, we have to ask how it can be provided more economically. I suspect that the answer to the question of how to provide higher education efficiently is not to replace the live lecture with the cinematic or televised lecture. I do suspect that lectures will play a much smaller role in the university of tomorrow than the university of today. We will find new methods, some of them grounded in the emerging information technology and all of them grounded in our new understanding of learning processes, that will make the student a much more active participant in the process than he or she is today. I propose that as the goal toward which all of us should be working.

REFERENCES

Anderson, J. R., Corbett, A. T., Koedinger, K., & Pelletier, R. (1995). Cognitive tutors: Lessons learned. *The Journal of Learning Sciences, 4,* 167–207.

Druckman, D., & Bjork, R. A. (Eds.). (1994). *Learning, remembering, believing: Enhancing human performance.* Washington, DC: National Academy Press.

Simon, H. A. (1998). Scientific opportunities of learning and intelligent systems. *Proceedings of the National Science Foundation June 1996 Symposium on Learning and Intelligent Systems,* (pp. 27–33). Arlington, VA.

Singley, M. K., & Anderson, J. R. (1989). *Transfer of cognitive skill.* Cambridge, MA: Harvard University Press.

Chapter 4

The Art and Science of IT Infrastructure

José-Marie Griffiths
Alan McCord
University of Michigan

INTRODUCTION

*I*nfrastructure is a frequently used term that is rarely defined in detail. Many think of infrastructure as buildings, roads, telecommunications systems, and so forth. When applied to information technology (IT), infrastructure is usually thought of as simply the telecommunications infrastructure, although it is rarely funded in the same way as other campus infrastructure components such as buildings, water supply, and power distribution systems. However, in practice, IT infrastructure is much more complicated and contains many more components than just the cable and wiring systems used to transmit voice, data, and video signals.

Infrastructure is variously defined as "the basic framework or features of a system or organization;"[1] "the underlying foundation or basic framework (as of a system or organization);"[2] or "basic support services for computing,

---

[1] *Hypertext Webster Gateway*, WordNet 1.6.

[2] *Webster's New Collegiate Dictionary*, 8th edition, 1979.

particularly national networks."[3] For the purposes of discussing the relevance of IT infrastructure for academic environments, a broad definition will help ensure that essential, but often invisible, components are not overlooked. My colleague and I define the campus IT infrastructure as including the physical infrastructure, facilities and operations, middleware and enabling services, as well as the core applications and services available to all members of the campus community. This chapter first describes the overall campus IT environment from the perspective of the technology itself, using a layered model that includes physical infrastructure, facilities, enabling applications, core applications, and specialized applications. Then follows a discussion of the broader sociopolitical perspective as illustrated by:

- How campuses are organized to provide technology services;
- How IT infrastructure enables the provision of application services;
- How IT infrastructure is perceived by faculty, staff, and students; and
- How CIOs and senior university administrators frame infrastructure needs and agendas.

Having established a broad definition of IT infrastructure to support the evolving learning environment, the IT infrastructure components are discussed in more detail along with associated issues and futures. These components include:

- Cable and wiring plant, including fiber and wireless services;
- Network electronics;
- Internet access, including the growth of commodity Internet traffic, the impact of Internet2, and the emergence of electronic commerce services;
- Facilities, including computing center facilities, public-access computer labs, training facilities, resale centers, and staff offices;
- Central computing hardware and operating systems, including a discussion of life cycles, scaling, and vendor diversity versus economies of scale;
- Middleware services, including directory services, access and authentication, on-campus versus remote access, and the impact of roaming users on campus; and
- E-mail services, including scaling issues and management.

---

[3]*The Free On-line Dictionary of Computing*, February 1998.

In addition to these pure technology infrastructure components, we will discuss support services that are essential to the smooth operation of a campus IT infrastructure. These support services are generally perceived by faculty, students, and staff as part of the IT infrastructure, and include:

- Problem and change management practices;
- Help desks, including automated help desk tools and central versus distributed help desks;
- Faculty and student training, including computer-based training tools, noncredit short courses, and training on demand; and
- Publications and documentation, including automated help facilities, search engines, and context-specific help.

As enterprise resource planning (ERP) systems, electronic commerce applications, and sophisticated online learning environments evolve and are used by greater numbers of faculty and students, issues of scale emerge to impact the IT infrastructure. Scaling issues for infrastructure components include:

- Networking, including network management, availability, and intrusion detection;
- Security, including directory services, identification, authentication, and authorization;
- Computing cycles, including centralization and economies of scale; and
- Help and training services, including distributed help facilities.

As IT becomes ubiquitous and pervasive, and as the learning environments are more readily recognized as mission-critical, more attention should be given to planning and cultural issues related to change management. Issues discussed here include:

- Importance of linking infrastructure planning to academic planning and application planning;
- Infrastructure investments as prerequisites to value-added services;
- Technology watch lists and other methods of tracking new technologies;
- Life-cycle considerations in making infrastructure decisions;
- Mindset changes to help facilitate consideration of infrastructure issues; and
- Federating campus infrastructure services.

Finally, issues associated with infrastructure funding and financing are presented, including:

- Bandwidth growth;
- Life cycle funding for infrastructure components;
- Objectives of various funding and chargeback models;
- Alternative funding and recharge models;
- Outsourcing campus IT infrastructure services; and
- Linking funding and chargeback models to campus priorities and directions.

The chapter concludes with remarks on the importance of IT infrastructure to the campus and to the CIO.

THE UNIVERSITY OF MICHIGAN ENVIRONMENT

This chapter frames IT infrastructure issues faced by Chief Information Officers (CIOs) and academic administrators serving a diverse group of campuses. Some campuses are very small, while others have multiple sites spread across a wide geographic region. Some campuses have been built from the ground up in an isolated area, others have clearly defined boundaries, some consist of century-old buildings loosely coupled in an urban neighborhood, and others change their footprints frequently through property purchases or leases. My colleague and I endeavor to point out the technological, sociopolitical, and scaling dimensions associated with each issue so that needs can be evaluated in light of general principles. By providing a brief overview of the technology environment at the University of Michigan, the reader can better understand the perspective from which we approach the issues discussed in this chapter.

The University of Michigan is the nation's leading research institution in terms of research budget, with 19 schools and colleges and a large medical complex.[4] The university is subject to many complex policies and rules imposed upon it by federal and state regulatory bodies. The university has 36,700 undergraduate students, 15,200 graduate students, and 34,000 faculty and staff on campuses in Ann Arbor, Flint, and Dearborn. Budgeted revenues approximate $3 billion with the major components being tuition, government grants, contracts, state appropriations, and revenues from hospitals and other medical activities. The Ann Arbor campus is spread across seven miles of the city, with 214 major buildings and 221 student apartment buildings having a plant value of more than $2 billion.

The University of Michigan maintains a very large and complex network and computing infrastructure. The Ann Arbor campus is served by a fully

---

[4]For more information on the University of Michigan, please see http://www.umich.edu.

redundant ATM OC-12c[5] backbone to carry IP[6] traffic, three large 100Mbps FDDI[7] rings to carry legacy protocols, and a Gigabit Ethernet backbone serving the Medical Center complex. More than 200 buildings are connected to this fiber optic backbone, and over 50,000 network Ethernet and ATM connections are supported by the network infrastructure. The three University of Michigan campuses are connected to the Internet via Merit Network Inc.,[8] of which the University is a founding member. Commodity Internet traffic[9] to and from the Ann Arbor campus averages more than 200 Megabits per second. The University also maintains an OC-12c connection to the Internet2 Abilene network[10] for research purposes. Point-to-point T-1 circuits[11] and Asynchronous Digital Subscriber Line (ADSL) circuits[12] provide network connectivity to leased buildings in the Ann Arbor area that lie outside the footprint of the campus.

The University of Michigan owns and operates a Nortel SL-100 telephone switch and 20 remote switches, providing over 45,000 voice circuits to the Ann Arbor, Dearborn, and Flint campuses. A SONET[13] fiber optic ring carries voice traffic on the Ann Arbor campus, and microwave links provide voice services to the Dearborn and Flint campuses. Point-to-point T-1 circuits connect remote medical clinics to the Ann Arbor campus. Numerous network connections to Ameritech and long-distance providers are also maintained.

Several administrative and academic units provide IT services to the Ann Arbor campus. Information Technology Central Services (ITCS) is the largest of these service providers, and reports to the University Chief Information Officer. ITCS is responsible for providing technology infrastructure, telephony, data backbone, Internet access, video streaming, and cable television services to all administrative and academic units of the university. The Michigan Administrative Information Services unit (MAIS) provides PeopleSoft® enterprise resource planning (ERP) services to the campus. The Medical Center Information Technology unit (MCIT) provides administrative and

---

[5]Asynchronous Transfer Mode operating at 622 Megabits per second. By comparison, a standard Ethernet connection operates at 10 Megabits per second.

[6]Internet Protocol.

[7]Fiber Distributed Data Interface operating at 100 Megabits per second.

[8]For more information on Merit Network Inc., please see http://www.merit.net.

[9]Commodity Internet traffic supports most typical uses of the Internet: browsing at other collegiate and business sites, file transfers from other institutions, and most commercially available services.

[10]For more information on the Abilene high speed Internet project, see http://www.ucaid.edu/abilene/.

[11]Digital circuit operating at 1.5 Megabits per second.

[12]ADSL circuits provide a digital data connection over a conditioned telephone line. Connection speeds range from 128 Kilobits per second to 1.5 Megabits per second.

[13]Synchronous Optical Network.

professional networking and computing services to the University of Michigan Health System. The Computer Aided Engineering Network (CAEN) provides networking services to the School of Engineering. Other schools, colleges, and units maintain significant information technology service organizations that offer unique networking and computing services to their constituencies in addition to the campuswide services provided by ITD.

DEFINITION OF IT INFRASTRUCTURE: THE TECHNOLOGY PERSPECTIVE

Because most people tend to take infrastructure in any form for granted, the full range of infrastructure requirements, issues, and concerns are understood only by the providers—the professional staff who develop, install, and maintain the infrastructure and provide the services that rely upon it. Effective strategic decision-making regarding IT investments requires an informed community. In particular, CIOs need to help administrators understand what is necessary to build and maintain a robust, efficient, and effective IT environment. This understanding begins with IT infrastructure.

For most colleges and universities, the development and use of new learning technologies represents the first truly mission critical IT application. Where IT is routinely used to support student learning, campuses are expected to provide a much more robust, reliable, and functional IT environment. Faculty and students need and expect access any time, from anywhere, without any excuses. CIOs and administrators need to address the concomitant question: should this be provided at any cost?

At the University of Michigan, we have developed a layered architectural model of the campus IT environment, which is shown in Fig. 4.1. This model, which we refer to as *the wall*, is used primarily as a means of communication with the campus community. The model comprises five separate layers: physical infrastructure, facilities and operations, middleware and enabling technologies, core applications and services, and specialized applications and services. For the purposes of this chapter, the campus IT infrastructure is defined as consisting of the lowest four layers of the model. Specialized applications and services are discussed briefly in this chapter, as is the permeable membrane separating this layer from the four layers of IT infrastructure.

Physical Infrastructure: Linking the Components Together

The lowest layer of the IT architectural model includes the components that are traditionally thought of as IT infrastructure—the physical telecom-

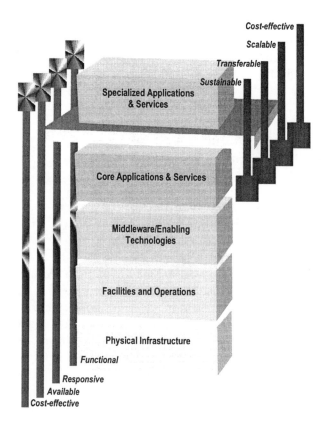

Cost-effective
Scalable
Transferable
Sustainable

Specialized Applications & Services

Core Applications & Services

Middleware/Enabling Technologies

Facilities and Operations

Physical Infrastructure

Functional
Responsive
Available
Cost-effective

FIG. 4.1. Michigan model of information technology.

munications channels that link campus computing resources and users. This layer includes the voice, video, and data communications systems—the wiring, fiber, routers, hubs, controllers, and switches that are hidden underground or behind building walls. In today's environment, we also include the IT infrastructure to support wireless communications in this layer.

Facilities and Operations: Where the People and Machines Are

Facilities represent additional hard structural components that are essential for campus IT service delivery. Facilities include data centers, public access computer laboratories, classrooms, training rooms, and performance spaces. Because IT is applicable to virtually every aspect of the campus learning mission, the relationship between the physical environment and the technology environment becomes more complex and critical. Campuses are faced with the need to balance ubiquity, reliability, flexibility, diversity, and costs.

Middleware and Enabling Technologies: The Forgotten Layer

Middleware and enabling services are the least understood layer of the architectural model. They are essential for any of the core or specialized IT applications to work. This layer is significantly impacted by increased user demands and by the advent of closely integrated and dependent applications. Included in this layer are directory services; identification, authentication and authorization services; and security services. Although colleges and universities have provided such services to their communities for many years, they have not always been implemented to ensure robustness and scalability on a campuswide, around-the-clock basis. Colleges and universities embody a culture of openness and knowledge sharing that must be balanced with the need to provide secure access to individual and institutional data, transactions, and applications. Although securing data and applications is a relatively recent requirement, in today's environment, security and privacy needs are priorities that require serious campuswide attention.

Core Applications and Services: What Everyone Can Expect

Core applications are defined as the IT applications that are provided universally to the campus community. These applications include such services as e-mail, Internet access, word processing and office productivity tools, statistical applications, mathematical subroutine libraries, access to library resources, and access to administrative information systems supporting such functions as student records, financial transactions, and personnel records. All individuals in the campus community should be able to assume that these services are available to them by virtue of their employment or enrollment. As new learning technologies evolve into ubiquitous services, they also fall into this layer. Clearly, the actual components comprising this layer vary from campus to campus, and the components change significantly over time.

Specialized Applications and Services: Serving Special Needs

This layer includes all other user applications—those that serve the needs of specific units or clusters of units, demonstration systems, and pilot projects. Examples of these applications might include parallel computing resources, geographic information systems, music composition systems, and medical instruments. Many campuses are now experimenting with online learning technology applications, and these applications initially reside in this layer. If the use of a specialized application spreads broadly across the campus, then that application is moved down to the core applications layer of the model. Before moving the specialized application to the core application layer, however, the impact of the application on all lower layers of the model must be fully understood so that infrastructure performance can be maintained. In some cases, significant upgrades will be needed to the lower layers of the infrastructure to support the migration of a specialized application into the core application layer.

The Permeable Membrane Separating Specialized From Core Applications

The interaction between the specialized applications layer and lower layers is represented in our model as a *permeable membrane*. The infrastructure, facilities, enabling applications, and core applications layers must be functional, reliable, responsive, available, and cost-effective. These layers must be scaled to support a degree of experimentation and testing of new specialized applications. With the IT infrastructure securely in place, specialized applications can be safely built on top of it. Specialized applications can migrate to the core services layer when they are able to meet the requirements of being sustainable, transferable, scalable, and cost-effective.

At the University of Michigan, we have provided our community with more definition to the layers by specifying the individual bricks that comprise each layer of the wall. Each brick represents a specific IT service or application, defined in user terminology. Various views of the wall can be produced, showing costs, funding sources, numbers of users, numbers of transactions, and unit costs for each brick. In this way, the IT architectural model provides the campus community with a common understanding of the IT infrastructure and a common vocabulary for discussing related issues. This chapter explores in depth some of the individual bricks that comprise the wall and offers advice to CIOs and administrators regarding the selection of specific brick to build an appropriately designed wall for their campuses.

DEFINITION OF IT INFRASTRUCTURE: THE SOCIOPOLITICAL PERSPECTIVE

It is easy to think that IT infrastructure decisions, particularly those with strategic implications, are the sole responsibility of the CIO and can be made with little regard for the broader academic mission, campus culture, or politics. However, the nature of IT and its relationship to the broader institution requires that IT planning be integrated into the larger context of campus strategic planning. This is starting to happen on some campuses but is by no means universal. The recent Y2K coordination efforts made IT issues a priority for administrators on many campuses, although they sometimes pushed IT out of the spotlight again when few significant problems were encountered.

Several forces require CIOs and administrators to reassess how their campuses are organized to provide IT services. These forces include:

- Moving from a monolithic and relatively unresponsive service model to a more flexible and entrepreneurial model that can respond quickly to new challenges;
- Moving from a one-size-fits-all service environment to an environment that can deliver customized and focused services;
- Moving from an exclusively centralized service model to a decentralized model where multiple providers collaborate to provide a broad portfolio of services;
- Moving from one relatively simple mainframe computing environment to a more complex distributed environment with fewer integrated management tools;
- Moving from an environment of delivering services based on the resources available to the IT providers to one driven by the needs of the campus community;
- Moving from a culture dependent on homegrown applications to one dependent upon vendor-provided solutions and services; and
- Moving from an IT culture focused on design and development to one that focuses on high availability and customer service.

These driving forces are applied to IT infrastructure decisions within a broad sociopolitical environment comprised of many constituencies and agendas, grounded in campus history and myths and bounded by institutional values and cultural norms. Decisions about the organization, governance structure, customer service standards, and even the look and feel of the IT environment are influenced by the sociopolitical environment as much as by the technical options available to the campus. One campus culture, for example, may value the autonomy of deans or department heads to the extent that it is politically impractical to implement an efficient standard network infrastructure. Another campus culture may value the appearance and aesthetics of their historic campus buildings and mandate that all technology be invisible to students, faculty, and staff. Yet another campus may not value investing in IT infrastructure because the president believes that technology should not be used to deliver classroom instruction. Still another campus may be the victim of a power struggle between a campus IT organization and a 1970s era physical plant that defined a practice of maintaining separate rather than shared underground facilities between buildings.

These few examples represent the breadth and depth of sociopolitical relationships on the campus that CIOs and administrators face in developing the IT infrastructure agenda and in designing strategies to build support for infrastructure investments. Using the previously mentioned wall analogy, the sociopolitical environment sets the boundaries for the size and shape of the wall, the color or texture choices for the bricks that comprise the wall, and perhaps even the color of the mortar that binds the bricks together.

Each of the sections that follow, while providing an outline of significant issues and options for IT infrastructure services (the science of designing and delivering IT services), must be viewed through the lens of the campus sociopolitical environment (the art of IT leadership).

Organizing Campus IT Services

On many campuses, various components of the IT infrastructure have been the responsibility of individual IT service providers, resulting in islands of development, implementation, and operation. The degree of IT centralization or decentralization varies widely between campuses. With increasing interdisciplinary activity among faculty, students taking courses in multiple departments or on remote campuses, and new ERP systems accessible via Web browsers by most members of the campus community, there is a growing awareness of the need to reconsider how IT infrastructure services are organized.

One of the more recent trends in this area is a movement towards federating the IT service providers within an entire institution. The University of

Michigan established the U-M Information Technology Federation in January 1999.[14] The federation includes all 1,700 IT professionals at the university, and is governed by an executive committee composed of the directors of the major campus IT service providers and representatives of the smaller IT units. The early goals of the IT Federation include information sharing, cooperative planning, and providing opportunities for staff to collaborate on specific projects affecting all IT Federation members. The members will then define IT standards and architectures for the campus.

A critical question for today's CIOs and campus administrators is to determine which IT services are best provided centrally and which are best provided using a decentralized model. Increased expectations and user demands tend to drive the provision of IT services toward a decentralized model. Central IT organizations find it difficult to support the diversity of needs and expectation of immediate service in multiple academic departments. On the other hand, decentralized models increase the chance that services will be duplicated, thereby raising overall costs and decreasing funds available for strategic initiatives.

Both centralized and decentralized IT organizations offer unique benefits. Centralized organizations can provide one-stop-shopping for users, can better exploit economies of scale, can more readily provide round-the-clock service, and can more effectively allocate scarce and specialized human resources. Decentralized organizations, however, are much closer to their respective user communities and can therefore be more responsive to their specific needs. Some campuses are experimenting with a shared services model, where centralized competency centers provide infrastructure services to decentralized IT providers, who in turn package those services for their users. For example, a centralized data center may provide operations services for single or multiple servers at reasonable costs, freeing decentralized units from having to hire operations staff and enabling them to provide round-the-clock service to their users. Outsourcing these shared service components is another approach to providing individual infrastructure components to decentralized units without requiring them to take on more activities than they need to.

Increasingly, the campuses with highly decentralized IT operations are moving toward using a common IT infrastructure to support all campuswide IT services. Having a common IT infrastructure reduces the need for maintenance, focuses user services efforts, and increases vendor discount opportunities. On the other hand, the academic culture typically values diverse

---

[14]For more information on the University of Michigan Information Technology Federation, see http://www.cio.umich.edu/itum/fed/index.html.

technology choices for individual faculty and students. These choices, however, are focused more on specialized applications and services and less on the lower layers of the IT infrastructure. By moving toward a more homogeneous and efficient IT infrastructure, more attention—and often more funding—can be applied to the layer of specialized applications, which more directly affects the academic mission.

Enabling Provision of Application Services

Recent changes in information technologies, especially the personal computer, client-server computing, and the Internet, have changed the needs and expectations of faculty and students. Users now assume that campus IT services are available 24 hours per day, seven days per week. Service unavailability or degradation are met with frustration and anger—usually targeted at the central IT organization regardless of where the problem actually lies! Faculty expectations for IT become even more critical as routine classroom use of IT increases. In this regard, the new learning environment is much more mission-critical than an ERP system—while a purchase order can just be processed 10 minutes later if the campus ERP system encounters a network problem, a lost classroom experience is not often recoverable.

The IT infrastructure needs to be strengthened and made more robust as user expectations grow. Because each layer in the infrastructure model is built upon the layer below it, the infrastructure should be strengthened from the bottom layer upwards. IT organizations are faced with the need to increase their focus on operation and maintenance of IT infrastructure, core applications, and basic services, often at the expense of developing new specialized applications. In fact, our IT architecture model supports the development of new specialized applications in decentralized units. Some IT professionals resist this shift in focus, but faculty and students expect robust and reliable IT services as a given on today's campuses. IT staff may resist this shift because it represents a movement away from the traditional one-to-one relationship between IT provider and user to a commodity relationship in which the user can choose between a number of relatively anonymous IT providers. Staff may also resist this shift because it represents a shift in relative power away from the IT provider and toward the user. Some highly technical staff may even believe that users do not possess the technical competence to manage their own IT environment. Still others are challenged by the requirement to develop and maintain IT services at much higher levels of availability and reliability than previously required—this is very difficult work and sometimes exceeds the capabilities of IT staff.

User Perceptions of IT Infrastructure

While IT professionals are most concerned about how to provide robust, reliable, and cost-effective IT services, the sociopolitical perspective requires that we also consider the perceptions of those who use these IT services, for perception is reality to the campus community.

Virtually all faculty, students, and staff use the IT infrastructure, but they are generally unaware of which specific services they use. For example, the e-mail user does not consider the details of the various underlying components—network services, directory services, authorization services, and so forth. Whereas, in one sense, this is the way it should be—users should focus their attention on what they need to do not on the technology itself—this transparency results in a view on the part of the user (and from a funding perspective) that IT infrastructure is simply not important. It is easier for users to support funding for specialized applications, since these seem to be the real uses of IT. Ironically, infrastructure usually becomes visible to the campus community only when it does not work well. The dilemma facing CIOs, therefore, is to build support to adequately fund a very robust IT infrastructure—one that is designed with a zero tolerance for unavailability, degraded performance, or slow response time—while dealing with the fact that IT infrastructure is largely invisible to both users and administrators. Making the case for investing in IT infrastructure requires CIOs to first educate administrators regarding the components of the IT infrastructure in terms they can relate to, and to then articulate the risks of not building and maintaining a solid infrastructure.

Framing Infrastructure Needs and Agendas

The extent to which CIOs and administrators jointly engage in IT planning varies from campus to campus. However, it is safe to say that most campuses struggle with issues of long-term IT financing and with recruitment and retention of qualified IT professional staff. Most recently, CIOs and administrators have been able to focus collectively on the Y2K challenge and the related needs to upgrade or replace legacy administrative information systems. The campus network also receives some degree of coordinated attention, but often this is only in response to a capacity or performance crisis. Upgrades to core IT applications are generally considered on a case-by-case basis—for example, what is required to implement a new ERP system—but often do not account for the implications of the new system on network traffic or on the number of calls to the campus help desk.

More attention needs to be focused on the enabling application layer to ensure that all components of the IT environment work together with a minimum of effort by users. The other important area that requires coordinated effort is the classroom and computer laboratory environment. As students and faculty move from one classroom or lab to another, they need assurance that their IT applications will work properly regardless of where they are.

Many colleges and universities have a campuswide faculty-student IT advisory group and an IT strategic plan. The establishment of CIO positions on many campuses has tended to improve communications between the campus community and IT providers. This improvement particularly occurs when CIOs are directly involved in strategic decision-making at the administrative level or report directly to the president.

INFRASTRUCTURE COMPONENTS, FUTURES, AND ISSUES

Infrastructure is the foundation upon which advanced IT services are built. Similar to the more traditional concept of public infrastructure, the IT infrastructure is typically represented by behind the scenes activities: underground cable plants, wiring systems located behind locked doors, secure operations centers, and technical support to help campus users effectively use campus IT resources. As IT applications become more sophisticated, services that were previously considered to be part of the higher layers of the IT architecture model shown in Fig. 4.1 are moving downward to the lower layers. Directory services are a good example of this phenomenon. User directories historically have been maintained in both mainframe and local area network environments to authenticate sign on and authorize access to various resources located within the core applications layer of the model. As mainframes and local area networks became incorporated into a wide area network, however, the focus of directory services expanded to give all users access to a broader range of IT services operating on many different platforms. This conceptual change necessitated the invention of more robust directory services that operate in the middleware and enabling services layer of the model.

Our view of the campus IT infrastructure as shown in Fig. 4.1 begins with the wiring and cable plant over which data streams are transmitted between users (clients) and various IT services (servers). The cable plant provides physical access (using network switches, hubs, and routers) to a variety of basic computing, voice, data, and video services operating on standards-based platforms. Supporting this suite of basic services are technical and operational support staffs, help desk and consulting services, and information services that document the use of the infrastructure. This base set of re-sources comprises our definition of infrastructure. Note that this definition does not include specialized applications that support specialized research and instructional activities, although these applications are enabled by the infrastructure components.

When CIOs approach issues relating to the campus IT infrastructure, they should evaluate those components from several perspectives in light of the campus sociopolitical environment. These perspectives include, but are not limited to:

- The depth and scope of the core services provided to the campus;
- The importance of specialized services provided to the campus;
- The robustness and capacity of the current infrastructure;
- The age and life expectancy of the components;
- The anticipated growth of campus technology use;
- The long-term cost of owning and operating the infrastructure; and
- The degree to which improvements to the IT infrastructure can result in efficiencies within the larger IT organization or other campus units.

In the sections that follow, we provide an overview of each infrastructure component along with a discussion of issues that CIOs may face in address-ing needs in each area. For those readers who want to understand some of the specific issues about each of these bricks in the infrastructure, they should continue reading this section. For those who want a broader under-standing of infrastructure, they should go to page 108—*Infrastructure Scaling Issues.*

PHYSICAL INFRASTRUCTURE

Cable Plant

The cable plant forms the core of the campus IT infrastructure—the lowest layer shown in Fig. 4.1—providing high-speed access between the various facilities that house basic IT services and the various buildings on the cam-pus. Because of the interrelated nature of today's IT applications and the necessity to connect desktop computers directly to the Internet, the cam-pus cable plant must provide very high availability and reliability to each building. Ideally, each building on the campus should be able to connect to resources in another building by at least two routes to ensure a backup path in case of a component failure. Because of the critical nature of the cable plant, it must be constructed to ensure protection against environmental incidents and unauthorized access.

The central cable plant is typically composed of multiple strands of single-mode and multimode fiber optic cable to provide very high bandwidth connections and flexible network design between campus IT facilities and buildings. Wherever possible, the cable plant should be installed in underground facilities such as transportation tunnels or utility ducts. Fiber should be installed in protective conduits to avoid damage from water leaks, steam leaks, temperature changes, or vandalism. In many cases, the campus data backbone conduits are installed and maintained concurrently with campus utility services. Where tunnels or steam ducts are not available, the cable plant can be installed in trenches using high-density plastic or concrete ducts for protection. These ducts are used to connect individual buildings to the campus backbone, or where the backbone network needs to cross rights-of-way owned by government agencies, businesses, or individuals. The high cost of digging trenches and constructing underground ducts dictates that these facilities be designed with significant excess capacity to accommodate future growth, and for the migration of data and telecommunications services to future shared network architectures.

Where underground facilities are not feasible, aerial fiber connectivity is possible through cooperation with local utility companies. Aerial fiber generally provides adequate reliability, but is more subject to environmental damage than underground facilities. Sources of environmental damage include wind, ice storms, traffic accidents, and construction crews working on or near aerial poles. Because of the potential for environmental damage, it is important to provide a redundant point of attachment for buildings served by aerial fiber.

Two types of fiber optic cable are most often installed today: 62.5-micron multimode fiber and 50-micron single-mode fiber. Until recently, most fiber optic data communications were carried over multimode fiber, with single-mode fiber used primarily to carry video signals. Today's higher-speed data communications services, however, require single-mode fiber. Cable plants built only a few years ago with predominantly multimode fiber are now constrained by the emergence of single-mode uses. It is likely that both single-mode and multimode fiber will continue to be used in the future, but it is impossible to predict which will dominate. The conservative solution, therefore, is to install both multimode and single-mode fiber in quantities greater than anticipated for the next several years. Another option is to use air blown fiber technology that facilitates the reuse of fiber conduits by pushing new fiber strands through the conduit using compressed air. This adds some cost to initial installation of the fiber optic network, but it may be less than the cost of building additional conduits or installing additional fiber in the future.

Network hardware and software chosen to manage the campus backbone must be able to manage very high volumes of traffic, measure historic network traffic, and facilitate diagnostics and error correction. Most campus backbones are implemented using either Gigabit Ethernet[15] or Asynchronous Transfer Mode (ATM) technologies. The recent deployment of the high-speed Internet2 Abilene network using SONET technology has sparked interest in using this technology for very high-speed campus backbone applications. At the University of Michigan, we have chosen to deploy our current technology backbone network in parallel with our legacy backbone network. We carry IP traffic on an ATM OC-12c backbone, and carry our legacy Novell® IPX and AppleTalk® traffic on our legacy FDDI 100 Mbps backbone. Plans are underway for next-generation backbones using higher-speed ATM technology and Gigabit Ethernet technology.

The backbone infrastructure must also facilitate the deployment of new services such as Internet2 multicast video, wireless data networking, multipoint videoconferencing using the data network, and the migration of voice services to the data network. The campus backbone should also be capable of configuring high-speed virtual local area networks on demand to support the consolidation of services between far-flung offices. All campuses should consider deploying an advanced fiber optic backbone network to serve as the foundation for current and future technology services. Although many campuses have already invested in fiber optic technology, some have not been able to implement fully redundant data networks due to inadequate or poorly located underground facilities. It is prudent to carefully evaluate the campus cable plant to ensure that it is capable of supporting the high-volume, mission critical transactions of the future—online learning, electronic commerce, and real-time research—that will not tolerate failure or degradation of the network fabric.

Building Riser Systems and Horizontal Cabling

Riser cabling refers to cables that link equipment in the main building distribution facility (BDF) with equipment in the local distribution facilities (LDFs) on each floor—commonly referred to as *communications closets*. The riser cabling connects individual workstations to the campus backbone through network electronics located on each floor or in the BDF. Wherever

---

[15]Ethernet operating at speeds of 1 Gigabit per second or higher.

possible, redundant connections should be provided between the BDF and the backbone network.

Local distribution facilities are generally located above one another on each floor and are directly connected to the BDF using large metal conduits. Most modern buildings are constructed with building networking in mind, with spacious BDF and LDF facilities. Adequate space should be included to accommodate network expansions and upgrades. The distribution facilities should not be designed for multiple uses, and should be physically secured to prevent unauthorized access. Some older buildings do not provide adequate distribution facilities or riser conduits, and should therefore be upgraded during renovation projects to correct these shortcomings. IT staff should collaborate with the physical plant department to develop standards for riser systems based on the number of building occupants, the number of floors served, and the uses envisioned for the building in the future.

Both BDF and LDF facilities should include adequate ventilation and cooling to support network electronics, and each facility should be protected with an uninterruptible power supply (UPS). Cooling is often overlooked even in new facilities, yet it is especially important when upgrading older buildings. UPS units can be mounted within communication racks to protect LDF facilities or can be integrated into the building electrical system to provide power protection from a central location. Some critical facilities—medical facilities, animal laboratories, computing facilities, public safety facilities, and so forth—may require more sophisticated power protection such as stand-alone generators to provide a continuous power supply in the event of a lengthy power outage. Such generators would provide protection to the entire complex, including the data network. Other riser cabling system issues deal with vertical and horizontal wiring.[16]

---

[16]Between building floors, the riser cabling system should provide both fiber optic and "Enhanced Category 5" (Category 5e) unshielded twisted pair (UTP) copper cables. This configuration provides maximum flexibility in deploying network electronics in the future, giving network engineers the option of linking network components on the upper floors of the building directly to the campus backbone with fiber optic cable, or linking individual network components together into a customized local area network. In new construction, it may be advantageous to deploy an exclusively fiber riser infrastructure to reduce the need for floor-level distribution facilities and to improve network manageability and physical security. Placing fiber optic cable between the building distribution room and each floor will limit the distances needed to carry Gigabit speed applications over Category 5e copper circuits between the local closet and the desktop. If the telephony infrastructure is constructed independently of the data infrastructure, Category 3 cabling can also be installed. If a separate coaxial video infrastructure is deployed on the campus, then RG-6 coaxial cabling should be installed in the vertical riser system to support connectivity on each floor. Electronics exist to integrate these various wiring systems into a common framework, but are quite expensive and not compatible with some existing telephone or video distribution systems.

Horizontal wiring refers to cabling that links local communications closets to customer outlets in offices and other workspaces, usually pulled through raceway conduits. Category 5e unsheilded twisted pair (UTP) cable is adequate for today's 10BaseT, 100BaseT Fast Ethernet, and 1000BaseT Gigabit Ethernet connections, and will likely support higher transmission speeds in the future. (Ethernet connections operating at 10 Megabits per second, 100 Megabits per second, and 1 Gigabit per second respectively.) Category 5e cable can also support high-speed digital videoconferencing applications. Pulling three Category 5e cables to each station will support two voice and two data connections to the desktop, while five Category 5e cables will support two voice and four data connections. Both single-mode and multimode fiber optic connections can be pulled to high technology laboratory or classroom settings where equipment will be permanently installed.

Many CIOs are considering the use of fiber to the desktop as a standard for network installations. At this time, the per-port cost of a fiber optic interface is still more expensive than a copper interface, but some environments support the use of a pure fiber optic infrastructure. These include high-technology and laboratory facilities where greater-than-Gigabit desktop connection speeds are required, or where significant electromagnetic interference is expected. The resulting reduced footprint requirements for local distribution facilities may create some savings in new construction. CIOs considering this option should remember that today's commodity student laptop machines and faculty desktop machines will likely be equipped with copper interfaces for the near future, so deploying fiber to the desktop will require additional expenditures for fiber optic network interface cards.

Wireless Network Infrastructure

Wireless networking is becoming commonplace on today's campus. It is likely that laptop and palm computers will be equipped with standard wireless interfaces within the next two years. The availability of low-cost wireless base stations (transceivers) will facilitate wireless networking in homes and apartments. As more students acquire laptops and palm PCs, it is likely that the current emphasis on wired public spaces will be supplanted by a focus on wireless public spaces.

While competing standards are still used, the basic principles of wireless communication and related infrastructure requirements are well understood. Wireless networks can be quite effective in line of sight environments such as open foyers, lobbies, and classroom spaces with relatively few users. They are less effective in walled settings, outdoor spaces, or high-traffic environments. Wireless transceivers must be mounted at strategic locations to ensure adequate connectivity and to minimize dead spaces. Truly the placement of wireless transceivers is often more art than science. As wireless transceivers are connected to the campus backbone through copper circuits and fiber optic cable, implementing a wireless environment does not fully remove the need to build and maintain a more traditional infrastructure.

While they provide adequate connectivity for basic data services such as e-mail and Internet browsing, wireless technology is not yet speedy or reliable enough to support more sophisticated applications such as high-speed streaming video, or to support large numbers of bandwidth-hungry users. Copper circuits are still more economical to serve workstations installed at fixed locations such as business offices. Fiber optic and copper circuit networks that can support higher-speed connectivity with higher reliability are more appropriate for file servers and other infrastructure devices. On the other hand, wireless networks offer great promise for convenient network access in areas such as faculty and graduate student offices, residence halls, library public access spaces, campus computing laboratories, student unions, and lecture halls.

Outdoor wireless transceivers can be used to provide rather broad coverage for areas such as courtyards or quadrangles. Unidirectional transceivers can be used to focus wireless networking service into outdoor areas, local coffeehouses, or bookstores by simply pointing the antenna at the desired location. Unidirectional high-bandwidth transceivers can connect remote buildings to the campus backbone. While not providing the bandwidth available with a fiber connection, multiple wireless signals can provide adequate connectivity for general-purpose applications at a relatively low cost.

When deciding whether to build a wireless infrastructure, CIOs should keep in mind that today's wireless technologies must be constructed on top of a wired network and must be linked to the campus backbone to allow connections to other users and to the Internet. While there are opportunities in new construction projects to dramatically decrease the number of horizontal cables needed to serve the building, vertical riser facilities and some horizontal cabling does need to be installed to connect the wireless base stations to the campus backbone. In addition, the building itself still needs to be served by fiber optic cable through underground or aerial facilities.

Despite its present limitations, wireless networking represents the future of connectivity for users both on and off campus. The migration from desktop computers to laptop computers has been a relatively slow process. We expect that the rapidly improving capabilities of palm computing devices, however, will result in a dramatic movement away from desktop to palm devices in the future. This potential for discontinuous change would result in an immediate demand on campuses to construct and maintain a robust wireless network infrastructure. CIOs should therefore proceed with the assumption that building a wireless infrastructure is a necessity rather than a luxury.

FACILITIES AND OPERATIONS

Voice Services

Traditional telephony services are another significant component of the campus IT infrastructure, and are the first of a set of components represented within the facilities and operations layer of Fig. 4.1. The campus telephone infrastructure provides users with three levels of basic service: on-campus calls, off-campus calls to the surrounding community, and long-distance calls. The traditional campus infrastructure supporting voice services typically consists of a mixed fiber optic and copper cable plant, with Category 3 copper cabling serving individual office telephone sets.

Campuses may purchase telephony services from their local regional Bell operating company (RBOC) or from a competitive local exchange carrier (CLEC). Campuses may also choose to purchase and operate their own telephone switch or switches to meet the needs of the campus. As most calls are made on campus, operating your own telephone switch may in some cases lower the total cost of telephone service. Campuses operating their own switches need to negotiate service agreements with their local RBOC or CLEC to provide calls to the local community, long-distance calls, and inbound and outbound toll-free services. These services are typically provided to the campus through *primary rate interfaces* (PRIs)—T-1 speed copper circuits connecting the campus telephone switch with the external service providers.[17]

Many campuses are now implementing *Voice over IP* (VoIP) services. This technology converts telephony signals into IP data packets and carries those packets over the data network to a special IP telephone attached to a data circuit. A gateway device connects the VoIP network to the traditional telephone network provided by the RBOCs or CLECs. Some VoIP imple-

---

[17]The traditional private branch exchange (PBX) solution—essentially a large specialized mainframe computer—is evolving to a server-based network referred to as a private communications exchange (PCX). In a fully distributed system, voice switching is handled by an integrated set of file servers performing specialized functions. In a hybrid scenario, many of the applications resident on the mainframe switch are migrated to servers, while components of the central switch are retained. Distributed systems are quickly evolving to compete with legacy PBX solutions in the areas of availability, reliability, and richness of features.

mentations require the use of special IP telephone sets, while other implementations use traditional telephone sets connected via standard telephone wiring to a hub, which is in turn connected to the network. Other VoIP implementations focus on carrying long-distance traffic over the data network, perhaps to connect two regional campuses.

VoIP provides the opportunity to build one network infrastructure rather than two, but with the added cost of VoIP network gateways and IP telephones. Today, VoIP makes economic sense when providing services to off-campus locations using the data network. VoIP services can also be considered when new buildings are constructed, or when the campus expands to areas not previously served by either the voice or data network. CIOs should recognize, however, that the future of what we now call telephone service lies with VoIP technology. VoIP promises to lower, or at least control, the long-term cost of providing telephone service by lowering the cost per minute of telephone service and improving the efficiency of network and device management. VoIP also supports the migration to a unified campus network infrastructure consisting of a very robust fiber optic backbone network and either fiber or copper circuits to the desktop. Therefore, CIOs should seriously consider the significant one-time investment that is required to enter the VoIP arena to be an essential strategic investment for the future.

Wireless voice services are being developed in parallel with wireless data network services, but the two services can be expected to merge over time. Wireless telephone technology enables a mobile handset to become a wireless extension of the campus telephone system. Wireless telephony transceivers have similar implementation issues to wireless data transceivers. Several vendors offer unlicensed products that do not require interaction with a public carrier, or products that use frequencies assigned to cellular and PCS carriers. The latter solution enables users to maintain a telephone conversation when moving outside their campus building by automatically shifting their call to a commercial cellular service provider.

Video Services

Most campus video services still focus on distributing television signals over a dedicated coaxial cable network. Video services are generally provided over a number of dedicated channels with content provided from a central head-end facility that schedules and directs content from various sources onto any cable television channel. Content can be provided from videotape, live camera broadcasts, satellite downlinks, or private connections with local cable television providers.

The campus video infrastructure can also provide support for point-to-point videoconferencing between special conferencing stations connected to the network. A multipoint conference unit (MCU) can enable a number of users to participate in a single videoconference. Conferencing can occur using Integrated Services Digital Network (ISDN) lines with the H.320 protocol, or directly over the data network with the H.323 protocol; both protocols should be supported to ensure that users can communicate with colleagues on other campuses that may be restricted to a single protocol.

On-demand video services can be provided using special scheduling and control devices. Content can be stored on large hard drive arrays, on CD-ROM jukeboxes, or on robotic videotape servers. Users interact with the scheduling software to request that specific content be streamed to a particular location on the network at a specific time. These digital video streams can be multicast to many simultaneous network users from on-campus or off-campus locations. Note that multiple video streams place a great strain on traditional campus networks, as an independent data stream must serve each user. The deployment of multicast support for backbone routers allows a single video stream to be carried to the edge of the data network, where it is then sent to the individual stations participating in the stream.

CIOs should carefully consider the importance of new video technologies to academic programs. Today's video technology is very expensive and typically is more difficult for faculty members to use than personal computers and LED projectors. Most faculty require professional IT support to effectively use video as a critical component of their instruction. As with most technologies, however, we can expect that video services will soon become much easier to use. At that point, video will have an immediate impact on the campus IT infrastructure as faculty grow to use video on a routine basis.

Facilities

Facilities to house IT infrastructure services include data center facilities, network and telephone switch facilities, network and operations management offices, and office space for technical and support staff. There is an advantage to maintaining multiple data center facilities to provide protection against failure on large campuses, but facilities should not be constructed with only this consideration in mind. Some facilities can be designed for lights out operation but still require a centralized network and operations management center to be available elsewhere on campus, linked via secure and reliable data connections. Redundant services can be located in rather small spaces depending on the nature of the service.

Environmental problems—cables cut by backhoes or animals, overheated facilities or electronic components, power failures or fluctuations—account for a significant percentage of IT infrastructure outages. Data facilities should be protected with robust uninterruptible power supplies and emergency electrical generators to ensure continuous power supply. Electronic switches should be installed to control generator startup and shutdown. Air handling systems should be designed with redundant components. Environmental monitoring devices with Simple Network Management Protocol (SNMP) can provide technical staff with real-time environmental data by passing that data to network management systems. Wherever possible, hardware should be equipped with self-diagnostic and communication capabilities to notify technical and vendor staff of problems.

Interior spaces of data facilities should be designed to facilitate the installation of new equipment or repurposing of the facility. Electrical service should be overdesigned to provide adequate circuit capacity for future growth. Some equipment still requires underfloor cooling and cabling, so a raised floor is necessary for most facilities. An overhead grid of network and power supplies, however, can serve most modern network and computing hardware. Adequate clearance spaces and passageways should be designed into the facilities.

In addition, all facilities should be designed to support the needs of the technical staff and vendor partners who support the infrastructure. Facilities should be adequately secured to control access and protect the safety of technical staff. Card key access systems coupled with video security systems are appropriate to control access to most facilities. Special attention must be paid to controlling access to loading docks and other areas where vendor partners and delivery personnel interact with technical and support staff. All facilities need to include adequate delivery, storage, and assembly space.

Central Computing Systems

Central computing systems are a component of the facilities and operations layer of the IT architecture model. These systems represent the production engines that deliver basic computing services—e-mail, web pages, administrative applications—to the campus. These systems should be housed in air-conditioned space and operated by professional IT support staff. Some campuses still maintain components of their central computing systems in unconditioned and sometimes even unsecured space—the classic problem of system developers maintaining systems beneath their desks. CIOs should establish management practices to ensure that all production systems are appropriately housed and managed to protect the campus IT infrastructure and services.

Central computing systems should be selected with reliability, scalability, systems management, security, and standards in mind. Vendor offerings should be carefully evaluated to ensure that appropriate growth paths are available and that a broad range of integrated hardware, software, and professional support services are also available. All central computing systems should be professionally maintained and serviced to ensure rapid resolution of system problems. Maintenance contracts should include aggressive response and repair time requirements, and can include requirements to house critical spare parts on-site. Systems that use *hot spares*—redundant components that can assume processing without requiring a system shutdown—can significantly improve system availability.

Some campuses struggle with the question of vendor diversity for IT infrastructure hardware. At the University of Michigan, we have made a conscious decision to support diversity for our workstations and specialized applications. The cost of diversity can be quite high even for a seemingly mundane item such as ensuring that both PC-compatible and Macintosh® computers can access our Institutional File System.[18] Nevertheless, user choice is a campus value, so we recognize and fund that additional cost.

CIOs should work with administrators to evaluate campus values and decide the extent to which they are willing to absorb the costs associated with maintaining those values. A careful evaluation of values can sometimes result in practices that at first glance appear in opposition. For example, we at the University of Michigan have decided that our campus IT infrastructure— network equipment, Unix servers, mainframe computers, disk storage systems, and so forth—will be supported by a very small number of vendors. This decision is appropriate because our campus values teaching, learning, and research rather than IT infrastructure for its own sake. The economies of scale and the benefits of working with leading industry vendors help ensure that our IT infrastructure is cost-effective, available, and reliable. These two seemingly contrary positions—ensuring diversity of choice for users while employing single-vendor solutions for the IT infrastructure—focuses proper attention on the academic experience and encourages the central IT providers to provide cost-effective, standard services.

Problem and Change Management

Problem and change management are closely linked methodologies that help improve the availability and reliability of infrastructure services. We view these services as components of the facilities and operations layer of

---

[18]IFS is an implementation of Carnegie Mellon University's Andrew File System.

Fig. 4.1. The goal of problem management is to improve availability and service levels through timely resolution of technology problems. The goal of change management is to improve availability and reliability through effective implementation and management of changes to the IT environment.

An effective problem management system provides a single point of contact for technology questions and problems. Problem management can be fully integrated into the campus help desk or may be established as a separate organization. Incoming problems are generally assigned a severity level based on the nature of the problem, such as:

- High—systemwide component failure, significant service impact, no alternative services are available;
- Medium—component down or degraded, moderate service impact, alternative or degraded services available;
- Low—component down or degraded, low service impact, alternative or degraded services available; and
- Nominal—component inconvenient to use, but little impact on service levels.

Each severity level should have an associated procedure for problem resolution. These procedures include escalation rules to refer problems to more senior technical staff and eventually to management if are not resolved within specified time frames. In addition to basic problem management procedures, it is important to develop emergency response or disaster recovery procedures to cover events such as fire, weather emergencies, civil disturbances, employee work stoppages, or vendor default.

IT staff should track and report all problems from recognition to resolution and maintain consistent and accurate measures of problems and their responses. This is important from several perspectives. First, problem analysis is an excellent indicator of the robustness and reliability of your IT infrastructure. Second, problem analysis can help identify previously unknown flaws in infrastructure design. Third, it will show how IT staff are deployed to resolve problems. Problem management staff generally provide first level problem determination and resolution to shield technical staff from addressing these problems. Problem analysis can help determine if technical staff are resolving relatively simple problems, or if front-line staff require additional training to handle a wider range of issues.

The movement of today's technology products to use industry standards has increased the potential for automated problem reporting and recovery systems to help manage the campus IT infrastructure. Infrastructure devices can often "phone home" or interact with SNMP-compliant software tools to report potential or actual faults, automatically activating an incident for staff to investigate and resolve. These systems enable technical staff from across the campus to use a common database of infrastructure incidents and to develop common protocols for addressing outages.

An effective change management system tracks all changes to the IT infrastructure and schedules those changes to occur at optimum times. This is important because of the increasing complexity of linked systems and the high visibility of IT applications to students, faculty, staff, and the outside community. Infrastructure changes should not be scheduled until adequate testing and sign-off have occurred. Changes to the IT infrastructure environment are generally versioned to schedule a set of related changes at once, usually at fixed intervals throughout the year.

Ideally, change management staff organize and schedule changes, announce upcoming changes to affected users, and track the outcomes of changes by cooperating with problem management staff who may observe problems associated with the changes. Change management staff also track and report the outcomes of all planned changes to the infrastructure environment.

As you can see, both management practices need to be closely coordinated and controlled in order to be effective. The availability and reliability of a campus IT infrastructure depends on problem and change management systems that are themselves available, reliable, and well coordinated. Few problem and change management systems operate across the broad range of technologies that comprise the IT infrastructure, so several systems are generally required—which must themselves be integrated. The CIO faces further challenges on campuses where IT infrastructure services are provided in a highly decentralized manner, and in cases where problem and change management practices vary widely between provider organizations. CIOs should consider the significant benefits afforded by mandating close coordination or consolidation of these important services.

Middleware and Enabling Technologies

Middleware includes a broad range of infrastructure that enables users to access computing resources—the middle layer shown in Fig. 4.1. This includes directory services, authentication services, file services, e-mail transport services, and certificate services that authorize users to access various resources.

Directory services act as the repository for information about users, groups, and campus resources such as classrooms and computing services. Unique identifiers and passwords for users can be managed as part of the directory service or separately. An authentication service manages the ownership and use of individual users' authorization to access various network applications. Network file services provide centralized storage for user files, web pages, and other information. E-mail is distributed to users' file storage areas by virtue of routing information stored in the directory service.

The suite of middleware services deployed by a campus should support easy access to a wide variety of computing resources, perhaps through a single sign-on environment in which an initial authentication session with the data network provides not only access to the network itself, but appropriate authentication tokens to access the various services available to the user across the network. These access and authentication services must work over wide area networks and across a variety of client platforms. Special challenges exist to ensure that access and authentication services function via dial-up connections as well as through direct on-campus network connections.

Security concerns cut across all layers of the IT architecture but are most predominant in the middleware layer. Traditionally, security was a concern only in the core application and services layer, with users having to remember multiple passwords for various systems. Today, components of the security architecture are implemented in the middleware, facilities and operations, and physical infrastructure layers as well. This is necessary because security pressures such as network hacking incidents continue to increase in both frequency and sophistication. Denial of service and other attacks can diminish the performance of the campus network and can significantly affect the security of institutional and individual data stored on the network. Scanning software should be employed to identify vulnerabilities on the network backbone and on servers connected to the backbone. Establishing practices to refresh system images can help ensure that operating systems are protected at the most current level. At the network level, intrusion detection and firewall systems can be deployed to minimize the damage caused by hacking attacks. Some vendors are incorporating intrusion detection and firewall capabilities into their backbone network devices. Firewalls can also be installed on the edges of the network or on individual servers or workstations that are particularly vulnerable to attack. Virus detection software also should be made available on a campuswide basis to ensure that individual workstations are protected from viruses transmitted via e-mail and file transfers.

CORE APPLICATIONS AND SERVICES

We define *core applications* as the user applications that are provided universally to the campus community—the layer just below the permeable membrane in Fig. 4.1. While some might argue that pure technology infrastructure ends at a lower layer of the model, we choose to include core applications and services as IT infrastructure for several reasons.

First, implementing any core application places a significant burden on the lower layers of the infrastructure to maintain acceptable performance levels. Before an application is deployed across the campus, the infrastructure often must be upgraded to just support it. Second, moving a specialized application down to the core application layer generally involves scaling and perhaps redesigning the application system to accommodate a larger number of users, higher transaction rates, and increased storage requirements. Third, a system migrating into the core application layer will often be handed off from the original IT provider to another that is better suited to administer the application at a production-service level. Finally, it is common that the funding available for operating a specialized application is not sufficient to supports its migration to production status. A commitment to move any service into the core application layer must be accompanied by thoughtful budgeting decisions to ensure the long-term viability and performance of both the application and the infrastructure needed to support it.

At the University of Michigan, we have defined a set of core applications and services as part of the basic computing package available to all faculty, staff, and students. The applications in the basic computing package include:

- A unique user account and Kerberos password
- Electronic mail service with 20 Megabytes of storage
- Access to general purpose Unix computing services
- An Institutional File Storage account with 10 Megabytes of storage
- Access to campuswide directory services
- Laser printing in the campus computing sites (400 pages per term)
- Dial-in access (100 hours of prime time use per term, unlimited night and weekend access)
- Internet access, including Usenet News
- Web-based computer conferencing
- Use of networked workstations in any of 14 campus computing sites
- Help desk, documentation, and online help services

The services in the basic computing package are designed to provide adequate services for 95 percent of the campus population, with specific service levels negotiated between the CIO and the Provost. Users needing additional services can purchase them at a marginal cost.

In addition to the basic computing package, two other core applications and services are funded centrally. The University Library, with the CIO providing operational support, funds the university's automated library system. The Provost and Chief Financial Officer mutually fund the university's administrative computing systems.

Clearly, the components of the core applications and services layer will vary widely from campus to campus and will change significantly over time. It is important to establish a long-range plan for the implementation of new campuswide core applications, their anticipated use over time, their retirement, their life cycle-cost, and the impact they will have on the underlying layers of IT infrastructure. Some core applications may be deployed at the unit level rather than campuswide, but CIOs need to be aware of these plans as well, as many of these applications are Internet-based or are dependent on other campuswide infrastructure services.

Help Desk, Documentation, and Training Programs

In addition to the IT infrastructure and the technical staff required to maintain its components, a certain amount of consulting, documentation, and training is required to ensure that infrastructure services are efficiently and effectively used. Most infrastructure services are often underutilized. Poor selection of infrastructure elements, inadequate integration among the elements, and substandard availability and reliability of the elements all contribute to this underutilization. However, many users also are not sufficiently knowledgeable about the infrastructure services available to them, and have not been trained to use them effectively. Most users know how to use only a few of the many IT tools available, and generally are familiar with only the basic features of those tools.

For example, many users are not familiar with how to maintain their campus directory entry, which reduces the accuracy and effectiveness of the directory. Many users do not know how to transfer an incoming telephone call to another telephone number, forcing the caller to place a second call to reach their intended party. Few users know how to establish and maintain a distribution list of e-mail addresses, and therefore select individual names from the directory each time they need to send a group message. Some do not know how to effectively manage their electronic mail or voicemail in-boxes, raising disk storage requirements. Others may spend time developing inefficient work-arounds in response to relatively simple problems. While each of these examples represents an extremely small suboptimization of the campus IT infrastructure, the net effect of many such incidents reduces the return on the investment required to build and maintain the IT infrastructure.

Help desk, documentation, and training programs can help the campus realize additional benefits from its investment in IT infrastructure. These services help users stay connected to the network, effectively use access and authentication protocols, better manage their e-mail and files, and use Internet search tools to improve their productivity. These services also reduce demands on technical staff by reducing the number of problems active at any one time—what can be referred to as the level of background noise in the campus IT infrastructure. All of these subtle improvements in user skills result in a more effective use of campus IT resources.

Most campuses maintain at least one IT help desk for users, and many maintain help desks within individual colleges or departments in addition to central help desks. In most cases, the primary mission of these local help desks usually is to provide user support for the various specialized applications that are unique to a school, college, or department—the applications comprising the top layer in Fig. 4.1. In some cases, however, these local help desks also attempt to provide support for core applications and services, help users connect to the network, and troubleshoot other problems in the lower layers of the IT architecture. In these cases, help desk services typically are not well coordinated with each other or with the central technical staff who support the campuswide IT infrastructure. This can result in a proliferation of standard procedures, the use of multiple diagnostic tools, and situations where multiple parties are—unbeknownst to each other—working to solve the same problem. The net impact on the campus is less efficient help desks, and less effective operation of the campus IT infrastructure.

Using automated help desk software can help coordinate the activities of multiple help desks by keeping track of user problems, usage trends, and problem history. Such systems can also help identify problem areas in the campus IT infrastructure requiring broader attention. For example, if half the calls arriving at the help desk involve problems establishing dial-in connections to the campus network, this area would appear ripe for attention by technical and help desk staff to correct technical problems, improve documentation, or develop new training programs. Effectively tracking all problems to closure is central to improving the overall effectiveness of the campus IT infrastructure. Because a problem may need to be addressed by multiple parties before it can be resolved, automated help desk software can track referrals and ensure that problems are resolved within standard time limits.

Automated help desk software also supports a closed loop problem management system where user problems are tracked to closure, ideally with a positive acknowledgment of problem resolution from the user before the problem is officially closed. Often, technical staff will declare a problem to be closed while the user is still experiencing a problem. Usually this gap between technical and user closure is due to documentation, training, and communication. Without hearing from the user that a problem is resolved, then by definition the problem still exists and the effectiveness of the IT infrastructure is diminished. By returning responsibility for problem resolution to the help desk staff after the technical issues have been addressed, help desk staff are able to work further with users to ensure that they have the information and skills to accomplish their tasks. Users who experience IT problems value the personal help of professional IT staff to resolve their problems. Establishing an effective help desk service where each contact results in the user saying, "Thanks for helping me solve my problem!" will significantly improve user satisfaction with campus IT services.

Note that the help desk service should be closely integrated with self-help facilities and online documentation. This aspect is more for the benefit of help desk staff than for users, as many users do not take advantage of the documentation and training materials available to them online. Establishing an online knowledge base and training your help desk staff thoroughly in its use, will improve the reliability of the advice provided to users. A search engine attached to an online knowledge base does not ensure that the information in the knowledge base is appropriately organized and indexed. Campus library professionals can help ensure that the information is appropriately organized, indexed, and displayed for users and help desk staff to find the information needed to solve problems.

User training programs should be directly associated with help desk and documentation services, with IT infrastructure capabilities and problem analysis reports used to help develop the training agenda. Training programs can take many forms, from non-credit short courses to informal brown-bag sessions to computer-based training programs. Training should be provided in several forms and at several venues to maximize the possibility that a program will match the learning styles and schedules of your users. All publications and documentation associated with training programs should be made available in multiple formats and integrated with the online knowledge base available to users and help desk staff. There should be no such thing as privileged information when it comes to user training.

Performance and Service Metrics

We believe that you can best manage what you measure. Infrastructure services can be significantly improved by instituting a thorough program of service level measurement. CIOs should select appropriate metrics to accurately reflect the quantity and quality of IT infrastructure services delivered to the campus. Metrics can be used to report service quality to users, identify areas for infrastructure improvement, and verify the effectiveness of support activities such as problem and change management. Examples of useful performance metrics for infrastructure services include graphs or tables showing:

- Network performance statistics (traffic, response time at de-fined intervals);
- Availability percentages for core applications;
- Number and type of problems reported, resolution rate, and time to resolution;
- Type of changes implemented, success rate, and effort measures;
- Historic and current number of LANs, workstations, and other network devices;
- Number of work orders completed, in progress, and waiting to begin;
- Maintenance level for each service, installed date, next mainte-nance level, and projected date;
- Distribution of problems to physical infrastructure, facilities, and core services; and
- User satisfaction based on the overall perceived level of perfor-mance and responsiveness.

INFRASTRUCTURE SCALING ISSUES

Additional challenges are placed on the IT infrastructure as usage and com-plexity increase. Systems designed to support several hundred users generally cannot process the amount of data generated by several thousand. The use of streaming audio and video may significantly degrade a campus network de-signed to handle only traditional data traffic. Availability and reliability lev-els that might be acceptable in a small department may not be acceptable when the service is deployed to the entire campus. The performance of some infrastructure components degrades gradually as usage levels increase, while the performance of other components will degrade dramatically when a cer-tain level of usage is reached. The integrated nature of IT infrastructure com-ponents results in situations where the degradation of one component can cause another component to fail completely. These are several examples of the complex problem of scaling IT infrastructure—designing infrastructure to handle significantly greater levels of use over time.

Scaling issues affect all layers of the IT architecture, because all of these components are interrelated. Encountering a scaling issue with one compo-nent may negatively impact the effectiveness of one or more of the other service components, thereby impacting the entire IT infrastructure. A scal-ing issue within the data network, for example, may cause middleware ser-vices to degrade, which may then result in failure of an e-mail system due to lack of authentication. In addition to the loss of e-mail service, the degrada-tion may also generate hundreds of calls to the campus help desk, degrading its service levels. Technical staff working to resolve the original problem with the data network may be pulled away to address the other related symptoms, thereby slowing resolution of the original problem.

The practice of capacity planning can help ensure that the appropriate IT infrastructure is in place to meet anticipated demands. To effectively address scaling issues, each component of the IT infrastructure needs to be thoroughly analyzed to determine its optimum capacity and identify the technical alternatives that are available when additional capacity is needed. The interrelationships between services then need to be evaluated to determine what additional requirements may be placed on each component when another component is degraded, upgraded, or replaced. The usage levels of each component need to be carefully tracked to allow IT staff to predict when individual or multiple components need to be upgraded or replaced. Finally, there is a need to predict both continuous change—the expected growth in usage and complexity—and discontinuous change—the entry of a new technology that may unexpectedly disrupt the IT infrastructure. As you can see, there are elements of both art and science in capacity planning.

A good case study in the need for capacity planning can be found in the explosive growth of network technologies over the past five years. During that time, Internet access grew quickly from a boutique service to an indispensable part of the campus IT infrastructure. Internet use has transformed from viewing relatively small Web pages to accessing sophisticated search engines, library resources, and video archives. As campus administrative applications were migrated to the Internet and usage increased dramatically, so did the need for high availability, reliability, and performance. Network scaling issues include bandwidth management, network management, intrusion detection, management of virtual networks, and the impact of streaming audio and video over the network. As backbone traffic increases, the network architecture should evolve to use Gigabit Ethernet, ATM, and perhaps SONET technologies. More sophisticated network management software is needed to control traffic and isolate faults. As the network becomes more sophisticated, it is reasonable to move toward a single-vendor infrastructure to minimize network integration and management challenges.

In addition to the rapid growth of commodity Internet traffic, the development of Internet2 is demonstrating the potential for delivering full-motion video services using quality of service functions. Quality of service allows users to request that a particular network session be provided with specific levels of bandwidth, latency (the delay time in the network), and jitter (the variation in that delay over time). However because the price of commodity bandwidth is still high, the cost of Internet services to the campus is rising rapidly. Campuses with high traffic requirements should consider obtaining commodity Internet services from at least two suppliers to minimize the impact of regional or national network outages.

Advanced video services represent a significant challenge to the evolution of the campus backbone as well as in-building networks. Installing backbone hardware and software that support multicast video is essential to managing the heavy traffic associated with video streaming. Strategically placing storage caches for video and other network traffic will help improve the quality of service provided to the campus. Upgrading building riser and horizontal cabling systems will be necessary in those buildings where video streaming and other bandwidth-intensive activities are most likely to occur.

Storage, backup, and recovery are additional areas where increased utilization creates scaling issues. In the older mainframe world, one tape backup system could effectively manage the information of the system complex as well as all application system data. In the new client–server world, multiple servers with multiple backup systems—some without tape management software—can make it exceedingly difficult to restore a computing environment after a database outage. The development of storage area networks (SANs) should be followed carefully, as this technology provides the opportunity to create *storage farms* at distributed locations where IT staff can provide comprehensive backup and recovery services in support of a highly distributed processing environment. Of course, deploying a campus SAN will place significant demands on the campus backbone to transmit large volumes of data at high speeds.

As CIOs consider the scaling issues associated with IT infrastructure, it is sobering to consider the number of discontinuous technological changes that have occurred in recent decades. The advent of the personal computer radically changed the distribution of processing power on campuses, paving the way for the development of campuswide networks. The advent of local area networks altered the focus of campus IT providers from managing one data center to managing multiple computing sites, often without the advantages of conditioned space, appropriate management tools, or even on-site IT staff. The relatively sudden impact of the Internet strained campus network infrastructures and shifted more processing responsibility to individual workstations. Electronic commerce is just beginning to impact campus business processes and information security practices. Palm-based computing has yet to place significant demands on the campus IT infrastructure because of its limited processing and networking capabilities. This will undoubtedly change as users begin to see the benefits of new wireless networking capabilities for using e-mail and collaboration tools. Support for streaming audio and video will begin to blur the distinction between palm computers and CD-ROM entertainment systems. The additive effects of these discontinuous changes will challenge the CIO to design an IT infrastructure that is capable of maintaining acceptable levels of availability, reliability, and performance.

How should CIOs approach this environment of discontinuous and unpredictable change? First, they should base the campus IT infrastructure on a firm foundation of industry standards. Second, they must minimize the number of vendors that provide infrastructure components to reduce the complexity of integration and upgrade decisions. Third, it is important to make as few modifications as possible to core applications and services. Fourth, infrastructure plans should be based on life cycle funding and by assuming short life cycles. Finally, CIOs should consider taking a brute force approach of overbuilding the campus IT infrastructure as a hedge against future discontinuous change.

INFRASTRUCTURE PLANNING AND CULTURAL CHANGE

As mentioned earlier in this chapter, IT infrastructure planning cannot be effective if it is divorced from campus academic planning. In fact, IT infrastructure planning can only be effective if it is known what types of core and specialized applications the infrastructure is expected to support. Thus, IT planning must be integrated with academic planning and be at the center of planning for new application systems.

Funding for IT infrastructure can no longer be thought of as an occasional need that can be addressed by periodic attention. Instead, campuses should develop long-term financial plans for their IT environments. As both hardware and software life cycles shrink, decisions will need to be made about the frequency and synchronization of upgrades and replacements.

Investments in IT infrastructure also need to be made in the context of the role of infrastructure in supporting value-added services provided by core and specialized computing applications. Investment in the higher-level value-added services without parallel infrastructure investment could suboptimize the total campus investment in IT. At the same time, campuses should develop business plans that link investments in the IT infrastructure to corresponding improvements in campus business processes and efficiencies.

As more technologies and more variations of those technologies are produced, IT choices are becoming more complex. It is virtually impossible for a CIO to stay current in all technology areas, or to predict the impact of discontinuous changes on the campus IT environment. CIOs responsible for campus IT planning must share the task of monitoring technological developments. This type of activity can be supported with a federated IT organization or similar collaborative organization structure. Identifying a technology watch list and distributing responsibility for monitoring to a group of qualified technologists can help avoid needless duplication and support collaboration between team members. CIOs should also make use of outside consultants to validate their observations and conclusions.

Education is perhaps the most important effort needed to ensure the campus pays adequate attention to its IT infrastructure. The CIO needs to fully understand how the requirements, perspectives, and concerns of the academic community impact IT needs. The CIO should make the campus community aware of the work that occurs behind the scenes to link the academic mission to the IT infrastructure. Regular reminders of the scope and complexity of the IT infrastructure and associated success stories must be communicated in ways that are both understandable and meaningful to the academic community. Breakdowns in infrastructure services should be reported in the context of the larger academic environment. The CIO needs to clearly articulate the benefits of a robust and capable IT infrastructure to administrators and then define the risks associated with inadequate infrastructure investments.

Impact of the New Learning Environments on Infrastructure

Many case studies have described the new learning environments and their impact on instruction and on the life of faculty members. As most new learning environments have not yet been scaled to support the entire campus, the IT infrastructure required to implement them has not been completely identified. Examples of the impact of the new learning environments on IT infrastructure include:

- Implementing Web-supplemented instruction may require upgrades to the campus infrastructure, particularly to remote access facilities;
- Implementing comprehensive Web-based instruction will require hardened operations centers, more sophisticated server hardware and software, significant network upgrades, and improved faculty help desk and training services; and
- Implementing on-demand video streaming will require backbone and building network upgrades and significant investment in new server technologies.

To address these issues, CIOs and administrators should engage in a structured dialog to identify their preferred future learning environment and the possible use of new tools to support the environment. In other words, the dialog should identify those specialized applications that will likely be migrated into the core application layer of the architecture to support instruction. The existing IT infrastructure can then be thoroughly assessed to identify the impact of the new core applications on the physical infrastructure, facilities and operations, support services, middleware, and other core applications.

Once a vision of the future and an assessment of the current IT infrastructure have been developed, CIOs and administrators can create various scenarios that scale the new learning applications at different usage levels and rates of change. For example, instituting a pilot program in Web-supplemented instruction might not have a significant impact on the current network backbone, but requiring that all courses be taught using the Web would have an immediate and significant impact. Similarly, deciding to simultaneously institute pilot studies for both Web-supplemented instruction and streaming video could have significant effects.

Once a range of scenarios has been identified, the CIO and university administrators can make decisions to ensure that adequate infrastructure resources are in place before implementing the selected new learning applications. The parallel infrastructure upgrade and application implementation provides a framework for measuring the total costs and benefits of using the new tools.

FUNDING IT INFRASTRUCTURE

Funding infrastructure is a significant challenge to most campus CIOs and administrators. The high cost of implementing enterprise application systems may cause administrators to focus on reducing costs of other areas of IT operations, which often includes infrastructure. This approach is akin to a state government neglecting to maintain its transportation system and redirecting the funding to economic development—although economic development may depend on the transportation infrastructure in order to be successful. Many factors contribute to costing and funding challenges:

- The rapid growth of technology use at the campus has placed capacity and cost pressures on a relatively flat funding environment;
- General fund support for basic computing services has not kept pace with the radically increasing demands for those services;
- As campuses rely more on commercially available software (e.g. Oracle®, PeopleSoft®, Microsoft®) and single hardware vendors (e.g. IBM®, Cisco®, Sun®), the need for campuswide coordina-

tion of investments, life-cycle costing, and site licensing has increased;

- The cost and time required to implement today's enterprise resource planning (ERP) systems have resulted in many campuses continuing to support a legacy mainframe environment while making greater-than-anticipated investments in ERP systems;
- Many IT funding models were built using economic assumptions that are no longer valid. For example, some campuses fund IT infrastructure upgrades from long-distance calling revenue margins. Falling long-distance rates have now removed the ability to capture a reasonable margin on these services; and
- Most campus IT planning is still handled on an adhoc basis, with reliance on one-time funding sources such as capital allocations, discretionary funds, gifts, and grants. The 1997 Campus Computing survey reported that only 29 percent of campuses have a working financial plan for IT. More than 70 percent of universities continue to fund most of their equipment, network, and software expenses with one-time budget allocations or special appropriations (Green & Jenkins, 1998).

IT costing and funding models are primarily used to help recover costs, but they also can be used to set direction and shape user behavior. There may be particular elements of campus IT usage that administrators may feel are desirable to shape, including:

- Encouraging faculty to use new learning technology tools to improve instruction;
- Ensuring that new specialized or core computing applications are successfully implemented;
- Encouraging use of the most current versions of desktop productivity tools;
- Ensuring that IT providers deliver core computing services at the lowest possible unit cost;
- Shaping or controlling demand for high-cost technology services such as Internet2 access or streaming video;
- Deciding to use a single vendor to provide certain core computing applications rather than relying on multiple competitive providers; or
- Selecting a suite of common good applications that are provided to all members of the campus community.

Many IT infrastructure services fall into the common good category—those services that can be provided to the campus community at predetermined service levels and funded centrally without recharge to users. Such services may include data network services, directory and electronic mail services, access to the commodity Internet, and access to administrative application systems. Other campus IT services are more appropriately provided using a market-based model where users can choose IT services based on service levels and price, such as choosing whether to use long-distance telephone service. New specialized IT services need to be introduced and deployed so that early adopters are not responsible for bearing the fully loaded cost of the service. The funding and chargeback model selected for a particular IT service will change as it moves from the specialized layer of the IT architecture model into the core applications layer.

If desired, the costs of providing common good services can be assigned to budgetary units using a cost allocation model. While such a model will be unique to each campus, examples of potential cost allocation metrics include:

- Total budget expenditures—where infrastructure use appears related to the overall budget expenditures of departments by virtue of advanced technology needs, demanding research programs, and so forth;
- Salary expenditures—where infrastructure use appears to be linked to the number of employees as well as to their compensation level, such as in medical centers;
- Faculty-staff FTE—where infrastructure use appears to be linked to the total number of hours that faculty and staff are on site and using the IT infrastructure, such as in administrative support units;
- Faculty-staff-student headcount—where infrastructure use appears to be linked to the total number of users of the IT infrastructure, such as in residence halls; or
- Square footage of facilities—where infrastructure use appears related to the size of facilities and perhaps to the traffic through those facilities, such as in computing labs or libraries.

Projected costs for common good services should be reviewed annually to validate the operating costs for the service, project the impact of additional users, identify necessary infrastructure upgrades, and approve infrastructure replacement plans. CIOs should benchmark the unit costs and service levels of common good services against commercial IT providers and other campus providers. The benchmarking process should be used to identify long-term efficiency improvements that can drive down unit costs of common good IT services.

Market-based products, such as monthly telephone service and long-distance services, must be priced to recover the full cost of providing the services yet still remain competitive with external providers. Again, benchmarking can help identify strategies for driving down unit costs over time. New market-based services can be funded through strategic capital allocations, from a reserve fund created by modest operating margins from core applications, from fully loaded user charges, or from a combination of sources. Regardless of the specific model chosen, new IT services should be costed on a life-cycle basis to establish rates for early adopters and, eventually, for the mature product operating in the core applications layer.

Most funding and chargeback discussions center on whether IT services should be priced at full or reduced cost and the extent to which users are able to choose their IT providers. In his award-winning *CAUSE/EFFECT* article, Oberlin (1996) addressed the *fee versus free* dilemma:

> The issue has never really been a question of fee versus free; instead, it is a question of fee versus subsidy—a much different issue with different implications. In this context, the issue becomes one of assessing the costs and benefits of the entire user community under each of the two possible cases. What is important is that under either of the two schemes there will be a different allocation of costs and benefits to the user community—although there is no clear answer yet as to who might benefit the most or by how much. However, where services are to be subsidized, the planning task is to determine the appropriate size of the subsidy as well as the primary audience the subsidy intends to serve. Given the growing demand, subsidizing all services to all groups will never be economically viable. (p. 29)

A funding and chargeback model, therefore, should provide the ability to subsidize those services believed to be in the best interest of the campus community. Conversely, the model should have the ability to define other services that are provided on a market-driven basis through full cost recovery. The extent to which any service is allowed to float freely in the market should be driven by campus values and academic objectives. The CIO can engage administrators in a dialog that helps develop funding and chargeback mechanisms that reinforce academic and IT objectives.

Funding new specialized or core application systems—what many campuses would call strategic projects—requires careful analysis of both implementation and operations costs. These costs should be fully disclosed before a rational decision can be made to fund the new project. GartnerGroup® (1998) estimates that 75 percent of users underestimate their total cost of implementing a large ERP system by as much as 50 to 75 percent. If strategic IT projects have such a high probability of exceeding their budgets, then identifying the linkages between implementation and operations—the result of moving new applications to lower levels within the IT model—is critically important. A risk factor should be incorporated into strategic projects to account for potential cost overruns or unanticipated impacts on IT infrastructure. In addition, CIOs should continually evaluate the impact of new application systems on the IT infrastructure as projects unfold.

Life-Cycle Planning and Funding

Life-cycle planning and funding helps ensure that the IT infrastructure evolves to meet the future needs of the campus. Effectively tracking technology life cycle costs helps control the long-term cost of IT services. If technology replacement is not built into a long-term funding model, then the IT infrastructure will not be able to deliver adequate service levels in the future. An aging infrastructure may then limit the ability of the campus to implement strategic IT projects.

Life-cycle planning and funding identifies the expected life of each component within the IT infrastructure. In its simplest implementation, the purchase price of the component is divided by its expected life to yield an annual reserve requirement that accumulates into a technology replacement fund against which future infrastructure upgrades are charged. Life cycles vary depending on the initial choice of technology, the rate of change of the technology market, the expected use of IT services, and the impact of discontinuous changes. For example, conduits designed to hold fiber optic cable might have a useful life of 20 years, as they may be reused for future generations of transmission media. Fiber optic cable will have a longer life cycle than twisted pair wiring. Operating system software will have a longer life cycle than application software. Network electronics may have a life cycle of as low as three years. The life-cycle model can also be applied to professional IT staff for items such as equipment replacement, technical training, and expected length of retention.

In some cases, technological advances enable CIOs to improve capacity and service levels at lower-than-predicted replacement costs. In other cases, increased system complexity may result in higher-than-expected replacement costs. CIOs can adjust the reserve requirement over time to account for these changes. The life-cycle model assumes that a new IT service will continue to be used and that the supporting technologies will be replaced on a recurring basis over the expected life of the service. Stating the expected life cycle of proposed IT services up-front helps administrators understand and anticipate technology obsolescence and can help prevent the inefficient perpetuation of obsolete services.

OUTSOURCING IT INFRASTRUCTURE SERVICES

CIOs use a variety of techniques to improve services in an era of flat or declining budgets, and outsourcing is one of these tools. Outsourcing relationships can be defined along two scales—the extent to which IT services are provided by the vendor, and the strategic importance of the IT service to the campus:

- Support relationships—low vendor provision and low strategic importance;
- Reliance relationships—high vendor provision and low strategic importance;
- Alignment relationships—low vendor provision and high strategic importance; and
- Alliance relationships—high provision and high strategic importance.

Strategic thinking is necessary to ensure a successful outsourcing venture. Some of the reasons to outsource are described below, listed from the most farsighted to least farsighted:

- Improving organizational focus—enabling the campus to increase its focus on its core mission is the single most important long-term reason to engage in outsourcing;
- Accessing world-class capabilities—leveraging external resources to provide access to skills and technologies that the campus cannot afford to purchase or build on its own;
- Accelerating process improvement benefits—engaging an external partner to provide new technologies and services to make faster progress in transforming the campus;
- Sharing risks—engaging an external partner with more advanced skills to help the campus become more flexible and transform itself into a virtual organization that can respond faster to changing business needs; and
- Freeing resources for other purposes—outsourcing operations not central to the campus mission allows remaining resources to be more focused on the mission.

Outsourcing can also be used to accomplish tactical goals. The most common tactical goals are to reduce or control costs, to improve service levels, or to provide needed technical resources to the campus.

In deciding whether to outsource, CIOs must strike a balance between campus strategic objectives, business and financial criteria, IT productivity, and the political realities of outsourcing in general. The major advantages of outsourcing (potential cost savings and maintaining high service levels) must be balanced with the major disadvantages (potential loss of internal intellectual capital and control over the IT planning agenda). A thorough understanding of campus strategic objectives can find the balance between these forces. Overemphasis on short-term benefits is a clear warning sign that a potential outsourcing project will prove unsuccessful. In addition, using outsourcing to address perceived poor performance of the campus IT organization does not generally yield savings. Many problems can prevent a campus IT organization from performing efficiently and effectively. If these root problems are not addressed, then outsourcing alone will not improve the situation.

Advantages and Disadvantages of Outsourcing

The potential advantages and disadvantages of outsourcing can be grouped into four areas: cost, service levels, human resources and cultural issues, and political issues. As in any management decision, political and human resources issues often override quantitative analysis, so it is important to consider all four of these areas.

Outsourcing can help reduce or control costs by reducing the number of technology platforms supported by campus IT staff, removing capital budget components, or replacing personnel expenditures with service charges. Explicitly linking the acquisition of new IT services to additional charges from your outsourcing partner can help administrators see the link between academic objectives and IT investments. Outsourcing may, on the other hand, result in cost increases due to vendor overhead, additional networking requirements, conversion to vendor-supported systems, or unexpected price increases resulting from poor baseline service level measures or utilization projections. To negotiate prices with outsourcing vendors, CIOs have to understand the total cost of providing IT services. These cost components include personnel, equipment, telecommunications, space, utilities, supplies, administrative costs, and staff training. In a highly distributed campus environment where IT is supported by many providers using complex subsidy arrangements, determining the real cost of IT services can be a formidable task.

Improving service levels is often a major focus of outsourcing initiatives. Outsourcing can improve system reliability and availability, increase responsiveness, institute formal planning and forecasting models, and provide new specialized IT services. On the other hand, the level of service can decrease if user requirements are poorly defined, if service levels are based on current needs without considering future demands, and if the vendor defaults on its contractual service level commitments.

The human resources, cultural, and political advantages and disadvantages of outsourcing are often overlooked. Although outsourcing can help improve service levels without adding IT staff positions, it is possible to lose staff who possess critical knowledge of campus business processes. Restaffing the campus IT organization once an outsourcing relationship ends is also a major challenge. One advantage of outsourcing is increased budget flexibility, which allows CIOs to reallocate funding between services rather than between staff positions. As positions are eliminated, however, the flexibility to retrain and reassign staff is lost. Another disadvantage of outsourcing is that staff morale can be impacted by partially outsourcing services—remaining staff sometime feel like second-class citizens whereas former staff hired by the outsourcing firm may have conflicting loyalties and even resentment toward their former employer.

Because the decision to outsource IT services is likely be highly political, CIOs and administrators must be aware of political advantages and pros and cons. Successful outsourcing can lower real costs, improve service levels, and provide greater understanding of IT costs. However, the campus may react negatively to changes in historic funding or chargeback policies or to perceived difficulties in administering the contract. CIOs and administrators must carefully consider how they will regain control at the end of the outsourcing agreement, as well as how they will handle the political fallout if either the campus or the vendor defaults on the contract.

Outsourcing Decisions

Before deciding whether to outsource IT services, CIOs should understand what factors are driving the desire for outsourcing. Is the campus trying to solve its financial problems, improve IT service levels, implement best of breed technologies, or solve other problems? Next, it is necessary to establish rational decision points upon which the decision to outsource will be based and to enumerate the real costs of alternative outsourcing scenarios. These actions can lead to a clearer understanding of the true costs and benefits of providing IT services to the campus, and of the specific IT challenges facing the campus.

If a decision to move forward with outsourcing is made, the next steps include a further analysis of services to be provided, development of a detailed Request for Proposal (RFP), and a thorough evaluation of vendors and their proposals. Because of the human resources issues and the potential for either great success or great failure, outsourcing contracts need to be carefully drafted and negotiated with the help of experienced attorneys. Equally important, contracts need to be carefully administered once they are signed. Certain predictors of failed outsourcing agreements are the lack of clear contract metrics or the abdication of responsibility by the CIO and administrators after the contract is signed.

Outsourcing Management

Managing an outsourcing contract generally requires closer and scrutiny that differs from that needed to manage in-house staff. CIOs need to develop a comprehensive transition plan, including contingencies for dealing with possible problems. Along with this plan, a management team that includes a designated campus contract administrator should be established. This team will administer the outsourcing contract, monitor costs, track service levels, and project future needs. Constant monitoring of the outsourcing agreement should include evaluations solicited from the campus community and periodic reports on outsourcing performance to the campus. To ensure the appropriate level of management oversight, regularly scheduled service level and contract reviews should be conducted. Anticipated changes based on user demand, market forces, and new technology must be documented so the agreement can be amended as needed.

CIOs can view outsourcing as either an opportunity or a threat but should be prepared to consider it as one of a number of techniques to provide quality IT services to the campus. In addition to outsourcing, CIOs should evaluate the potential for renegotiating existing service contracts, in-sourcing to other campus service providers, establishing federated IT organizations, and re-structuring the IT organization to better reflect campus strategic objectives.

GUIDANCE FOR THE CIO

So why is IT infrastructure an important issue to CIOs and administrators? Infrastructure is invisible—it is most successful when users do not complain about network response time or system availability. Infrastructure is not exciting—it is often easier to convince administrators to invest large sums of money in a distance learning initiative rather than smaller sums to expand underground duct facilities to improve network redundancy. Infrastructure is not well understood—administrators are generally not equipped to discuss middleware or backbone networks, although they may be much more familiar with the specialized applications associated with their respective academic disciplines.

Despite these drawbacks, infrastructure is important to CIOs and administrators because it forms the foundation on which more visible technology successes can be built. Infrastructure is important because it enables the campus to operate predictably and reliably—to register students, engage in electronic commerce, exchange research documents with colleagues, and protect the privacy of its student and employee records. A robust IT infrastructure reduces the risks associated with IT on campus, and low-risk levels foster a decision-making environment that is more conducive to additional IT investments. Infrastructure is important because a well-managed IT infrastructure helps maximize the school's return on its IT investments, and demonstrates good financial stewardship by the CIO. Most importantly, IT infrastructure is important because it is necessary to support the primary mission of colleges and universities—teaching, learning, research, creativity, performance, and public service.

REFERENCES

GartnerGroup, 1998. The Impact of Packages Applications on Infrastructure and Data Center Operations. Presented at their conference, "Extending the Operations Center: A Survival Guide for the New Millennium." December.

Green, K., & Jenkins, R. 1998. "IT Financial Planning 101," *NACUBO Business Officer*, March.

Oberlin, J. 1996. The Financial Mythology of Information Technology: The New Economics. *CAUSE/EFFECT*, Spring, 21–29.

Chapter 5

The Disquieting Dilemmas
of Digital Libraries

Sara Lou Whildin
Penn State University

Susan Ware
Penn State University

Gloriana St. Clair
Carnegie Mellon University

R obert F. Munn, former acting provost and dean of the Graduate School of West Virginia University, wrote an article entitled "The Bottomless Pit, or the Academic Library as Viewed from the Administration Building," which became infamous in library circles. Among several cogent points, Munn alerted librarians that:

> Many academic administrators view the library as a bottomless pit. They have observed that increased appropriations one year invariably result in still larger requests the next. More important, there do not appear to be even any theoretical limits to the library's needs. Certainly the library profession has been unable to define them. This the Administration finds most disquieting. (Munn, 1989, p. 636).

Since Munn's article first appeared, college and university administrators have continued to be disquieted by the rising costs of libraries. In the past three decades the volume of published material has exploded, the cost of materials has outstripped inflation, and the demand for storage facilities has strained capital budgets. Strategies such as fund raising and costsharing through consortia have helped stretch resources, but libraries nationwide are purchasing a continually decreasing portion of the world's knowledge products. Even on campuses where administrators have attempted to support libraries by exempting them from the budgetary limits imposed on other units, there is growing concern that the traditional library is a luxury that higher education cannot afford. As educators have been digging deeper and faster, the walls of the bottomless pit seem to be caving in around us.

Into this environment of frustration comes the concept and early editions of the digital library—our ladder out of the bottomless pit. Several administrators confidently declare that we need no more paper collections, publishers are now an unnecessary evil, and we will have a library without walls. Indeed, most of that will be true—not as quickly as we might wish, but eventually. However, rather than the heralded gold mine, the digital library is an even more bottomless pit of the 21st century information landscape. Digital technology resolves very few of the dilemmas that have caused decades of disquiet for administrators such as Dr. Munn. This chapter defines digital libraries, describes the dilemmas facing them, and discusses how those dilemmas might be resolved.

DIGITAL LIBRARIES DEFINED

William Saffady found 30 definitions of the term *digital library* in literature published between 1991 and 1994 (Saffady, 1995). Robin Peek decries overuse of the term, as it has been applied to a variety of web sites, ranging from one offering just eight photographs to the entire World Wide Web as a whole (Peek, 1998). Peek urges us to confine our use of the term digital library to those organized collections of digital information that have the following characteristics:

- A digital library owns and controls the information;
- A digital library provides access to information, not just pointers to it;
- A digital library has a unified organizational structure with consistent points for accessing the data;
- A digital library has a reason for the information being there and, consequently, a responsibility for keeping it there.

If one accepts these characteristics as essential to the definition of a digital library, most so-called digital libraries are eliminated from consideration. In her definition, Peek excludes vendor databases and online bookstores whose purpose is to sell; web subject directories with pointers to other sites; and the multitude of web sites (including many mounted by traditional libraries) that only offer access to an online catalog.

IBM's Fred Mintzer, who has been involved in the creation of several heralded digital libraries, wrote:

> The term digital library is not yet well defined in either the popular or the technical literature, but is generally used to describe systems that manage very large collections of data and provide abundant search tools and other library-like information services. Indeed, the two characteristics that most fundamentally distinguish digital libraries from other information management systems are the large size of the target collections and the abundance of search tools (Mintzer, 1999, p. 72).

His "reasonable measure" of large is one terabyte.

Common to the Peek and Mintzer definitions is the idea that a random grouping of information does not constitute a library. The concept of a sizable, organized collection of information—implying that someone selected and structured it—is critical to the idea of a library, whether traditional or digital. Implicit in the concept of an organized collection of information is an assumption of purpose and storage, and an expectation of value-added services to facilitate retrieval for continuing use.

Michael Lesk, who predicts that half of the materials accessed in major libraries will be digital in the early 21st century (Lesk, 1997, p. 264), offers the clearest explanation of digital libraries and why they hold such promise:

> Digital libraries are organized collections of digital information. They combine the structuring and gathering of information, which libraries and archives have always done, with the digital representation that computers have made possible. Digital information can be accessed rapidly around the world, copied for preservation without error, stored compactly, and searched very quickly.... A true digital library also provides the principles governing what is included and how the collection is organized (Lesk, 1997, p. xix).

Under these definitions, many projects (such as The Making of America, underway with Cornell University, the University of Michigan, the University of California at Berkeley, Pennsylvania State University, and the New York Public Library) qualify as digital libraries, especially if they are taken in aggregate with other projects that those libraries support. The Making of America collection is organized, can be searched and copied, and was developed with a set of defined principles. Conversely, the Internet, which has no organization, cannot easily be copied or stored, and does not have principles for inclusion of materials, is not a digital library.

The digitization of information is exciting for academic library applications because it has enabled more compact information storage, easier retrieval, and wider and faster distribution. However, most of the dilemmas facing academic libraries operate beyond those limited functions and threaten to continue in the digital world.

DIGITAL LIBRARY DILEMMAS

The dilemmas that have made a bottomless pit out of the traditional library also plague the digital library. In fact, the digital library presents some of these problems in disturbing new dimensions because of its distributed worldwide scope. The potential pitfalls facing the digital library in the academic environment include:

1. A lack of definition in users and their needs;
2. Lack of clarity in the role of digital libraries in the teaching-learning process;
3. Inadequate reference and instruction services;
4. Competing priorities for collection development;
5. Continuing problems with collection preservation;
6. Territoriality associated with ownership and authorized use;
7. Economics of information;
8. Contention over copyrights and fair use;
9. Cost factors—a constituency perspective implicit in all of these issues; and
10. Cultural implications.

Dilemma One: Lack of Definition in Users and Their Needs

The most fundamental problem facing libraries is a lack of definition of their users and the needs of those users. The inability to answer the questions, "Who are our users?" and "What do they need?" has led to the high costs associated with libraries. Most academic libraries serve parent institutions that have consistently avoided placing limits on their missions, programs, or clientele. Consequently, traditional academic libraries have always faced competing demands from their potential users: faculty, students, staff, alumni, citizens of the surrounding community, visiting scholars, the clientele of other libraries, and future generations of scholars. Depending on the mission of the parent institution, libraries have attempted to serve these varying constituencies to a greater or lesser extent.

In the most comprehensive of research institutions, which strive to be all things to all people, libraries for some time attempted to acquire everything just in case someone needed it. As the information explosion progressed, this hopeless goal gave way to a cooperative attempt to share collection responsibilities among libraries, arranging for material to be delivered if and when a user needed it. The digitization of information makes this just in time access to collections an even more viable alternative to institutional ownership of collections. Full-text databases of periodical literature are the best examples of providing access to far more material than any single library could own.

Still, the problem of identifying the user and defining user needs remains critical in a digital environment because it determines what digital information should be available and how it should be organized for retrieval. Indeed, this problem is aggravated in a digital environment because digital information can be retrieved by a wide spectrum of users in far-flung corners of the globe. For whom are we building or providing access to a digital collection? For research scholars, graduate students, or undergraduates? Only those in our own institution, or only those associated with institutions in our consortium? Will a member of the community, a professional, or a K-12 student be able to access it? How wide is our community if we accept state or federal funds? Will persons with different languages, religions, or sensory capabilities use it? Will these people be members of our distant learning community? For those who license access to digital libraries, the answers to these questions are key to determining volume of use, simultaneous demand, adequacy of resources, and pricing. For those creating digital collections, the answers will suggest different organizing principles, searching mechanisms, and retrieval capabilities that need to be taken into consideration for design. If the missions of colleges and universities continue to broaden, we may not be able to define who is not a user of the digital library. We should anticipate that the cost of serving anybody, anywhere, anytime will be as great or greater than the costs of a traditional library.

On the other hand, digital technology may provoke us to better define our users and their needs. Digital technology gives us the ability to monitor use and develop more realistic profiles of users. Providers of digital information expect us to define our clientele and reimburse them according to potential or actual uses of information. This, in turn, requires us to authenticate users and ensure that only authorized and accounted-for members of our community have access to licensed resources. The authentication process offers us the ability to monitor use and tailor information to user preferences and patterns.

One question that has surfaced more recently is whether we will have to forego sophisticated data collection on users and usage patterns to honor concerns about privacy. Assuming we can ensure privacy for individuals, we can expect digital information providers to give us feedback on volume and patterns of use that will still enable us to make wiser use of our resources. With use-driven costs and better information about use, perhaps we will be able to make the tough political decisions: Will we deny access to external clientele? Will we be able to publicly identify subjects that generate little or no demand, and cease to support them? Will we divert support to those units that do generate usage, regardless of their relatively low prestige within the academy? If not, Dilemma One will continue undaunted in digital libraries.

Dilemma Two: Lack of Clarity in the Role of Digital Libraries in Teaching-Learning

Digital libraries hold the prospect of dramatically impacting teaching and learning, but how this may happen is unclear, and it may happen in unexpected ways. Champions of the digital library envision a world of information at the fingertips of every curious learner. As Metzl said in 1996, "the virtual library will be a miracle of access. It will open the doors of the Bodleian [Oxford University] and Widener [Harvard University] not only to students wanting to work at home, but to aspiring Mongolian academics, Namibian journalists, and anybody else with the proper equipment and a little money." (Metzl, 1996, p. 153). Assuming the current technical problems in delivering this reality will be solved, will there be demand for the digital information universe? Maybe not from learners—and maybe not from education providers, either. We explain this hesitation.

Nothing about the digitization of information necessarily motivates learners. Most will continue to seek paths of least resistance, and an increasingly customer-oriented higher education establishment will respond to the demands of the marketplace. Therefore, while technology could offer vast digital libraries for students to browse and search, it will likely deliver electronic reserves and custom information modules supporting specific assignments, designed into course packaging. Students may not need to define their information needs, formulate search strategies, and retrieve relevant materials from the digital universal library. Unless learning how to conduct those activities is a specific goal of the course assignment, there will be no need to engage in such information seeking. Even while Metzl dreamed of desktop access to the Bodleian Library, he admitted, "the computer-facilitated ability to search so quickly and directly for so precise a piece of information seems, in contrast, inherently threatening to the idea of the book as an integrated whole ... We feel ourselves being conditioned to think of articles and books less as integrated narratives and more as groupings of small bits of information that can be accessed independently." (Metzl, 1996, p. 154) Conditioned by links to focused, just-in-time, prepackaged fast food for thought, students will demand relevant information be incorporated into course design. Educational providers will likely respond to this demand not only to satisfy customers, but also to reduce costs of providing a wider range of information just in case it might be needed.

On the other hand, providing embedded information directly to students as part of course design may mean that more students successfully access and use relevant information. The digital world allows the same information to be available to all students in the course; no longer will the professor's recommended reading be available only to the first student to get to the shelf. Students can spend more time evaluating, using, and presenting information, rather than identifying and retrieving it.

At the same time, course designers will have to recognize that a worldwide clientele may require them to be sensitive to cultural mores and taboos when selecting information. Just as textbooks vary by state, digital libraries may have to be customized (or sanitized) for audiences to avoid controversy. It might well be that digital libraries in support of worldwide learning would not offer the rich diversity of information we envision, but rather a homogenization of safe information. Digital libraries have the potential to offer students more information but, depending upon political and economic decisions, students may actually have more restrictions on the information available to them.

The digitization of information does not have to lead to prepackaged, embedded information nor to circumscribed exposure to information for learners. It has the potential to be customized to meet the unique needs of individual learners, or what Toni Carbo has described as the just for you digital library:

> What we are moving toward is customized, individualized service that is "just for you." For example, if a person is a whole-part learner and better with visual images than text information, presentation may be customized for those needs. If a person cannot see and therefore must have a voice recognition system and software that will read the material aloud, customized delivery can be tailored for that individual. (Carbo, 1998, p. x)

Of course, such individually tailored delivery assumes we can define and track users' needs, learning styles and preferences. The possible pitfalls associated with such an assumption were discussed as a part of Dilemma One, and continue to be relevant here.

Digital information makes possible just in case, just in time and just for you scenarios. Which of these we choose to implement requires a clearer understanding of the role information is to play in specific teaching and learning assignments. If we cannot work with education providers to develop that understanding, we can not ensure the return on our investment in digital libraries, any more than in traditional ones.

For the next hundred years, faculty and librarians will be caught between the potential of the digital library and the reality of fully digital resources for education. Faculty teaching distance education courses will want to make sure that appropriate resources are available. Currently, in Penn State's World Campus, the course design team includes a librarian who can advise on appropriate resources, create links for a course home page, and cause appropriate materials to be digitized in support of curriculum. Librarians who want to provide just-in-time service will be attentive to requests—not only to have the course reserve materials digitized and mounted for courses, but also to begin the process of obtaining permission to scan ranges of more contemporary books for students to browse in the digital library. The advent of netLibrary, a resource filled with digitized scholarly press imprints, offers another alternative for adding content in support of instruction.

Dilemma Three: Designing Adequate Reference and Instructional Services

The proliferation of digital libraries will provide greater demands on reference and instructional services. As the demands for digital library information grows and matures in an anyplace, anytime format, new forms of designs for reference and instructional services need to be developed. Failure to develop both the technological aspects and the needed service components will lead to underutilized digital libraries.

The "Seven Principles of Good Practice in Undergraduate Education" provide a practical checklist for employing new technologies in higher education (Chickering & Ehrmann, 1996). They also provide guidance on the development of effective reference and instruction services in digital libraries. Distilled from the findings of more than 50 years of research on teaching and learning, the Seven Principles bring into focus the importance of interpersonal communication, collaboration, active learning, critical thinking, and respect for diversity in effective teaching and learning. These values and goals also define the historical tradition, theory, and practice of library reference services. As digital libraries seek ways to integrate technologies to provide a full range of traditional services over an electronic network, these timeless values must be retained.

According to the Seven Principles, the best teaching practices encourage: (1) student–faculty contact, (2) cooperation among students, (3) active learning, (4) prompt feedback, (5) time on task, (6) high expectations, and (7) respect for diverse talents and ways of learning. Academic learning communities, a common feature of technology-enhanced courses, are notable examples of the powerful role technology can play in support of principles one through four. Thomas Angelo characterizes academic learning communities as environments in which faculty, students, and academic support services work collaboratively toward shared academic goals. In learning communities, all participants have both the opportunity and responsibility to learn from and help teach each other (Angelo, 1997). Advances in communication and networking technologies are providing exciting opportunities to create dynamic learning communities in which participants can communicate and collaborate using email, computer conferencing, Internet resources, and the growing store of information and resources in digital libraries. Unparalleled in their potential as interdisciplinary teaching laboratories, digital libraries will be rich with a mix of scholarly research, images, archives, data, classical texts, and popular culture.

Librarians are joining dynamic learning communities as coaches and collaborators, guiding students through the complex maze of print and digital resources, teaching them how to search effectively, and helping them judge the quality and usefulness of the information they encounter. Collaborative teams representing learning communities from community colleges and liberal arts colleges, as well as large state and private universities, have showcased such innovative projects as the New Learning Communities Conferences (1994–1997), sponsored by the Coalition for Networked Information (www.cni.org/projects/nlc). In particular, the 1996 conference theme was "Librarian Leaders in New Learning Communities," which focused on special efforts being made to ensure that, in the midst of emerging technologies, traditional library values of high quality and personalized service are maintained (Ferguson & Bunge, 1997). At Penn State, Project Vision began with a library studies course where students interacted asynchronously with and were taught and supported by librarians in conjunction with discipline faculty. In that learning community, students also provided peer support for each other. As digital library support of technology-enhanced learning grows and matures, so will the service expectations of users seeking assistance at anytime, from anywhere, through a wide range of media and networks. Librarians' high standards of service and their proclivity for spending a great deal of time to answer student questions make them excellent participants in these learning communities.

Of all of the desired features of digital library reference services, real-time transaction log analysis is the most challenging. While historical studies of internal database transaction logs are common in academic libraries, real-time analysis of both private and commercial database logs is not. Digital libraries must begin to negotiate for real-time access to the transaction logs generated by the host of databases that have become a basic feature of digital libraries. These transaction logs should reveal the keywords, search fields, search syntax, and hit rates of prior searches. With the ability to view search histories, librarians can detect patterns of errors that searchers may be unaware of or unable to describe fluently during reference negotiations. With real-time transaction analysis, digital libraries would have the potential to match the quality of reference interviews that is now only available face-to-face. Winstar Telebase, a commercial information database service, has captured real-time database transaction information through its live help desk service. Search histories captured by the help desk give some insight as to why some patent searches fail: Some do not follow the required syntax, while others fall victim to poor spelling and typing. Currently, most log analysis tools are in the hands of corporate information providers, although some are being proposed as part of an ambitious new initiative called Library.org. The research questions associated with that project will provide a large data set of interest to human computer interaction and cognitive psychology researchers as well as librarians.

As yet, there are no formal guidelines, standards, or national networks for the electronic delivery of reference and instruction services through digital library networks. However, much work is in progress. Librarians are conducting research on the influence of technology on the nature of reference service, the Library of Congress and individual academic libraries are designing and testing digital reference prototypes, and a growing number of library professionals are discussing digital reference issues at national conferences and on professional listservs (Rieh, 1999; Ferguson & Bunge, 1997; LaGuardia & Mitchell, 1998; Lipow, 1999).[1] Though ongoing, the general consensus of these discussions is that the model digital reference service should be real-time, interactive, staffed by professionals and avail-

---

[1]http://lcweb.loc.gov/rr/digiref/; DIG_REF listserv (a forum of information specialists discussing the reference needs of Internet-based users and setting an agenda for re-defining reference services in the Internet context), http://www.vrd.org/Dig_Ref/dig_ref.html.

able at any time, from anywhere. Personal service at the time of need remains the goal as libraries enter the digital age.

Both the traditional library and the digital library share a strong instructional mission to teach students and faculty about:

- Assessing their own information needs,
- Identifying appropriate sources to meet those needs,
- Retrieving information,
- Evaluating information, and
- Using information to transmit or create knowledge and works of imagination.

The traditional library does this through regular instructional courses, instruction in discipline courses, brief workshops on subject searching, and regular individual reference desk contacts. The digital library attempts to meet these same objectives through interactive web pages, web tutorials, and e-mail reference. The Library.org group is seeking NSF funding for the creation of a science chat room to determine whether science education can be improved through 24 hours a day seven days a week reference service. Transaction logs from such a service will provide a capacious resource for a variety of researchers and may even offer feedback on science teaching.

Computer-assisted instruction and intelligent tutoring systems hold promise for supporting the teaching mission of digital libraries. They serve well as examples of the use of technology to enhance the good practice principles five through seven. Computer-mediated instruction modules can be self-paced, graduated to teach from basic to highly advanced levels, and designed in a wide range of formats that accommodate diverse learning styles. Intelligent software agents have been designed to assist users interactively and to continue to provide personalized assistance autonomously after learning from the user's activity and responses (Lieberman, 1997).

However, technology has its limits. Instructional software sophisticated enough to substitute for the work of library professionals must involve problem-based learning, complex projects, critical thinking, reflection, and discussion. Such modules are difficult to design, labor intensive, and require frequent updates to keep the content fresh and challenging. With any computer-mediated instruction, support services are needed to assure that the hardware and software are available consistently, in proper working order, and compatible with routine changes and upgrades in computer operating systems and interfaces (Ehrmann, 1995). Used alone, intelligent agents fall short, as well. They cannot communicate interpersonally with a user who is stalled or confused, and they cannot draw on diverse professional and personal experiences to make intuitive associations and judgments. Moreover, computer-based agents cannot access resources that have not been indexed or digitized, and only human intermediaries can conduct personal negotiations to acquire restricted materials (Nardi & O'Day, 1999). Humans and software agents make an effective team, but one cannot substitute for the other.

Chickering acknowledges the power of new technologies and the significant contributions they can make to the advancement of the Seven Principles for Good Practice in Undergraduate Education. Yet, he warns that institutional investment in professional development, training, and staffing will be necessary if the learning potentials of technology are to be realized (Chickering & Ehrmann, 1996). A liberal arts college president warns more explicitly:

> One mistake made by many information technology advocates is to sell information technology on the basis of cost reduction. At no point in our experience has the information revolution led to cost savings. Rather it has led to increased expectations from faculty and students, to demands for ever more rapid shifts of equipment and software, and to an ever mounting increase—almost Dilbert-like—of staff to support the effort. (Williamson, 1996, p. 40)

Ultimately, institutional support of reference and instruction in digital libraries presents no exception to the demands of new technologies in the delivery of higher education. In fact, digital library services may require more support than most academic units. Fifteen years ago, William Miller declared that academic reference service was at a breaking point (Miller, 1984). So many new functions were being added to the responsibilities of reference librarians that burnout and a decline in the quality of service loomed darkly. Tyckoson (1999) reexamined the state of academic reference services and declared that the crisis had gotten worse. The addition of digital reference and instruction services to an already overburdened system remains a dilemma.

Dilemma Four: Competing Priorities for Collection Development

Because digital libraries hold such promise for improvements over traditional methods of storing, retrieving, and distributing information, why do we not digitize everything and solve a lot of problems? Probably the biggest reason that we have not taken this route is that it is not easy to find $3 billion to fund the conversion of 100 million books to electronic form, plus the additional (probably larger) amount that we would need to compensate the copyright owners for most of those books (Lesk, 1997, p. 3). Despite the fact that the technological costs of conversion and storage continue to decline, not every piece of nondigital information is likely to be converted to digital format. Most academic institutions cannot afford the costs of accessing all the information already produced in digital format. Consequently, digital libraries still must contend with the dilemma of competing priorities for developing digital collections. What should be the priority for conversion to digital format? What should be the priority in licensing access to digital libraries? Some of the competing options include:

- *Information that needs to be preserved because of deteriorating physical condition, regardless of the demand for such information.* Because much of the deteriorating material is older and therefore out of copyright, many libraries have digitized such collections. The strategic benefit is that when information is available digitally, wear and tear on precious originals can be reduced or eliminated. As an added benefit, projects such as the Library of Congress's work with documents related to the founding of the United States and similar efforts in many other countries will also contribute to greater cultural understanding.

- *Information in high demand by lots of users.* One of the first targets for digitization in many academic libraries has been materials put on course reserve by professors. Because every student is expected to read the same articles and book chapters, and because many students wait until the night before the reading is due to even begin, these materials are not only heavily used but also in contention for use. Student reaction to digitization of reserves has been very positive. They enjoy the convenience of having unlimited access to reserves around the clock from their dormitories and apartments.

- *Information in demand by users dispersed over a wide geography.* Institutions like Pennsylvania State University, which has 23 locations spread over a state of 45,333 square miles, have benefited greatly from the advent of digital resources. Penn State can serve its 81,000 students equally through the provision of electronic, full-text versions of *Science, Nature,* and major newsmagazines.

- *Information that is likely to generate income or funding by sponsors.* Some large digitization projects have been the result of significant gifts. Carnegie Mellon's HELIOS (http://heinz1.library.cmu.edu/HELIOS/) provides digital versions of the papers of the late Senator H. John Heinz III. HELIOS is unusual among digital projects in that it accesses relatively recent resource materials. This was possible because the Heinz papers were government property and thus in the public domain. With almost 800,000 pages, HELIOS is also one of the largest full-text projects to date.

• *Information that is not covered by copyright or other ownership issues.* Projects mentioned above indicate that material without copyright implications are attractive targets for digitization efforts.

• *Information that is of intellectual value.* Project Gutenberg, which is included in the Universal Library (www.univlib.org) focused on making classics such as the work of Charles Dickens available on the Web. Resources were scanned and sometimes typed in without information identifying the source of the text. While this practice testified to the universality of the classic, students who want to use these resources in the production of term papers find the lack of publication data disconcerting.

• *Information that is complementary to national or international digital initiatives.* Iceland, England, Norway, Denmark, Sweden, and a host of other countries all make their most precious founding documents available via the web.

• *Information that is easier to use in digital format.* Indices were among the first materials to be made available digitally. The added functionality of keyword searching makes them much more useful than they were in paper format. Few English scholars, for example, wish to return to the arduous task of using the Modern Language Association indices in paper form. Similarly, popular reference works, such as *Numerical Recipes in C*, have also flourished in the online environment.

"In creating digital products, libraries are called upon to balance the competing worlds of boundless promise and limited resources." (Hazen, Horrell & Merrill-Oldham, 1998, p. 1) Value judgments are no easier to make in the digital library environment than in a traditional library environment.

Dilemma Five: Continuing Problems with Collection Preservation

Of all the dilemmas that carry over from the traditional library to the digital library, the continuing problems with collection preservation are often the most surprising to academic administrators. It is widely believed that digitizing information preserves it. It does, but for only a little while. No digital medium currently in use will preserve information for more than 50 years. At present, most information can be preserved for 5 to 30 years. Magnetic media, from the floppy disk to the digital audiotape, may lose portions of their information in just a few years. CD-ROMs have a 50-year life expectancy. "At present there is no storage medium in sight that would eliminate the need to recopy." (Lehman, 1996, p. 311) In his film, *Into the Future: On the Preservation of Knowledge in the Electronic Age,* Terry Saunders reports that the 20-year-old magnetic tape holding the records of the Mars mission is decomposing, and efforts to recopy it are suffering a 10 to 20% error rate due to the decomposition (Saunders, 1997).

In addition to the durability of the storage medium, there is also the problem of longevity in coding systems, software, operating systems, and hardware. We are moving through generations of these tools in a year, or even months. If the storage medium persists, the equipment and programming necessary to run it may not—unless they, too, are archived and preserved in operating order. One can imagine the need for the digital equivalent of the Rosetta Stone to decipher early versions of digital libraries.

Assuming we will evolve technologies to help migrate digital information from one format to another, we still need to secure institutional commitments to developing and implementing the routines necessary to preserve the rapidly evolving digital record. Donald Waters of Yale University lists two organizational imperatives to insure preservation of digital information: First, we need experts who understand systems and how to migrate them; second, we have to have routines in place for migrating information from one format to another as ordinary events in our daily lives (Saunders, 1997).

Jeff Rothenberg, in his report to the Council on Library and Information Resources, *Avoiding Technological Quicksand,* argues against an effort to constantly migrate data to new software and hardware formats. Instead he calls for a "long-lived solution that does not require continual heroic efforts or repeated invention of new approaches every time formats, software or hardware paradigms, document types, or record-keeping practices change." (Rothenberg, 1999, p. 30) Rothenberg calls for research into and implementation of an emulation approach that would enable future computers to encapsulate documents with their attendant metadata (annotations, descriptors, indexing), software, and emulator hardware specifications.

Whether the solution is migration, encapsulated emulation, or some other innovation, storing large digital libraries will be expensive. The very nature of a distributed network of digital libraries suggests there must be agreements among institutional consortia regarding the standards and routines for the creation, preservation, and migration of digital information. Because materials will be so easily available from one institution to another, it will make even more sense for there to be divisions of responsibility around which institutions steward which sets of material. Further, the system we create should be extravagantly redundant, so that a disaster at a single institution or in a single region of the world will not have a devastating effect on digital knowledge.

In spite of all these negative comments and concerns, some members of the digital library community are increasingly confident that digital collections can and will be preserved. Whereas a book can be neglected for a century or so, then picked up and immediately used, digital files will probably not endure such treatment. However, universities that make it their business to preserve the large digital collections they create will be able to migrate them successfully from system to system far into the future. New software and hardware will pose problems, but computer scientists will write programs to migrate materials to them. Best practices in this area will include the use of standardized and widely accepted formats for the creation of materials, and annual attention to digital archives. In the same way that librarians pay regular attention to their paper collections, they must also steward their digital ones.

Finally, libraries need to make decisions about the types of digital records they will preserve. Should the digital archive include e-mail, listservs, discussion groups, bulletin boards, web sites? What will be the basis for inclusion and exclusion? Given the highly interactive and frequently updated nature of some of these forms of discourse, which version of an electronic document will be preserved? How can we insure that the site we preserve is as its author intended, rather than as a visitor amended? Paper libraries have been very exclusive in their choices; digital libraries also need to be selective.

Recognizing that too much information (which cannot be found and retrieved) is as bad as none at all, Deanna Marcum, President of the Council on Library and Information Resources, urges selectivity. "A good collection, like a good book, is made in the editing. Individuals don't save every scrap of paper in their files—tax records, restaurant receipts, dry-cleaning tickets—and deed them to their descendants with the injunction that they be kept forever. That would be irresponsible, self-centered, and lazy." (Marcum, 1998, p. A11) The scholarly heritage, long the purview of academic libraries, clearly must be preserved—but the more popular culture should perhaps survive only in samples. "The long-term preservation of digital publications is frontier country." (Lehmann, 1996, p. 319) Traveling in frontier country requires courage and caution; it is exciting, but there are rocks and holes—even bottomless pits.

Dilemma Six: Territoriality Associated with Ownership and Payment

In order to achieve a golden information age, as much information as possible should be made available at no charge to the individuals who want to use it. Many visionaries believe that scenario could be attained with appropriate government support and a commitment by scholarly authors to share their knowledge as broadly as possible. Large digital collections could be shared cooperatively either by copying them into disks at other institutions or by allowing access via the Internet. As digital libraries begin to develop, however, the feasibility of establishing the kind of barter system that could enhance teaching and learning at comparable institutions seems difficult to achieve. The Digital Library Federation, a group of about 25 institutions that believe the future of libraries is digital, is currently debating whether to negotiate an implicit barter arrangement and open their digital collections to one another, or to work out a system of payments among the members.

The existing library model is the interlibrary loan system, which operates in an environment of both trust and suspicion. Some libraries make their book collections available at no charge to a certain group of partners, such as the members of the Research Libraries Group or the members of a state or regional consortium. Libraries from outside these stated groups are charged a fee for each transaction. All academic libraries typically charge corporate libraries. Some states, such as Pennsylvania and Texas, subsidize a certain number of libraries to serve the rest of the state at no charge. In the digital environment, Digital Library Federation members (all of whom have significant digital collections) might allow free access to those collections among themselves, but charge all other libraries for access.

Paper library models continue to dominate both librarian and educational administrative thinking. It is not easy to discount decades of being ranked in terms of the sheer number of physical volumes. Building similarly impressive numbers of online resources is now fashionable. Such collections would be safer if they resided simultaneously on a dozen sites rather than just one, and the cost of that expansion would be small. But the Universal Library project at Carnegie Mellon, which has offered to copy collections and host them at no charge, has had no acceptance. Clearly, ownership still involves physical control.

Cooperation among libraries has always been easy to discuss but difficult to achieve. Colleagues from India, China, Japan, Mexico, Scandinavia, and Saudi Arabia all agree on this difficulty. The difficulties arise from a fear that another educational institution will gain at the expense of the home institution. These institutions compete for students; for funding through grants, foundations; the government; and for faculty. It is not difficult to see why the libraries find cooperation somewhat unnatural, in spite of its many benefits.

Cooperation in the digital environment is cheaper and faster but just as hard to effect. As librarians realized that they could not collect everything they needed to support their students and faculty, interlibrary loans among academic institutions grew, became more efficient, and offered substantive supplements to local collections. However, charging for interlibrary loans also became an accepted practice. Typically, a college or university will have a list of no-charge partners—those who have significant collections to share in return—and will only charge institutions outside that cadre. Because for-profits do not have such collections, they have traditionally had to purchase their interlibrary loan services. One unpleasant truth about interlibrary loan is that, until recently, the cost of collecting the charges often exceeded the amount collected.

Universities' economic environment has changed enormously over the years. Recognition of corporate sponsors; activity fees; and charges for telephones, refrigerators, and data connections in dormitories have all provided new sources of revenue to academia. In the 21st century, micropayments will become a reality. While credit card holders typically charge 3 to 5% to vendors for processing payments, micropayment vendors (who will deal in fractions of cents) are contemplating charging 30%. While visionaries hope that micropayments for information will truly be micro (i.e., extremely small), having to pay a 30% surcharge will drive up the cost of information for digital library resources. And while micropayments for information would be consistent with universities' growing appetite for charging students for services, the question of the effect on learning deserves further discussion. Just because we can charge micropayments for information does not mean that charging them will support the best learning environment.

The typical paper library in a traditional university pays for the information used by its faculty and students. The just-in-case collection and just-in-time interlibrary loans are both funded by the institution's central administration. That practice encourages faculty and students to use as much information as necessary. As with all free and third party payer situations, some waste probably exists. In contrast, for-profit universities often provide students with an allowance for information. The effect of this rationing has yet to be assessed, but the two types of institutions' goals are so different that a one-on-one comparison would have limited value.

Only the simplest studies exist around the issue of charging for library resources. Early studies of charging for online searching and for the provision of interlibrary loan indicated that students would not pay additional charges for information. However, every library's long history with photocopiers proves that students will pay for the convenience of copying. Many universities are now finding that students will also pay for printing. If micropayments can appear to students to offer added convenience and truly be as small as the charges for photocopying and printing, the pricing of information for students in traditional institutions might begin to change without adverse effect.

Still, many students are relatively poor and will not have the resources to pay for the information they need, even though they know that they need it. These disadvantaged students will be further penalized in an environment where out-and-out payment is expected on top of tuition and other fees. Education historically has had a positive societal effect by enabling individuals to move from poverty into wealth. Charging for information will discourage that transformative effect. Further, some entire nations are poor and can benefit in the same way that individuals do from the free flow of information. Finally, some nations do not regard intellectual property as property, and cannot understand why they should not benefit fully from the increased knowledge being developed in all parts of the world.

The practical and expedient decision about charging for information via a micropayment system may not be the best decision for the long-term achievement of learning objectives, either. The philosophy behind libraries, both public and academic, has been that free access to information engenders progress on the individual and societal level. It is possible that creating a freely available, internationally accessible digital library can advance society significantly.

Dilemma Seven: The Economics of Scholarly Information

An overwhelming problem with the paper library at the traditional university is the escalating cost of information. David Shulenburger, provost of the University of Kansas, has summarized the problem: From 1986 to 1996, the consumer price index increased 44% while the price of health care went up 84%, both increases that are viewed as relatively significant. Meanwhile, the cost of scholarly journals outpaced both—increasing 148%, more than three times the rate of inflation. The bottom line is that libraries would need two and a half times their present budgets to stay current.

Several factors contribute to these untoward price increases. Faculty, whose research creates scholarly information, want to share it as widely as possible; they want it to be a free good. Yet the transfer of copyright gives much scholarly information to commercial publishers, whose market strategy is to maximize their profits. These publishers often make profits of more than 40% based on information that they received free from research faculty. The library operates as a third party payer, in which the library itself is not the customer; rather, the faculty member is. However, each faculty member considers only personal need and not the good of the whole university. Therefore, faculty are unwilling to reduce their own subscription lists because neither they nor their department is paying the bill. Further, journals do not substitute for each other, so the consumer cannot pick a lower-priced information source. A recent letter to the *New York Times* pointed out that the journal *Brain Research* costs more per pound than a Mercedes, and the marketplace does not provide a Ford-priced alternative (Published, but not paid, 1999). Normally, a marketplace with inflation at this rate will correct itself as consumers move to lower-cost alternatives, but such a correction has not corrected in the academic marketplace.

"To Publish and Perish" (Zemsky, 1998, p. 2), a special issue of *Policy Perspectives*, discusses issues around this continuing challenge and methodologies for resolving it.[2] Universities must collectively engage in several coordinated actions in order to ensure the future of a healthy scholarly communications system. *Policy Perspectives* recommends these actions:

- *End the preoccupation with numbers.* University promotion and tenure mechanisms need to focus on quality rather than quantity. Because faculty believe that the number of articles published is all that counts, they divide their research into its smallest components and publish as many articles as possible. This practice drives the proliferation of journals and raises costs. Publishing fewer articles of higher quality would alleviate part of the problem.

- *Be smart shoppers.* Libraries need to value agility over the sheer number of volumes and journal subscriptions and must work to shape a more coherent market for scholarly materials.

- *Get a handle on property rights.* Faculty need to be educated so that they can be agents of solutions around questions of copyright and publication.

- *Invest in electronic forms of scholarly communication.* The fundamental changes brought by the Internet offer the academic community an opportunity to engage in steady and fundamental change.

- *Decouple print publication and faculty evaluation for the purposes of promotion and tenure.* Scholars need to be able to submit major papers to either leading journals or relevant scholarly society referees for certification and electronic publication, with the knowledge that promotion and tenure committees will value the two means of dissemination equally (To Publish and Perish, 1998, pp. 5–10). If scholarly

---

[2]*http://www.arl.org/scomm/pew/pewrept.html.* Cosponsored by the Association for Research Libraries, the Association of American Universities, and the Pew Higher Education Roundtable. Discussed the challenge of maintaining access to research and scholarship when the price of information has increased three-fold in the last decade and the volume has also grown significantly. W. K. Kellogg foundation, The Pew Charitable Trusts, and the Gladys Krieble Delmas Foundation provided the funding for this incisive discussion of this critical issue facing the higher education and research communities.

societies would referee materials and mount them on the web instead of putting all of them through print publication, costs could be reduced and access increased. However, for this practice to take hold, refereed web articles must count equally with paper publishing for promotion and tenure.

All of these initiatives relate to the creation of the digital library and the transformation of higher education through technology. The most important and promising solution is the last one, involving the decoupling of print publication and faculty evaluation for the purposes of promotion and tenure. Implicit in this idea is the assumption that web resources and refereed electronic journals could begin to replace the print offerings, whose prices escalate so rapidly. Provosts at the California Institute of Technology conference (where the decoupling idea was developed) believed that universities were already spending enough money on scholarly communications to allow for a barter or gift exchange arrangement at no additional cost. However, it now seems that micropayments of some kind are a more likely alternative for financing this transformation (St. Clair, 1997). Certainly, as traditional and for-profit universities diverge, the for-profits are unlikely to produce resources that can be bartered and the traditional are unlikely to want to subsidize them with free knowledge.

Dilemma Eight: Copyright and Fair Use

Another serious dilemma surrounding the creation and success of digital libraries is existing copyright law. The purpose of copyright is to foster progress in the sciences and useful arts. Until 1976, U.S. copyright protection extended for 28 years; the author could then extend protection for another 28 years. The limit was later expanded to 75 years and, more recently, to 95 years because Disney Corporation's Mickey Mouse character was about to pass into the public domain. Colleagues in other countries report that their difficulties with copyright are just as serious as those in the United States. Around the world, the length of time that materials are likely to be out of print but still in copyright creates a serious barrier for the creation of a digital library.

Many libraries have begun their digital efforts with archival projects because they retain the rights to those materials. Others have focused their digital projects on older, out-of-copyright materials. The Digital Library Federation's Making of America project features materials from the Gilded Age (1870–1898); the Library of Congress's project digitizes materials related to the founding of the United States; and the University of Virginia's project deals with early American fiction. Carnegie Mellon University scanned the papers of the late Senator H. John Heinz III. All of these materials are in the public domain because of their dates or their origins, and can thus be scanned and made available for use by the scholarly community. In many disciplines, however, no such materials exist. Computer science, materials science, acoustical engineering, and many other disciplines have all developed since the 1920s. None of their most essential resources are yet in the public domain.

Circulation patterns in paper libraries indicate that more recent materials circulate more actively, and the shelves of most bookstores are filled with current works. Based on these findings, it seems that being able to scan in more recent materials is essential to the success of digital library initiatives. At Carnegie Mellon University, the Universal Library project mounted the texts of over 2,000 books published by the National Academy Press, the publishing arm of the National Academy of Science. These resources were difficult to read online and slow to print. As a result of this effort, the Press's sales, facilitated by a *Buy* button on the web site, rose 200%. The University of Pennsylvania is now engaged in a similar initiative with Oxford University Press.

Libraries need to engage in several initiatives around the legal copyright barrier. A Carnegie Mellon research project is currently taking a random sample of 400 books from the online catalog and contacting publishers to see whether they can obtain permission to scan them. Michael Shamos, director of the Universal Library project, is also considering the value of a copyright law provision that allows the creator to withdraw the copyright after 35 years have passed. Shamos, a copyright attorney as well as a computer scientist, thinks that the *Titanic phenomenon*—the sudden salability of books on a single topic because of a successful movie or event—will keep publishers from granting permission for copying until they can see the economic value.

Most books go out of print within two or three years of their publication. Thus, books published in 1999 may be out of print but under copyright for over 90 years. A system of micro payments might provide the correct incentive for publishers to allow such books to be digitized. Many faculty would favor this practice because desirable texts to support courses are often no longer available. Along these lines, the music industry currently uses a model of small payments back to the publisher and author, both from new arrangers and from performers. This payment system works well in the industry and has potential for application to other venues. Its acceptance in academia, however, would depend on the resolution of a number of the issues discussed above.

Dilemma Nine: Cost Factors—a Constituency Perspective

Costs are prohibitive in the digital library. The high prices charged by commercial sci-tech publishers who want libraries to subscribe to both paper and online copies of their journals, continue to rise. These publishers are eager to charge for the use of individual articles. Some have proposed an undiscounted rate of $30 per article. While the abstract would not be charged for because it is in the public domain, any browsing of the article itself would incur the charge. When science and engineering department heads at a prominent technological university were consulted about subscribing to the resource, they were offended at the $30 charge, especially because $20 of it is labeled as a copyright fee. Few scholarly authors, whose work fills these journals, see any part of this revenue. Large new sets in the humanities are equally expensive. The *New York Times* reports that the purchase price for the digital version of the complete *Early English Texts* will be $93,000 (Beamish, 1999); only the most affluent universities will be able to afford such resources, even though they will be in great demand.

A more comprehensive issue around costs is how publishers and other providers will charge for these commercial online resources. Understanding licenses, what to expect from licenses, how to negotiate them, and when to modify them is a new competency required of librarians. The vendor community has yet to settle on a model or group of models for selling digital resources. Two favored alternatives are based on the number of campus constituents (faculty, students, and staff) and by the number of simultaneous users. Both of these allow resources to be priced to the projected or actual needs of individual campuses. Other alternatives, which are more difficult to understand, are charging the same price for everyone regardless of size, pricing by geographical location, and pricing by individual use. Librarians are most reluctant to begin to pay by individual use because of the difficulties in being able to predict demand and, therefore, budget effectively. A recent pricing alternative from a major sci-tech vendor has caused some libraries to buy the resource but not make it available for campuswide use.

The cost of converting materials in existing paper formats is also high. Librarians have traditionally told their administrators that it cost $100–$500 per book to digitize materials. The arrival of a new generation of scanners in 1999 made librarians hopeful that disbound books could be scanned, have optical character recognition performed, and have bibliographic and identifying data attached for around $25 each. Experiments continue to reduce costs of scanning from paper.

Costs are also declining in other areas relevant to the digital library. Servers and, especially, storage are now much more affordable. Computer scientists believe that digital versions of all the information ever published in the world would fit onto a petabyte of disk storage. This petabyte would cost about $30 million at today's prices and would handily fit into a head librarian's office, but—as discussed in the opening chapter—the cost of such storage is expected to drop significantly over the next several years.

Despite the costs, if a cost-benefit analysis were to be performed on the digital library, it would seem cheap indeed. A book digitized for $25 and mounted on the World Wide Web, free to read, can be used by everyone around the world. Carnegie Mellon is currently making a popular title, *Numerical Recipes in C*, available free to read through its Universal Library project, where about six people an hour access it. Costs per use are infinitesimal and the benefits to those who regularly use this text are enormous.

Dilemma Ten: Cultural Implications

Four cultural issues are dilemmas in the full realization of digital libraries. First, faculty on promotion and tenure committees around the country must accept electronic refereed journals as equivalent to their paper counterparts. Hundreds of electronic journals in a variety of fields already exist. Yet, it is difficult to get faculty to agree that they are as prestigious as the paper journals. Even though their editors and editorial boards may be just as impressive, e-journals are not as old as their paper counterparts, their track records are not as well-established, and they lack the essential thump quality for tossing onto the desk of the department chair. In addition, faculty are skeptical that the online journals will be as permanent as paper, even though technological universities such as Carnegie Mellon believe that migration from system to system will preserve the full functionality of electronic materials into the future. Many faculty are taking this wait-and-see attitude about electronic journals at a time when libraries can afford to buy fewer and fewer journals in paper form.

A second cultural issue is the continued difficulty of reading from a computer screen. In 1999, the first e-books became commercially available. The products are interesting but they continue to be heavy, have poor screen contrast, and require proprietary formats for downloading resources. Nevertheless, e-books are here, and within five years will demonstrate that they can have greater functionality in many ways than their paper counterparts. This cultural problem will probably be resolved far sooner than faculty acceptance of electronic publication.

Related to the readability issue, on a positive note, is the convenience of online information. Students today are accustomed to fast-food restaurants, stop-and-go markets, personal TVs, and cell phones. They have little patience for traditional library service. The inconvenience of reading from the screen or printing what they want to read is greatly preferable to the inconvenience of going to the library during the hours it is open. As full-text online resources became available at different universities, the student response was extremely positive. They quickly demanded that indexes indicate which articles were available in full text so that they could go directly to them. Being able to work on their own timeframes and from their dormitories and apartments greatly increased their appreciation of convenient service.

A third cultural dimension of the digital library is its potential democratizing effect. Because information is power, it follows that democracies will demand equal access to information. In the same way that emerging societies have gone directly to satellite telephones rather than building telephone lines, they will also want to create digital libraries. With large bodies of quality scholarly information freely available worldwide, the next century may produce a hundred Einsteins instead of just one.

A fourth, more perplexing, cultural question is the complex issue of the future of traditional higher education (see chap. 2). Although many faculty and administrators wish otherwise, the entry of for-profit universities and the advent of computer-enhanced distance education will have profound and transformative impacts on the core nature of higher education. Affordable public and higher-priced private residential institutions dedicated to educating traditional-aged students will be increasingly threatened by these for-profit alternatives. The four-year regimen for traditional-aged students provided more than an education in a core curriculum and a traditional major. It also socialized the student into the cultural mores of middle class life. Its emphasis was more on building educated citizens than on creating employable workers, even though employability continued to be a parental concern.

Throughout the 20th century, statistics reinforced the value of a college education by indicating how much more a college graduate typically earned. The bachelor's degree provided a certificate that admitted holders into higher salary ranges. Having the degree was a prerequisite for being able to apply for many jobs, even though the company still might need to train the individual. As more and more jobs have shifted into the computer area, college certification has become less important, and competency has become the basis for hiring into high-paying positions. While some become competent through their own individualized study and experimentation, and others continue to earn college degrees in technical areas, many others seek education focused on giving them the precise competencies required in the marketplace. This shift fosters the success of for-profit education vendors.

As discussed above, the traditional college or university offers a traditional library, filled with books and journals that have been selected by librarians just in case students or faculty want to use them. In spite of all the changes in providing library services, the system of ranking libraries based on the number of volumes, the dollars expended, and the number of librarians and staff continues around the world. These just-in-case libraries also offered gracious spaces for learning and study and trained librarians dedicated to one-on-one instruction so students could learn how to find and use information. The just-in-time provision of resources through interlibrary loan became a powerful and essential supplement to traditional library collections.

In contrast, for-profit universities do not create just-in-case facilities, with inviting spaces and nurturing librarians. Instead, they often contract for the provision of online services, encouraging students to select materials from online databases, such as OCLC's FirstSearch, and to have resources delivered directly to them. Relying on just-in-time provision of resources in this way doubtless satisfies students' known and immediate demands, yet it offers no opportunities for the serendipity of considering the dozen books on the shelf beside the one identified from the online catalog. It bypasses that interaction with the librarian who is not only answering the stated reference query but also helping socialize the student to the discipline's scholarly communications structures and helping the student explore different methods of information seeking.

For-profit universities also implicitly rely on the World Wide Web to meet student information needs. Student information-seeking on the Web is perilous compared with that in the just-in-case library. Only five percent of resources on the Web are refereed in a discipline and, therefore, appropriate for use in traditional scholarly endeavors. Because students prefer to use digital information, this paucity of appropriate materials threatens both for-profit and traditional educational institutions. Many traditional libraries offer tutorials and instruction on discerning the better resources, and many faculty assign papers and projects that limit or preclude use of the web. Even though for-profits often teach in technological areas where refereeing is less entrenched, the reliability and validity of information are still important. The famous *New Yorker* cartoon, "On the Internet, nobody knows you're a dog" (Fleishman, 1998) continues to provide a succinct metaphor for the ability of individuals to represent themselves on the Web in any way they please.

Creating digital libraries that combine the convenience and accessibility of online information with the strict adherence to the value of discipline refereeing and librarian selection should be a priority for higher education. Such libraries offer the convenience and cachet that appeal to students, allow for worldwide access, can foster democratization of information if the economics are right, and could make the information age a golden age for the improvement of societies world-wide.

Despite the strong promise digital libraries hold, the paper library still has some strengths that should be recognized:

- *Socialization.* The traditional library was a place where students could socialize with each other, with their teachers, and certainly, with librarians and library staff who could assist them with their information-seeking behavior. Some librarians have argued that the library was a place where students could learn the knowledge-creating behavior of their discipline.

- *Serendipity.* Many scholars praise the traditional library for the serendipitous experiences they had there. By browsing in open stacks, they ran across books and journals whose contents mingled with their preconceived search results and created a far richer mix.

CONCLUSIONS

Ten dilemmas stand between our present state and the realization of a digital future, but the challenges of each can be overcome.

- Users and their needs will be defined as digital libraries progress and as user demands for more and more digital information are accepted.

- Research into the role of digital information in the teaching and learning process will demonstrate both its values and its drawbacks.

- A broad-based network of digital library reference librarians will offer round-the-clock service that is fully integrated into the fabric of technology-based teaching and learning.

- Priorities in collection development will be set locally, consortially, and internationally as the demand for digital libraries grows.

- Creating and preserving a viable archive to carry digital resources into the next millenium (Y3K) will become an important new academic library responsibility.

- New models of ownership and payment will evolve; the educational value of no-charge information should outweigh the expediency of charging micropayments.

• The scholarly communications system will be reformed to allow information to flow more freely; decoupling print publication from faculty evaluation and allowing for refereed web presentation will be an important step.

• Innovative alternatives will be developed to allow materials that are out of print but still under copyright to continue to serve their purposes.

• Creating the digital library is expensive, yet the breadth of its benefits will justify the expense.

• Cultural factors, such as promotion, tenure-committee acceptance of electronic publications, readability, the democratizing effect of digital libraries, and the changing higher-education landscape, will continue to evolve.

The factors drawing libraries into digitization are infinitely more powerful and sustainable than are the barriers to a digital future. The potential of access, the demand for convenience, and the cultural advantages of digital libraries outweigh the many difficulties and costs. Libraries have been bottomless pits in the paper environment, but digital libraries can become shining towers that broadcast information to stimulate the spread of democracy and the flowering of genius. The costs of making all information available to everyone digitally are staggering, but the benefits to society should justify them from every academic administrator's view.

REFERENCES

Angelo, T. A. (1997). The campus as a learning community: Seven promising shifts and seven powerful levers. *AAHE Bulletin, 49*, 9, 3–6.

Beamish, R. (1999). On-line archive will preserve earliest English books. *New York Times*, July 29, p. 7.

Carbo, T. (1998). Preface. In M. T. Wolf and others (Eds.), *Information imagineering: Meeting at the interface*, (p. x). Chicago: American Library Association.

Chickering, A.W., & Ehrmann, S. C. (1996). Implementing the seven principles: Technology as lever. *AAHE Bulletin, 49*, 2, 3–6.

Ehrmann, S. C. (1995). Asking the right question: What does research tell us about technology and higher learning? *Change, 27*, 20–27.

Ferguson, C. D., & Bunge, C. A. (1997). The shape of services to come: Values-based reference service for the largely digital library. *College & Research Libraries, 58*, 252–265.

Fleishman, G. (1998) New Yorker cartoons to go on line. *New York Times*, October 29, p. 10.

Hazen, D. C., Horrell, J. L., & Merrill-Oldham, J. (1998). *Selecting research collections for digitization*. Washington, DC: Council on Library Resources.

LaGuardia, C., & Mitchell, B. (Eds.). (1998). *Finding common ground: Creating the library of the future without diminishing the lilbrary of the past*. New York: Neal-Schuman Publishers.

Lehmann, K. (1996) Making the transitory permanent: The intellectual heritage in a digitized world. *Daedalus, 125,* 307–330.

Lesk, M. (1997). *Practical digital libraries: Books, bytes, and bucks*. San Francisco: Morgan Kaufman.

Lieberman, H. (1997). Autonomous interface agents. *ACM Conference on Computers and Human Interface, CHI 97.* March 22–27, 1997, http://lieber.www.media.mit.edu/people/lieber/Lieberary/Letizia/AIA/AIA.html.

Lipow, A. G. (1999). "In your face" reference service. *Library Journal, 124,* 50–52.

Marcum, D. B. (1998). We can't save everything. *New York Times,* July 6, p. A11, col. 3.

Metzl, J. F. (1996). Searching for the catalog of catalogs. *Daedalus, 125,* 147–160.

Miller, W. (1984). What's wrong with reference: Coping with success and failure at the reference desk. *American Libraries, 15,* 303–306, 321–322.

Mintzer, F. (1999). Developing digital libraries of cultural content for Internet access. *IEEE Communications, 37,* 72–78.

Munn, R. F. (1989). The bottomless pit, or the academic library as viewed from the administration building. *College & Research Libraries, 50,* 635–637.

Nardi, B. A., & O'Day, V. L. (1999). *Information ecologies*. Cambridge, MA: MIT Press.

Peek, R. P. (1998). Miss web manners on digital libraries. *Information Today, 15,* 36.

Published, but not paid. (1999). Letter to *New York Times,* March 7, p. 14, col. 6.

Rieh, S. Y. (1999). Changing reference service environment: A review of perspectives from managers, librarians, and users. *Journal of Academic Librarianship, 25,* 178–186.

Rothenberg, J. (1999). *Avoiding technological quicksand: Finding a viable technical foundation for digital preservation*. Washington, DC: Council on Library Resources.

Saffady, W. (1995). Digital library concepts and technologies for the management of library collections. *Library Technology Reports, 31,* 221–380.

Saunders, T. (Writer, Producer, Director). (1997). *Into the future: On the preservation of knowledge in the electronic age*. American Film Foundation, Saunders & Mock Productions in association with Commission on Preservation & Access and American Council of Learned Societies.

St. Clair, G. (1997). Innovations for a scholarly communications system. *Editorial in Journal of Academic Librarianship, 23,* 355.

Tyckoson, D. A. (1999). What's right with reference? *American Libraries, 30,* 57û63.

Williamson, S. R. (1996). When change is the only constant: Liberal education in the age of technology. *Educom Review, 31,* 39û41.

Zemsky, R. (Ed.). (1998). To publish and perish (Special issue). *Policy Perspectives, 7*(4).

Chapter 6

Creating Organizational and Technological Change

Paul S. Goodman
Carnegie Mellon University

University A offers extensive training to its faculty in using technology to enhance learning. Workshops and materials are available on multimedia applications, Web-based courses, and so on. However, six months after the training, there is little evidence of any change in learning inside the classroom or out.

University B has announced a grant program to support professors in developing new technology-based learning. The program is announced and publicized. Proposals are received from 1 to 2 percent of the faculty. The projects are completed, and most lead to changes in learning environments. The program is continued for two more years, with similar levels of participation and results. Although the completed projects have changed specific learning environments, their effects remain isolated, and there has been little diffusion of knowledge or applications from those projects.

University C has established a new center for learning. The goal of the center is to stimulate and redesign new learning environments. Over a three-year period, the center has produced some new educational software and helped redesign portions of courses. However, a majority of the administration and faculty are either unaware of the center or do not see how its work is related to the work of teaching in this university.

*T*hese are three actual cases about changes in university settings designed to improve education and learning. The motivation behind each was to improve the university's effectiveness at utilizing new educational and technological environments. The results of these change interventions were less than expected. Time, resources, and people were invested, but the goals of improving education and learning at the university were not realized. Creating effective organizational change with new technology that enhances organizational performance is difficult. Quite frankly, there seem to be many more accounts of failures than successes. But there are solutions.

This chapter is about creating effective change in educational institutions. The organizations in question are universities or other tertiary institutions. The object of change is new learning environments shaped by technology. The goal is to improve effectiveness in education and learning. I approach this goal by acknowledging that creating effective change is difficult to begin with, and creating effective changes in universities is even more difficult.

In working with different universities around the world, I have found some central questions university presidents ask about change:

- *Students.* In what ways will technology facilitate or inhibit learning processes? Will the student be a more active designer and participant in the learning processes? Will technology permit new forms of learning? How can I get students to work effectively in nontraditional classrooms? How will new technological environments affect the social aspects of learning? Do we need new approaches to assess these effects?

- *Professors.* What will be the professor's role? How can I encourage my faculty to experiment and adopt new forms of technology for the classroom? How can I get them to change?

- *Institutions.* How do I change the physical and technological infrastructure of the university to meet the needs of faculty and students? How can we obtain resources in the light of constantly changing technology? How should the structure and governance of the university change as technology permits learning opportunities that bridge space and time? How will the deliverers of postsecondary education change as a function of new technology?

You should note that these frequently asked questions often focus only on faculty, students, or infrastructure as objects of change. Commonly, people thinking about change only think about changing people or objects and not about changing the broader system of the university as the object of change (e.g., its culture, reward systems). It is important to think about changing the university as well as the other stakeholders.

Other, broader, questions that underlie this discussion about creating change in universities include:

- What will or should our university look like 5 to 10 years from today? What is the changing market for postsecondary education? How do I move the university toward that future state?
- What are the critical learning processes, and how will technology change these processes? What are effective change strategies to create these new learning environments?

I present all these questions and the cases to provide an initial way to frame the problem statement for this chapter. I want to sharpen the understanding of creating change in a university setting. To accomplish this, a set of conceptual tools will be presented, drawn from the extensive literature on organizational change (c.f., Argyris 1985, 1990; Beer, Eisenstat, & Spector, 1990; Lawler, 1986, 1992; March, 1991; Mohrman, Mohrman, Ledford, Lawler, & Cummings, 1989; Nadler, Gerstein, & Shaw, 1992; Nadler, Shaw, & Walton, 1995; Pfeffer, 1994). My focus will be around creating new technology-enhanced learning (TEL) environments. I think of these TEL environments very broadly. They may include a computer-based demonstration of cell structure in biology in a traditional classroom, an intelligent tutor in algebra, a virtual chemistry lab, a virtual university, asynchronous Web-based courses in software engineering, a graduate seminar across multiple time zones, digital libraries, and more. One wants to think more systematically about these different learning environments than simply generating lists. Chapters 1 and 2 and the following section provide some frameworks for organizing our thinking on this topic.

My focus also will be on tertiary institutions, with a particular emphasis on universities as organizations. Note that I use the term *universities* with some caution. In the United States alone, there are more than 10,000 postsecondary institutions. Within this group lie private and public institutions: two-year and four-year degree-granting institutions, some accredited and others not, some solely for undergraduates, some for graduate and undergraduate students, and others that are only graduate-level. From these, approximately 660 offer doctoral degrees, and a smaller set may be described as research universities. The basic idea here is to illustrate the enormous diversity we face. If one ventures into tertiary institutions in other countries, the number of institutions is smaller but the variety is the same. In thinking about the effects of TEL environments, organizational context makes a difference. At one level, creating change in a large public research university is different from creating change in a small liberal arts college. Creating change in a five-year-old university in Peru is probably different from trying to introduce new learning environments to a 100-year-old university in Chile. At a different level, there are some common issues and processes in creating change, and that will be our level of analysis. I acknowledge the diversity, but believe there are some common tools that will help the people who are responsible for creating change in these institutions, including the formal leaders of these organizations, the designers of new learning environments, and the faculty and students.

RATIONALE

Why worry about creating change in universities? Why focus on new TEL learning environments? Universities are remarkably stable institutions that, in many cases, exemplify the concept of institutional inertia. Despite predictions to the contrary from many of the futurists (Toffler, 1970), the basic structure and process of universities have remained relatively unchanged over many decades. However, whereas institutional inertia almost universally affects the postsecondary institution, there is a set of critical external factors that demand improvement in our ability to create effective change in these organizations.

First, the environment of universities is changing, and this is a powerful force for change. From chapter 1, you should have a dramatic picture of the changes happening in technology. These are fundamental shifts that create new opportunities to alter the basic structure and function of universities. The dramatic rise in computing power and corresponding drop in costs can change the equation of where, how, and when we get our education.

Another environmental change comes in the form of new competitors (see chap. 2). The proliferation of corporate universities represents one example. Some profit-oriented firms market and deliver university courses; others claim to be the content and delivery experts, while the university serves as the knowledge expert. The expansion and diversity of these content and delivery providers reflects, in part, changing customer needs. People are moving away from spending the four years between 18 and 22 in a single institution and are instead seeking knowledge at different times and in different places. Profit-making organizations will respond to this change and take away certain market segments from tertiary institutions. In addition to the new competitors, the old competitors—other tertiary institutions—will be armed with a new set of technology-driven tools that give them new access to the students and revenue that you once claimed.

Changes in demographics also put pressure on tertiary institutions to change. Potential new students, now and in the future, will have grown up in an *edutainment* environment. To reach these students, universities will need to change their traditional methods of delivering education. In the adult population, given the growing propensity toward more boundaryless careers, there is a growing need for education on demand. Will universities adapt to this form of learning? The forces in the tertiary institutions' environment are both powerful and evolving. Unless the educational institutions are able to change, the death rates of these institutions will rise.

Another motivator for thinking more carefully about organizational change is the *productivity paradox* (Harris, 1944). This paradox basically asserts there is little connection between investments in information technology and productivity benefits. Most of the research on this phenomenon has been in the industrial sector at industry and firm levels of analysis. Now, you might ask why is that finding relevant for understanding changes in universities? While research in this area is providing a better understanding where benefits might accrue, there are still many examples of where investments in information technology have not led to expected benefits. We are focusing on investments in new TEL learning environments in order to enhance the objectives of our institutions. Why should the productivity paradox not apply to educational institutions?

Recognize that the productivity paradox is a complicated phenomenon. Some of its contributing factors include the adoption of inappropriate technology, failed implementation of these new technologies, or the isolated introduction of technologies that had little impact on the organization as a whole. I need only remind the reader of the very large literature dealing with unsuccessful implementations of new technologies (c.f., Beatty & Gordon, 1988; Bikson, 1987; Bikson, Gutek, & Mankin, 1987; Cooper & Zmud, 1990; Ettlie, 1984; Lucas, 1981; Tornatzky, Eveland, Boylan, Hetzner, Johnson, Roitman, & Schneider, 1983; Walton, 1989). More recent literature (cf. Goodman, 2000) focuses on why successful changes in one unit or level may have no impact on the overall organization. The productivity paradox is relevant for educational institutions. For that reason, we need to understand the organizational change processes that will enhance the impact of TEL environments on the educational objectives of tertiary institutions.

ROAD MAP

This chapter is organized around several themes. First, we examine the context for change—the university and the TEL environments. Here, we explore the unique features of universities and the dimensions of new TEL environments. Next we explore some basic types of changes. These range from incremental changes to some fundamental changes in the identity of the educational institution. The second major section focuses on the change process. The chapter concludes with some critical dilemmas in creating effective change. Table 6.1 provides a brief overview of our framework for change—preconditions and critical processes.

PRECONDITIONS FOR ORGANIZATIONAL CHANGE

The University

Because our focus is on institutions of higher education, it is probably useful to remind ourselves about the features of these institutions. Earlier, we acknowledged the diversity in tertiary institutions. However, understanding the commonalities among them is clearly a critical precondition for creating effective change.

What are some features of universities, and how do these impact change? First, we can think of universities as a community of faculties, each of which is quite diverse. The work and education (i.e., the production function) in an art department differs from that of a physics department. The work of chemical engineers differs from that of marketing professors. These faculties also are often loosely grouped—the work of the physics department, for example, is fairly independent of the music department. This is not a tightly integrated organization moving in one unified direction.

Second, the principal producers—the professors—are relatively autonomous. Their work as educators has considerable freedom around what and how to teach. While the relative autonomy of the professor varies across institutions and countries, this concept of autonomy distinguishes professors from other occupations. They may show allegiance not only to a university, but also to an external professional community. This loyalty to one's discipline

TABLE 6.1 Framing Organizational Change

Preconditions for Change	Defining the unique features of a university—sources of inertia
	Identifying different learning environments
	Selecting a strategic form of change
Critical Processes in Achieving Change	Planning
	Implementation
	Institutionalization

weakens the university's ability to shape and change its professors. Attempts to change behavior, such as university reward systems, rarely produce major results. Indeed, the principal reward in the U.S.—tenure—reinforces autonomous behavior and eliminates the need for major changes in work.

Although some of a university's outputs are operational, such as the number of students graduated, other measures of effectiveness are more ambiguous. The quality of education provided to the class of 2001 is difficult to assess. It is also hard to quantify the time lag between environmental changes, organizational reactions, and their consequences for the university. The market forces that lead to sudden drops in market share or profitability in industrial firms seem absent in most university settings.

Universities are focused on creating knowledge in particular disciplines and serving as repositories for and presenters of such knowledge. The process of scanning and assessing a university's broader environment has not been well developed. Although there have been many dramatic changes in technology, globalization, and demographic composition in the last 50 years, universities have been slow to adapt to the world's changing needs and demands (Williams, 1999). This organizational inertia is due to the characteristics described above—the autonomy and loose coupling of faculty and departments, the tenure system used to reward faculty, dual allegiances to the institution and one's professional colleagues, etc. As former Carnegie Mellon University President Richard Cyert once said, "People say it's easier to move a cemetery than it is to move a faculty." (Changing Nature of Work Video Series, 1996) He might as well have said the same thing about universities.

These basic features and their implications for change should be self-evident. My goal is to make these features salient as educators work through the stages and dilemmas of creating change. The agent of change must think of these general features and how they take specific form in his or her own institution.

The Learning Environment

The second critical contextual element is the nature of the learning environment. In many conversations, meetings, and symposia, I have been struck by the ambiguity surrounding the concept of TEL environments. For many, it is a concrete thing such as a videoconference or Web-based course. Obviously, that is a restrictive picture. The map we develop about learning environments is another precondition for organizational change. There is not one map, but many legitimate different meanings. Earlier chapters by Raj Reddy and Paul Goodman (chap. 1) and Richard Larson and Glenn

Strehle (chap. 2) have provided some input for articulating forms of learning environments.

Let me suggest some dimensions for conceptualizing learning environments. The first is space and time. Figure 6.1 provides a simple view of where and when learning can happen, a preliminary map. Basically, this table provides a preliminary map of where and when learning can unfold. There are many options in each cell and in combinations across cells. The traditional classroom typically has been organized around the delivery-receiving mode (Cell 1), in which the professor delivers information and the students receive it. However, even in this traditional setting, computers can be used to provide students with opportunities to visualize phenomena that have, in the past, been presented only through words and text. Ruth Chabay's electronic hockey example (Chabay, 1995) provides a useful way to understand physics principles of Columb's law and Newton's second law, the superposition principle. Jack Wilson's studio concept (chap. 10) provides another example of innovative classroom learning. Cell 2 pictures students learning in distributed settings at the same time. On one hand, this is an old environment that first appeared in correspondence courses decades ago and appears today in courses that are delivered by video conferencing or as streaming lectures over the Web. Chapter 7 describes one of the most advanced virtual universities using these types of technologies. Cell 3 captures the role of computer-based systems for learning. Chapter 8 describes a computer-based environment for learning finance. Chapter 9 captures the role of intelligent tutors in improving learning and educational perfor-

TIME

		Same	Different
SPACE	Same	1 Classroom Learning	3 Computer-based Systems
	Different	2 Distributed Learning	4 Asynchronous Learning

FIG. 6.1. Learning environments by space and time.

mance. Cell 4 deals with asynchronous forms of learning. Here, students are distributed geographically and do their educational work at different times.

Figure 6.2 focuses on the second dimension of learning environments: what people are learning, not so much in terms of specific content but whether that learning is largely explicit or tacit (Nonaka & Takeuchi, 1995). Explicit knowledge is knowledge you are aware of and can articulate or explain to another person. The mode of delivery is based on transferring explicit knowledge. On the other hand, tacit knowledge represents things you understand that may be quite important, but cannot be articulated or presented to another. In developing a map for changing learning environments, the distinction between explicit or tacit knowledge is important, and so are the mechanisms for converting tacit to explicit or vice versa.

Let us think about learning to play an instrument. My teacher can give me information (explicit to explicit) about the structure of scales or whether I am playing a Chopin prelude at the right speed or sound. But other aspects of playing this composition cannot be explained, although my instructor understands them. Perhaps by watching and listening to others play this piece, I can either intuitively acquire new insights about playing this particular piece (converting tacit information into tacit knowledge) or, over time, I may be able to induce from observation some explicit principles used by my instructor (tacit to explicit). Additionally, by mastering several Chopin preludes, I may acquire some tacit ideas that may affect how I play other pieces by Chopin (explicit to tacit).

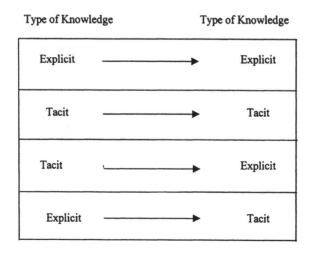

FIG. 6.2. Forms of knowledge conversions.

I introduce this idea of explicit-tacit conversions because it is fundamental to creating effective change. If you think about learning as the delivery of explicit knowledge, it leads you down one path toward change. If you think about learning in terms of the conversions in Fig. 6.2, you will create different change paths. These are not simply academic distinctions; they are important preconditions to effective change.

The third dimension related to mapping learning environments focuses on our basic assumptions about learning. How do people learn? Note that I do not expect change agents in universities to acquire complicated theories of learning. Rather, I want the reader to think about the question and be able to articulate some basic principles and their implications. In chapter 3, Herb Simon suggests some features underlying how people learn.

- Learning depends wholly on what the student does, only indirectly on what the teacher or university does.
- We must use technology only when we can see how it will enable us to do the educational job better.
- Information is no longer the scarce factor in human learning ... the scarce factor is human time ...
- In designing courses ... for our students, we must apply ruthlessly principles of sampling.
- Humans process information serially. Increasing mental loads inhibits effective learning

A very different perspective comes from the work of John Seeley Brown and his associates (Brown & Duguid, 1995). They argue that people learn in "communities of practice," typically informal, self-designed groups in which people share information, tell stories, and observe. As Brown says:

> A community view ... allows a more rounded view of what learning ... is and how it happens. A delivery view assumes knowledge is made up of discrete, preformed units, which learners ingest.... People don't become physicists by learning formulas.... In learning how to be a physicist—how to act as one, talk as one, be recognized as one—it is not the explicit statement, but the implicit practices that count. (Brown & Duguid, 1995, p. 9)

I could give other examples; however, the point of this section is that developing a map of learning environments is a necessary condition for effective change. It is probably not useful to think about learning environments solely as things (e.g., video conferencing, Web-based courses). As Fig. 6.1 illustrates, there are many types of environments. Figure 6.2 challenges you to be more clear about what you want people to learn. Finally, the discussion on learning assumptions pushes you to further clarify your map. If you believe the assumptions about communities of practice, your strategic choices about changing learning environments will be very different than they will be if you are grounded in the delivery-receiving mode of education.

The basic precondition for change is that one needs to be explicit about the intersection between the mode of delivery, the forms of knowledge (explicit-tacit conversions) and assumptions about how these people learn. Failure to understand this intersection will significantly harm any change effort.

Forms of change

The third precondition for change considers the form of change. Given an analysis of the organizational context of the university and the nature of the learning environment, one must consider the strategic form of change. The recent literature on organizational change has paid some attention to different forms of change (Nadler et al., 1995; Weick & Quinn, 1999). Figure 6.3 represents one typology (Nadler et al., 1995). One basic theme is that some organizational changes build on work already done, attempting to make small, incremental changes. Incremental changes represent the continuation of ongoing change within the organization and may require a large or small amount of resources. Another form of change, known as discontinuous change, occurs when an organization makes a fundamental break with the past and undertakes a major restructuring. Nadler et al. (1995) introduce a second theme based on whether the change strategy is reactive or proactive. Proactive means the organizations plan ahead and anticipate the need to make changes. Reactive strategies occur when changes in the environment, competitors, or other forces spur the organization to change.

As illustrated in Fig. 6.3, these two themes generate four different change strategies. Some strategies are incremental and proactive. Another strategy represents reactive-discontinuous change. In this case, changes in the environment cause fundamental changes in the environment. The other two cases represent reactive incremental change and proactive discontinuous change.

Why consider these types of change? First, it is one way to think about change in organizations. Second, the forms of change have different implications. In incremental change, the force of change can be internal, while in discontinuous change, one typically needs to understand major environmental forces and develop future strategies. In incremental change, the focus is on parts of the organization. In discontinuous change, the whole system is the object of change. The level of stress, trauma, and dislocation is much stronger in discontinuous change. The role of senior leadership is more fundamentally proactive in discontinuous change.

	Incremental	Discontinuous
Proactive	1	3
Reactive	2	4

FIG. 6.3.   Forms of change.

Why worry about discontinuous change? Universities are prime examples of institutional inertia, where discontinuous change seldom occurs. Are we not really talking about anticipatory or reactive incremental change when we focus on postsecondary institutions? First, I introduced this typology because I want the people responsible for change to think about alternative forms of change. Second, while changes in tertiary institutions have been incremental in the past, for some, more discontinuous change may be important for survival or effectiveness in the future. Earlier in the chapter, I noted many new competitors that are beginning to gain market share in areas previously considered the domain of universities. Changes in technology and demographic factors also call for more fundamental changes. Some universities already are spending more time recreating their identity in a fundamental way (chap. 7 captures a movement to discontinuous change models). In the future, discontinuous change may be an important strategic choice in order to offset the forces of inertia and respond to the changing environment. This third precondition is introduced to stimulate change agents in tertiary institutions to consider alternative forms of change. Perhaps in the past, the only strategic choice was around making proactive or reactive incremental changes. The future challenge for the university will be to consider all forms of strategic change.

CHANGE PROCESSES

We have explored a number of preconditions for change:

- Defining the unique features of a university and forces for inertia
- Identifying different learning environments
- Selecting a strategic form of change

The task for a change agent is to take a position on each of these three issues. In doing so, you must consider the unique features of your university and the inherent forces driving its inertia. What are the basic elements of the learning environment—is there an emphasis on explicit or tacit knowledge? What is the strategic form of change you want to produce?

The next step is to review some of the basic processes in creating effective change. While there are many processes discussed in the literature, I will examine three:

- Planning
- Implementation
- Institutionalization

For each process, I will provide a definition, selectively report some findings from the literature, and discuss both tactics and dilemmas in actualizing this process. I will use examples to illustrate these points. You should select some of your own to make the processes more concrete and accessible.

Let me add one other important observation. Change is not a linear rational process. It is chaotic and random, with many exogenous shocks. Phases begin and abruptly stop. We may move from phase one to phase two, before reverting to phase one even though some aspects of phase three are in operation. The problem in writing a chapter like this is that it is linear and seemingly rational. The phases of change do not work that way.

Planning

Planning is the basic process for setting up any change (see Table 6.2.) It comprises two elements: defining the appropriate stakeholders and aligning the organization for change.

1. *Defining the appropriate stakeholder(s) for change.* Before designing or implementing a new TEL environment, one must identify the critical players. The research literature on creating new technological environments (cf, Goodman & Griffith, 1991; Leonard–Barton, 1987,

TABLE 6.2   Summary of Change Process

Planning	Identifying appropriate stakeholders
	Aligning change interventions and the human, organizational, and technological systems
Implementation	Creating motivation-commitment to offset:
	— resistance to change
	— paradox of value
	Creating socialization processes to reflect and align:
	— different stakeholders
	— different types of learning
	— different learning mechanisms
	Creating feedback and redesign processes to recalibrate change
Institutionalization	Creating motivation and commitment to energize
	— new participants
	— old participants
	by finding new combinations of rewards and reward distribution mechanisms
	Creating socialization processes to reflect:
	— new participants
	— changing knowledge requirements
	Creating feedback and redesign processes to reflect:
	— unexpected external and internal changes
	— natural growth and evolution of the change processes
	Creating diffusion to extend the values, beliefs, and activities of the change to other parts of the organization

1988) has found that focusing solely on the end user will lead to ineffective implementation of technology. For example, we studied the implementation of a new technology that by any objective standard should have improved the effectiveness of a manufacturing organization (Goodman & Griffith, 1991). Millions of dollars were invested, but the new technology was never fully utilized. One explanation was that the change process focused solely on the users while many other stakeholders (e.g., designers, maintainers of the technology) should have been involved in the change process. These excluded stakeholders eventually undermined the company's investment.

In our context, let us say that we wanted to introduce the FAST system described in chapter 8 into a university setting. FAST is an exciting approach to teaching financial analysis that now operates in more than 15 countries. Yet I observed the attempted introduction of this learning system in another university, where it failed. One reason was the organization's failure to define the appropriate social system for making the change. Including the faculty person and the students was the right place to begin. But one also needed to include the other faculty members in this discipline, as well as technical support personnel, members of the university administration, alumni, and members of the financial community. Without the real involvement of these people, the introduction of this new learning environment was almost certain to fail.

There are some obvious questions. How do you know who should be in the social system? Do the appropriate stakeholders shift over time? There are no simple answers to these questions, but there is a research literature on change that provides guidance on selecting stakeholders. Just by doing a simple network analysis of the FAST learning environment or reviewing other applications of this learning model, it would have been possible to identify the key stakeholders.

2. *Aligning the organization.* I opened this chapter with a story about a university that trained its faculty in TEL, but experienced little change. This was an example of a single system intervention (training). A basic theme of the research literature is that multiple system interventions are likely to be more effective. But success is not contingent simply on the introduction of factors such as training rewards, support systems, and new technology, but also on the alignment of these multiple system interventions.

One dominant theory in the change literature revolves around sociotechnical analysis. The essence of this position is that it is better to change both the technical and social aspects of an organization rather than focusing on any one system. Some of the work by MacDuffie and associates (MacDuffie, 1995; MacDuffie & Pil, 1997) illustrates this point through the study of automobile plants all over the world. One interesting question this research addresses is whether investments solely in new technology improve productivity. The answer is generally no. If the plants changed both their organizational and technological environments, the change was more effective.

What do automobile factories have to do with universities? Actually, a lot. The basic principles of sociotechnical analysis are relevant. Figure 6.4 provides a simple representation of three aspects of sociotechnical systems. First, the human component deals with capabilities, defined in terms of knowledge, skills, motivation, and values. Second, the organizational components include strategy, organizational structure, decision-making systems, reward systems, training systems, leadership culture, etc. Finally, technology refers to the university's infrastructure and the platforms for the new learning environment. The basic principle is that these three factors need to be aligned before effective change can take place. For example, let us say we want to build a new collaborative learning community where people in distributed environments can work and learn. In this case, I am not talking about e-mail or chat groups, but a broader technological environment where people can have real conversations (not just exchange text), communicate their feelings, communicate both asynchronously and synchronously, talk in different languages but have real time conversations, and so on. (See Brown and Duguid, 1995, for a description of such an environment.) Figure 6.4 informs us that the human, organizational, and technological systems must align in order to achieve effective change. If the dominant organizational culture is hierarchical or individualistic, the reward or organization support systems primarily support a delivery-receiving

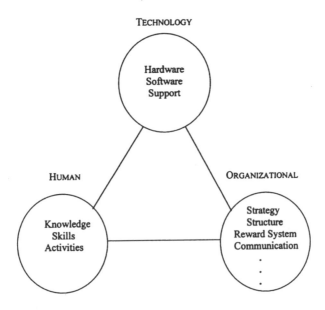

FIG. 6.4. A sociotechnical system.

mode of education, or the basic technological infrastructure is not supportive, the new collaborative learning environment is unlikely to survive. Also,
it will be difficult to build a collaborative learning environment with a
top-down change strategy.

Identifying the relevant stakeholders and designing change around the
alignment of human, organizational, and technological dimensions are the
key planning processes.

Implementation

This is probably the most-studied process in the change literature. It refers to
the process by which concepts, methods, or new learning environments are
put into practice. Although there is a long list of factors that may affect implementation success—the availability of resources, top management support,
nature of the technology, and organizational culture (Leonard–Barton, 1987,
1988; Ettlie, 1984), I will focus on a few processes that seem to drive the implementation. (See Table 6.2.)

> 1. *Motivation-commitment.* The simplest way to think about change is
> that it moves you from one state to another. An interesting concept
> proposed by social psychologist Kurt Lewin is that change starts by *un-
> freezing.* In other words, the forces keeping a person in one state are re-
> laxed and the person moves to another state. In the context of this
> chapter, let us say that unfreezing permits one to move from a deliv-
> ery-receiving mode of education to a collaborative mode of education.
> Another way to think about unfreezing is that motivators (positive
> and negative) hold a person in one state. When these motivators are
> changed, the individual moves to a new state and (depending on the
> motivating factors) may remain in the new state, or revert to the ear-
> lier state, or find another state.
>
> Let us be more concrete. Remember the three examples earlier in
> this chapter. Training was provided regarding new learning environ-
> ments, but there was no change in learning environments. Grants
> were provided to create new TEL innovations, but there were few tak-
> ers. A new center to support innovations in learning was created, but
> again, there were few innovations. In all of these examples, there was
> no unfreezing, and people remained in their current state.
>
> Motivation-commitment processes are central to any change effort,
> but they are particularly important at two points in the implementation
> process. The first deals with the above examples of unfreezing, and the
> second deals with moving to a new state.

When unfreezing does not occur and no new exploration is initiated, it is often labeled resistance to change. This is an unfortunate use of words, because it has a negative connotation and implies some level of irrationality. Actually, professors who do not change to new learning environments are acting quite rationally—such changes often bring outcomes that people experience as undesirable (e.g., uncertainty, more work). Based on the research on change (cf. Rousseau, 1995), we know that:

- Gains and losses are subjectively understood.
- Losses are more painful than gains are good.
- With change, losses often come before gains are realized.
- Losses affect important dimensions such as self-identity, competence, rewards, power, and social relationships.

All of this is not to say that change never happens. The essential thing is to understand the structure of and relationships between losses and gains. One implication for initiating change might be to focus more on reducing losses than on advertising the gains (a typical tactic in implementation). Another option may be to create a way that key stakeholders can actively scan the environment and learn about new learning environments. I use the words *actively scan* because people need to see, touch, and feel these environments in order to understand the gap between current and possible future learning states. Powerful opinion leaders within the university community can articulate and build some shared understanding about these new environments. The observed commitment of the senior administrators is another factor. These and other tactics might create the unfreezing and movement to another state.

Assuming that unfreezing occurs, another motivational-commitment issue arises when one begins operating in this new state or environment. This is called the paradox of value, and it is inherent in any change implementation (Sproull & Hofmeister, 1989). The basic argument is that in introducing new forms of change, there is a tendency to build expectations about the benefits and understate the costs. Because at least initially, the experienced costs are likely to be higher and benefits lower, this will lead to a discrepancy between expectations and experience. The greater the discrepancy, the more negative people will be about the change. The longer the discrepancy lasts, the less likely the change will be viable.

The initial levels of motivation and commitment within the organization will buffer the effects of any discrepancy. That is, people will be more tolerant of the discrepancy between expected benefits and costs. Finding ways to ensure high motivation and commitment levels is critical in the new learning environments. Some tactics to enhance commitment and motivation, which will offset some of the negative effects generated by the paradox of value, include participating in the design of the change process, serving as teachers, and facilitating diffusion of the new changes throughout the institution.

2. *Socialization.* Socialization is another key process in the effective implementation of new learning environments. This process deals with acquiring new knowledge, skills, and values to effectively operate in the new setting.

Consider the following case: At Carnegie Mellon, there is a learning environment that requires students to operate a company as a team. A complicated computer environment allows the students to make real-time decisions about production, marketing, and advertising in a world where they compete with other student-run companies. In addition, the companies negotiate with real union negotiators over a labor contract, go to banks for loans, and report to a board of directors. The goal of the game is to have students learn how to integrate the major business functions in a real-time decision-making context. At this time, the game is played by students who are colocated. The new change is to have students work in a virtual environment. Teams or companies will have people in different locations, a substantial challenge.

What is the role of socialization in this new learning environment? First, the targets of socialization need to be identified. This is the same as identifying the relevant stakeholders. The students, faculty, and technical support personnel are obvious candidates. The board of directors, union, and bank officials are other players. Administrators, alumni, and other university staff may also be relevant. Focusing solely on the immediate users will lead to an ineffective implementation.

Another issue, which is much more complicated, is identifying what you want the stakeholders to learn. Let us assume, to simplify the discussion, that people need to learn how to operate the mechanics of the game, to make strategic decisions, and to operate effectively in a virtual environment. These are all very different knowledge tasks. Learning the mechanics of the game is an example of explicit knowledge. Learning how to operate as part of a virtual team is more tacit in nature.

A third issue concerns the mechanics for socialization. Classroom-based training is most commonly used in implementing new technology. It is a formal and structural approach to socialization. However, there are many other learning mechanisms such as apprenticeship, observing others, trial and error, simulations, story-telling in communities of practice, etc. Using only formal classroom training limits the effectiveness of change implementation. It is critical to use the other learning mechanisms to achieve effective implementation. In summary, there are more robust ways to impart different types of learning.

The challenge in socialization is to fit the type of knowledge required by participants in the new environment with the specific mechanisms for imparting that knowledge. In our example of the virtual management game, the basic operating mechanics could be acquired through a classroom format or via some interactive, computer-based learning system. Knowledge about strategic decision-making may be acquired by working with an expert. Skills for operating in a virtual environment may be acquired by observing and analyzing with others the activities of one's own team and other virtual teams.

3. *Feedback and redesign.* These two processes are critical for implementation success. Implementation interventions are both complicated and dynamic, and often bring unintended negative consequences. For example, people may not behave as we expect, and as their experience grows, they can discover new opportunities for using the learning environment (chaps. 8 and 9 illustrate this point). All these factors suggest that it is necessary to initiate some formal procedures for measuring intended behaviors and both intended and unintended outcomes. A review of the change literature suggests that formally developing objects to measure, measuring devices, and a group to review results and indicate redesign steps does improve the chances of implementation success (Leonard Barton, 1987, 1988; Nadler et al., 1995; Ault, Walton, & Childers, 1998).

For our students in the virtual management game environment, we need to establish some standards and measures about the expected level of communications, the types of communications, and the types of analyses that are necessary, as well as performance indicators such as sales and profitability. In order to incorporate feedback and redesigns, we need to monitor behavior and make adjustments as discrepancies occur. There may be a decline in communication in some teams. Others may experience considerable conflict and find themselves unable to resolve controversies. Operating in this new learning environment will generate many unintended obstacles that must be observed and changed in order to make the change viable.

Institutionalization

The last process I want to explore is institutionalization. Institutionalization refers to a process by which the change persists over time and the new learning environments become part of the structure, norms, and values of the organization. The change becomes independent of any individual. A change that has become institutionalized can evolve and be modified over time. Whereas change is and will be a dynamic process, many of the functional features of the new environment remain the same.

In the literature on organizational change, much more attention has been attached to implementation, yet institutionalization is really key to long-term organizational effectiveness. In 1979, I wrote a book (Goodman, 1979) on assessing organizational change, which described a large-scale organizational change and positive outcomes over a three-year period. However, by year three, many of the basic structural changes (e.g., teams, rewards, and coordination mechanisms) had dissipated because the change had not been institutionalized. There are other accounts of successful implementations but failed institutionalizations (cf. Ettlie, 1984; Dean & Goodman, 1993).

How and why an institutionalization process succeeds or fails is an important question. In this section, I will sketch out four processes that are critical for explaining success or failure. (See Table 6.2.) The first three processes are the same as discussed for implementation, but the focus is different.

1. *Motivation-commitment.* Motivation and commitment are important throughout the change process. Earlier I focused on two critical motivational obstacles—unfreezing and the paradox of value. But over time, new obstacles appear. The inflow of new personnel introduces people who were not committed to the change efforts or were not even a part of them. Alternately, the initial commitment of members who were part of the change can dissipate. Certain rewards, such as those in the form of recognition, might be quite effective early in a change effort, but not later (Repenning, 1997; Sterman, Repenning, & Kofman, 1997).

The challenge, then, is to shift the distribution of and types of rewards. This will likely entail a movement toward rewards that are inherent in the new learning environment and rewards that are inherent in the organization's social norms and values. In my example of a change to a virtual team learning environment, institutionalization in part means the rewards are intrinsic to being a member of a virtual team and making decisions, solving problems, and coordinating the team's activities. It also means this kind of activity is not an isolated event. Rather, it is aligned with the educational strategy and structure of the university and is supported by a set of norms and values honoring this type of collaborative activity.

2. *Socialization.* I explored socialization as an important implementation process. It has a similar role in institutionalization. The problem

in many implementations is that there is a tremendous focus on acquiring new skills in the beginning of change, but this focus drops over time. Huge amounts of resources are allocated to get started, but not to sustain the change. The problem is that the knowledge and skills needed in the beginning are different from the knowledge needed over time. Again using the example of building virtual team environments, in the beginning, knowledge acquisition for the users and designers will revolve around the mechanics of the game and creating coordination in a virtual environment. Over time, the knowledge requirements may focus on how to create "swift trust" so members can learn how to work together faster and more effectively (Myerson, Weick, & Kramer, 1995). Or the new focus may be on improving strategic-decision making or fostering nonverbal communication in a virtual environment. The mechanisms for creating swift trust or processing nonverbal cues are likely to be quite different from the mechanisms to train people in the mechanics of the game. The basic idea is that over time, knowledge requirements change and the mechanism to transmit these requirements must also change.

3. *Feedback and redesign.* This mechanism continues to be important in institutionalization processes. The focus now is in terms of providing a long-term evaluation of the learning environment. In the case of the virtual team environment, there are likely to be contextual changes over time. The mix of universities participating in this activity may change, and the technology will surely change. At a more micro level, motivation and interests may wane. All of these changes bear on the life of this learning environment. Some formal mechanisms to assess learning procedures and outcomes and then redesign the environment are necessary for continued growth. In this particular example, where multiple universities will be participating, the responsibility for feedback and redesign should be collective.

4. *Diffusion.* This refers to the process by which the change is extended to other parts of the organization. There is a fairly extensive literature on how diffusion occurs (Rogers, 1983, Ault et al., 1998), but I include it here to discuss its consequences for change, rather than how to do it.

Change in institutions can be targeted to parts of the organization or the whole organization. Given the diversity and autonomy within universities, it is likely that change will be implemented in parts, not the whole organization. A problem in introducing change in one section of an organization is that if the form of change is different from the central practices and norms of the organization, it can be isolated and its effectiveness reduced (Ault et al., 1998; Trist & Dwyer, 1982).

Diffusion of the change to other parts of the organization signals its legitimacy and often generates more infrastructure support. Over time, as more people work in related new learning environments, they should develop more normative and value consensus around the change. In the case of our virtual team learning environment, it may remain as a stand-alone innovation within a more traditional environment, where the beliefs, norms, and values surrounding the change are not shared by others. In this scenario, long-term viability is uncertain. In contrast, if other forms of collaborative work appear in other parts of the focal institution and these different learning environments become part of a community of collaborative learning environments, our innovation in virtual teams has a higher probability for long-term survival and growth.

DISCUSSION

A number of critical themes underlie the intellectual arguments in this chapter. Although each theme has been considered separately and serially, they are really quite intertwined and dynamic in nature. Let us review some of these themes.

First, there are some preconditions to change. Failure to understand and work through these preconditions will lead to an ineffective change process. One requirement is to acknowledge the problem of organizational inertia that characterizes tertiary institutions. Another task, perhaps more difficult, is to develop a map of the learning environment you aspire to create. Most change agents, whether they are administrators, faculty, or external change agents, typically are not well versed in the three levels of learning environments developed in this chapter, yet this is a critical step prior to initiating change. Failure to think about the intersection among modes of delivering education, the type of knowledge to be acquired, and how people learn will lead to a mechanistic approach to change that is not likely to be successful. The third precondition is to articulate the form of change you are planning—is it an incremental form or a broader organizational transformation? In the past, we have thought only about incremental change in the university setting. In the future, we may need to think about discontinuous change as well.

Each of these preconditions is a necessary step in creating effective change. Different tertiary institutions will develop different positions relative to the three preconditions. The content of their positions is not as important as carefully considering each of these three questions.

The second basic theme concerns the phases in creating effective change—planning, implementing, and institutionalization. Whereas these phases, by nature, are quite general, they represent conceptual categories for creating change in university settings. To make these phases more useful, I have tried to identify a basic set of processes that are inherent to each phase. I tried to draw on the extensive literature on organizational change to identify some specific tools. For example, aligning the human, organizational, and technological dimensions in any intervention is a critical part of creating successful change. There is an extensive research literature across a variety of settings and types of change that supports the alignment concept.

In implementing any change, the paradox of value is also likely to be present. This means that the parties to the change effort are likely to initially experience fewer benefits than promised and to experience greater losses than expected. This discrepancy between expectations and experience creates an obstacle to change. Understanding this paradox and engaging in the activities suggested earlier in this chapter to minimize its effects is an important step in creating effective change. For both implementation and institutionalization, I presented a small set of processes, such as socialization, that need to be dynamically managed during the change. Table 6.2 lists the major components and possible actions over the three phases of change.

Whereas Table 6.2 may be a neat and orderly summary, it may be also dangerous to your thinking. Recognize that change is not a checklist, but a dynamic, chaotic process. Planning does not stop when implementation begins. Implementation and institutionalization are going on simultaneously. The target group and stakeholders are likely to vary over the course of the change. Many different forms of socialization are occurring for different constituencies at different times.

A number of dilemmas make change in universities more difficult. The lag between initiating an organizational intervention and experiencing the benefits of those interventions is not well articulated. In an automobile assembly plant, if I change the tooling, the results are known immediately. Unfortunately, that immediate feedback mechanism is not characteristic of significant organizational transformations, particularly in universities. Another dilemma concerns whether one should initiate change in a part of the organization or in the whole organization. In many interventions, the change agents often begin with parts of the organization that are more disposed to the change intervention, and early positive results are demonstrated. The problem with this strategy is that unless the change is quickly diffused to other parts of the organization, it will probably fail. Data from the change literature show interventions in subparts of the organization that are not incorporated by the whole organization tend to wither on the vine. On the other hand, diffusing the intervention to other parts of the university is a difficult task. Given the diversity of production functions within a university (art versus physics), it is also difficult to diffuse a common paradigm of change across these diverse units.

There are other dilemmas in sustaining change over time. In most change efforts, initially, there are few players. As benefits are observed, more people participate, which, in turn, accelerates the change effort. A positive feedback cycle of benefits—more players more benefits—drives the change for a period of time. However, one reaches a point of diminishing returns, where all people are participating and many of the benefits have been realized. Unless the change process itself goes through a major retransformation, the motivation and results surrounding the change are likely to decline.

I point out these dilemmas only to acknowledge the complexity and difficulty of change. The dilemmas are real and must be confronted both intellectually and in action, just as one must deal with the preconditions, phases, and processes set forth in this chapter. The challenge educators face is fairly clear. The environment of tertiary institutions is changing in significant ways. Unfortunately, most universities do not have good mechanisms to read and adapt to environmental changes. One could say that universities have persisted in this mode for thousands of years. Although that observation may be true, I think the form and types of changes are much more dramatic today. As a result, the need to initiate and to create effective change is much more critical. Hopefully, the tools developed in this chapter will provide some direction for creating effective change.

REFERENCES

Argyris, C. (1985). *Strategy, change and defensive routines.* Boston: Pitman.
Argyris, C. (1990). *Overcoming organizational defenses.* Boston: Allyn & Bacon.
Ault, R., Walton, R, & Childers, M. (1998). *What works: A decade of change at Champion International.* San Francisco: Jossey–Bass.
Beatty, C. A., & Gordon, J. R. M. (1988). Barriers to the implementation of CAD/CAM systems. *Sloan Management Review, Summer, 25–33.*
Beer, M., Eisenstat, R. A., & Spector, B. (1990). Why change programs don't produce change. *Harvard Business Review, 68,* 158–166.
Bikson, T. K. (1987). *Understanding the implementation of office technology.* Report No. N–2619–NSF, The Rand Corp., Santa Monica, CA.
Bikson, T. K., Gutek, B. A., & Mankin, D. A. (1987). *Implementing computerized procedures in office settings: Influences and outcomes.* Report No. R–3077–NSF, The Rand Corp., Santa Monica, CA.

Brown, J. S., & Duguid, P. (1995). *Universities in the digital age.* http://www.parc.xerox.com/ops/members/brown/papers/university.html.

Chabay, R. (1995). *Electric field hockey.* Raleigh, NC: Physics Academic Software.

Changing Nature of Work Video—University President, www.workvideos.com, 1996.

Cooper, R. B., & Zmud, R. W. (1990). Information technology implementation research: A technological diffusion approach. *Management Science, 36,* 123–139.

Dean, J. W., & Goodman, P. S. (1993). *Toward a theory of total quality integration.* Unpublished paper. University of North Carolina.

Ettlie, J. E. (1984). Implementation strategy for manufacturing innovations. In M. Warner (Ed.), *Micro-processors, manpower and society: A comparative, cross-national approach* (pp. 31–48). New York: St. Martin's Press.

Goodman, P. S. (1979). *Assessing organizational change: The Rushton quality of work experiment.* New York: Wiley-Interscience.

Goodman, P. S. (2000). *Missing linkages: Tools for cross-level organizational research.* Thousand Oaks, CA: Sage.

Goodman, P. S., & Griffith, T. L. (1991). A process approach to the implementation of new technology. *Journal of Engineering and Technology Management, 8,* 261–285.

Harris, D. H. (1994). *Organizational linkages: Understanding the productivity paradox.* Washington, DC: National Academy Press.

Lawler, E. E. (1986). *High involvement management.* San Francisco: Jossey–Bass.

Lawler, E. E. (1992). *The ultimate advantage.* San Francisco: Jossey–Bass.

Leonard–Barton, D. (1987) Implementing structured software methodologies: A case of innovation in process technology. *Interfaces, 17,* 6–17.

Leonard–Barton, D. (1988). Implementation as mutual adaptation of technology and organization. *Research Policy, 17,* 251–267.

Lucas, H. C., Jr. (1981). *Implementation: The key to successful information systems.* New York: Columbia.

MacDuffie, J. P. (1995). Human resource bundles and manufacturing performance: Organizational logic and flexible production systems in the world auto industry. *Industrial and Labor Relations Review, 48,* 197–221.

MacDuffie, J. P., & Pil, F. K. (1997) Changes in auto industry employment practices: An international overview. In T. A. Kochan, R. Lansbury, & J. P. MacDuffie (Eds.), *After lean production: Evolving employment practices in the world auto industry* (pp. 9–44). Cornell University Press.

March, J. G. (1991). Exploration and Exploitation in organizational learning. *Organization Science, 2,* 71–87.

Meyerson, D., Weick, K. E., & Kramer, R. M. (1995). Swift trust and temporary groups. In R. M. Kramer & T. R. Tyler (Eds.), *Trust in Organizations* (pp. 166–195). Thousand Oaks, CA: Sage.

Mohrman, A. M., Mohrman, S. A., Ledford, G. E., Lawler, E. E., & Cummings, T. G. (1989). *Large scale organizational change.* San Francisco: Jossey–Bass.

Nadler D. A., Gerstein, M. S., & Shaw, R. B. (1992). *Organizational architecture: Designs for changing organizations.* San Francisco: Jossey–Bass.

Nadler, D. A., Shaw, R. B., & Walton, A. E. (1995). *Discontinuous change.* San Francisco: Jossey–Bass.

Nonaka, I., & Takeuchi, H. (1995). *The knowledge-creating company: How Japanese companies create the dynamics of innovation.* New York: Oxford University Press.

Pfeffer, J. (1994). *Competitive advantage through people.* Boston: Harvard Business School Press.

Repenning, N. P. (1997). Successful change sometimes ends with results: Resolving the improvement paradox through computer simulation. Working Paper, Sloan School of Management, Massachusetts Institute of Technology, Cambridge, MA.

Rogers, E. M. (1983). *The diffusion of innovations.* New York: Free Press.

Rousseau, D. M. (1995). *Psychological contracts in organizations: Understanding written and unwritten agreements.* Thousand Oaks, CA: Sage.

Sproull, L. S., & Hofmeister, K. R. (1986). Thinking about implementation. *Journal of Management, 12,* 43–60.

Sterman, J. D., Repenning, N., & Kofman, F. (1997). Unanticipated side effects of successful quality programs: Exploring a paradox of organizational improvement. *Management Science, 43,* 503–521.

Toffler, A. (1970). *Future shock.* New York: Random House

Tornatzky, L. G., Eveland, J. D., Boylan, M. G., Hetzner, W. A., Johnson, E. C., Roitman, D., & Schneider, J. (1983). *The process of technological innovation: Reviewing the literature.* Productivity Improvement Research Section, Division of Industrial Science and Technological Innovation, National Science Foundation.

Trist, E. L., & Dwyer, C. (1982). The limits of laissez-faire as a sociotechnical change strategy. In R. Zager & M. P. Rosow (Eds.), *The innovative organization: productivity programs in action* (pp. 149–183). Elmsford, NY: Pergamon.

Walton, R. (1989). *Up and running.* Boston, MA: Harvard Business School Press.

Weick, K. E., & Quinn, R. E. (1999). Organizational change and development. *Annual Review of Psychology, 50,* 361–386.

Williams, J. R. (1999). *Renewable advantage.* New York: Free Press.

Part II

Applications

*T*his section is grounded in four specific educational applications that have exhibited long-term effectiveness. There are many possible applications that might have been selected. These were chosen because they have been successful, there is evidence of diffusion to other settings, and there is diversity among the applications. They represent concrete examples of new learning environments.

For each application, the learning environment is presented so the reader understands the context. Then the challenges, mistakes, and the evolution of these environments are explored. It is this learning evolution and redesign that represent the critical lessons from these chapters.

Chapter 7 presents the development of one of the best virtual universities. The setting is Mexico and the coverage is throughout Latin America. Over a 10-year period, the Virtual University of Instituto Tecnologico y de Estudios Superiores de Monterrey (ITESM) has evolved into a major center of learning. A series of 10 lessons learned from these experiences are explored. Some of these are the role of educational models and technology, quality, asynchronous and synchronous interactions, selecting the technology, customized learning, motivating professors, and academic regulations. The discussion of these topics is useful for people designing or redesigning virtual learning environments.

Chapter 8 is about a computer-based learning environment for teaching finance. We follow the development of FAST (Financial Analysis and Security Trading) tools originally designed for research purposes to a classroom setting, and then its diffusion throughout the United States and other parts of the world. A striking feature of this learning environment is that it trains people to operate in a financial world that is constantly undergoing change. These forces in the financial markets, in turn, drive the continuous evolu-

181

tion of the learning environment. Understanding more about the why, how, and what of this dynamic evolution is an important lesson for the future and for designers and administrators responsible for new learning environments. In 1996, FAST won the Smithsonian-Computerworld Award for innovative uses of information technology.

Chapter 9 examines a very different form of computer-based environment—intelligent tutors. Again, we follow cognitive tutors in areas such as algebra, geometry, and programming from early successes in a laboratory context to their dissemination throughout the United States. The lessons in this chapter are about why these tutors are successful with a particular focus on the transformation of the classroom, the role of assessment in new learning environments, and the critical factors explaining the widespread dissemination of this technology.

Chapter 10 presents an award-winning approach to redesigning the traditional science classroom into a studio design. The reader is first introduced to the idea of a studio as an alternative to traditional environments for teaching courses such as physics and the learning assumptions underlying the studio design. The facilities, equipment, and cost considerations required to build studios out of traditional classrooms are explored. We experience a typical day in the studio and learn about the deployment of the studio in many science and engineering disciplines.

Some impressive results of the studio on improving learning are presented. Also, the evolution of the studio in a virtual setting is explained. It is important to pay attention to the lessons from the studio concept because it has focused on changing the core or fundamental courses in most universities.

The goal of this section is to look for lessons learned that may be applicable to educational innovations.

Chapter 7

The Virtual University:
Customized Education in a Nutshell

Carlos Cruz Limón
Instituto Tecnologico y de Estudios Superiores de Monterrey

INTRODUCTION

This chapter's objective is to provide a foundation for understanding the application of distance learning and its importance in higher education. I will be sharing information, experiences, concepts, and ideas about distance learning, using the Virtual University as a basis for many of these discussions. It is both an honor and an important responsibility to expound upon the development of distance learning at the Instituto Tecnologico y de Estudios Superiores de Monterrey (ITESM) over the past 11 years, an evolution that has led to arguably one of the most important achievements in the history of this great university.

This chapter will first provide some essential background information about the ITESM and its Virtual University. It also discusses how educational models have evolved and how they have transformed education, especially in the context of distance learning. The educational model is fundamental in providing students with the desire to work, the opportunity to retain practical knowledge, and skills that will allow them to be highly productive in the workplace. Considering the important role that technol-

183

ogy plays in the teaching–learning process, especially in the context of distance learning, the chapter reviews the use of technology in education. Technology, however, is only one part of the equation for meeting the high demands of today's sophisticated consumer of educational services. With the emerging global market, everything has become more competitive than ever before, and users of educational services are more aware of the options available to them globally. Moreover, users both need and desire more convenience and flexibility in their educational pursuits without sacrificing quality and value. For these reasons, distance learning institutions must customize their degree and nondegree programs in order to meet the demands of today's students. This challenge is being confronted successfully at the Virtual University as is discussed in this chapter. Finally, we get to the big question of what distance learning will become in the future and, therefore, what model the Virtual University and other distance-learning programs will have to emulate to be successful. Accordingly, I discuss 10 lessons based on our experience at the Virtual University that might provide a basis for planning future distance-learning projects.

ITESM AND THE VIRTUAL UNIVERSITY

ITESM: The Institution

Quality Leadership has been the key to success at the Monterrey Institute of Technology (ITESM) since it was founded in 1943 by a group of Mexican businessmen led by Eugenio Garza Sada. These gentlemen had an interest in producing locally trained professionals at the highest academic level, in order to generate a solid human resources base that could bolster the development and growth of industry in the city of Monterrey. Today, Monterrey is considered the top city in Latin America for doing business, according to a recent article in Fortune (Kahn, 1999). Among the reasons given was the high level of engineering and scientific talent produced by ITESM.

A university with a reputation for academic excellence, ITESM is currently the largest privately run university in all of Latin America. It consists of 30 campuses in Mexico, a traditional student enrollment of nearly 85,000, and a faculty of approximately 6,000 professors. ITESM's presence is felt throughout Mexico, and its educational services are being extended to nine other Latin American countries by way of the Virtual University.

The Mission of ITESM is: "to educate students to be individuals who are committed to the social, economic, and political development of their communities and who are internationally competitive in their professional fields; and to carry out research and extension services, relevant to Mexico's sustainable development." This is not too different from what the founders had in mind for this institution more than 50 years ago. The real distinction between the ITESM of 1943 and the ITESM of today is the scope of its impact; it would like to do for the entire country, and to some degree Latin America, what it has done for the city of Monterrey.

ITESM believes that it has to meet six objectives in order to turn this dream into a reality. These objectives are the following:

- Carry out a reengineering of the teaching–learning process;
- Refocus activities associated with research and extension services;
- Develop the Virtual University (VU);
- Internationalize the institute;
- Maintain the process of continual improvement; and
- Promote the growth of the institute.

Lorenzo Zambrano, President of CEMEX and Chairman of ITESM's Board of Directors, when asked what he believed was the future of the Virtual University at ITESM, responded, "The Virtual University is the future of ITESM." As you can see, ITESM is acutely aware that in order to be successful, its future graduates must possess new abilities in research and information analysis via electronic media. At the same time, ITESM recognizes the importance of telecommunications, computer networking, and multimedia techniques in the development of new instruments that will have an important influence on both long-distance and on-site educational systems.

History of Distance Learning at ITESM

In the 1970s and early to mid 1980s, ITESM experimented with a geographical expansion that transformed it into a multicampus university with academic locations spread throughout Mexico. With this expansion, ITESM realized the need to consolidate the quality of its educational services and to strengthen its infrastructure, which supported this consolidation. The development of technologies and new educational options in the country allowed ITESM to achieve these objectives.

One of the first actions taken by the Institute in distance education was the integration of the ITESM through the BITNET network in 1985. This allowed students and teachers to use e-mail and transfer data internationally. In 1986, a fiber optic network was set up between the Monterrey and Mexico State campuses, which led to the idea of establishing a satellite system to transmit voice, visual images and data, and generally foster communication between all campuses.

In 1987, ITESM's multicampus system went through a process of self-examination in each location in order to eventually gain accreditation by the Southern Association of Colleges and Schools (SACS), a recognized authority on education in the United States. The SACS required that all professors have at least a master's degree, which at the time was not the case at ITESM on a systemwide basis. Due to the multicampus structure of ITESM, not every campus had the academic programs necessary for their professors to earn a master's degree on-site. Therefore, ITESM opted to use satellite technology to give all undergraduate professors the opportunity to pursue a graduate degree and thereby satisfy the requirements set forth by the SACS. By August 1989, ITESM had incorporated the use of satellite technology into its educational system, which allowed for simultaneous interaction between teachers and students in what was then a 26-campus university system.

By using the available satellite technology, ITESM believed that satellite technology could enable masses of professors across multiple campuses to achieve the required education level in a cost-efficient manner, while at the same time expanding the reach of the university's best professors. In addition, other advantages were also perceived, such as the development of a new level of interpersonal and learning skills as a result of distance work groups and a greater emphasis on self-learning and self-management. Hence, the Satellite Interactive Education System (with the Spanish acronym SEIS) evolved.

Transmission began on April 26, 1989, with a seminar on exporting goods to the United States; the first class with academic credit at the postgraduate level was broadcast in the summer of 1989; and as of August 1989, four hours of programming were broadcast on a daily basis. Included were five courses for two graduate programs, two classes for undergraduates, and several classes for teacher training. SEIS had two transmitting sites, the Monterrey and Mexico State campuses, which transmitted via satellite to the 26 campuses located throughout Mexico.

At the time, the principal characteristics of SEIS were the following:

- Students were exposed to better courses due to computerized animations, videos, slides, and photographs;
- Both undergraduate and graduate courses were available to students irrespective of their campus;
- Participants had the benefit of interacting with professors who were specialists in their subject area; and
- Students could communicate simultaneously with groups at different locations throughout the country.

The Virtual University: A New Beginning

In March of 1996, ITESM's Virtual University was created to support ITESM's mission. It was developed in accordance with two fundamental goals; the first was to expand the teaching core with the best professors from ITESM as well as from other universities, and the second was to bring high-quality education to new reaches and areas. Based on these propositions, as well as ITESM's basic mission of bolstering development in Mexico and Latin America, the Virtual University is committed to offering education through innovative educational models, combined with the most advanced electronic and telecommunications technology.

The Virtual University has the following objectives:

- Support the perpetual improvement of the educational processes of the many ITESM campuses;
- Extend educational services to persons both nationally and internationally;
- Enrich and amplify the learning process, while allowing flexibility in terms of time and space;
- Create and diffuse a new concept of learning that incorporates the reasonable use of technology;
- Promote the development of multidisciplinary and cooperative groups in the analysis of educational programs; and
- Advocate educational research.

The vision of the Virtual University is to be the bridge that brings together the most esteemed professors of ITESM and other universities around the world to students throughout the entire American Continent, by using the most advanced technologies in telecommunications and electronic networks. The Virtual University's mission is to offer education through innovative educational models and the most advanced technology in order to support the development of Mexico and Latin America.

The Virtual University creates educational models that help develop students' ability to generate their own knowledge and improve their own learning skills. All courses have incorporated educational models that transform the professor-centered process into a group-learning process, where the instructor goes beyond just teaching to design experiences, exercises, and activities that allow for and encourage group work. Through group learning, the goal is for students to learn by themselves, learn from their classmates, and solve problems as a group.

The Virtual University uses leading-edge telecommunications and computer networking technologies. It adopts a hybrid model composed of a satellite broadcast, videoconference transmissions, an online university, and an open university. As opposed to other universities, the VU is a combination of these technologies and the educational models associated with them.

Growth of the Virtual University

The Virtual University has experienced tremendous growth since its onset in 1996. Several important statistics demonstrate just how dramatic this growth has been over the last four years.

- In 1996, the Virtual University offered nine degree programs; today it offers 18 degrees in the fields of management, education, engineering, technology, and the humanities, including a PhD in Educational Innovations and Technology. Furthermore, many stand-alone courses and nonacademic programs have recently been added, including a high-level training program for municipal officers in Latin America.

- There were three satellite channels and two sites with videoconference on ITESM campuses in 1996; today, there are five satellite channels and 12 sites with videoconference. In addition, there are 18 associate videoconference transmitting sites at foreign universities in Latin America, the United States, Canada and the European Union.

- The Virtual University had 56 receiving sites in 1996 for all academic and nonacademic programs. Today, 1,457 exist throughout ITESM campuses, at universities in nine other Latin American countries, and at Mexican and Latin American companies.

- The number of students went from 4,028 in 1996 to 54,172 in 1999.

The VU has gone from an ordinary distance learning center to become an extremely advanced communications network that incorporates all of the available technologies, including satellite, videoconference, multimedia, and computer networking, so that students and professors have the necessary tools to accompany the innovative teaching–learning models applied in this environment.

FUNDAMENTAL ISSUES

In almost 10 years, the Virtual University has found 10 fundamental issues that should be considered in planning and implementing its academic programs. Following are the most important lessons learned from this experience.

TABLE 7.1   Ten Lessons Learned from the Virtual University

1. The educational model to be used in a specific program has to be selected carefully.
2. The selection of this model should be founded on quality.
3. Interaction is essential within the new learning–teaching processes.
4. It is advisable not to get married to a single technology. It is mandatory to consider both the inherent virtues and shortcomings as regards to the program.
5. Determine the right technological combination and teaching learning model.
6. Professors require additional support as they take part in these courses.
7. Students have a more active role.
8. The institution has to have strong, convincing and reliable leadership.
9. Flexibility in academic regulations is a facilitating element.
10. The use of computer networks contributes to develop citizens of the world.

Educational Models and Technology

It is critical to avoid the trap of believing that technology is the only way in which we will overcome the knowledge barriers that divide our societies. Educational institutions must cautiously select the appropriate educational model and technology for each program and be sure to design strategies that will allow students to obtain and validate information. These strategies should also encourage students to put their knowledge into practice, to develop new theses, and to debate and exchange ideas with their classmates.

However, saying all of this and doing it are two very different propositions. When VU first attempted to make the virtual classroom more interactive and began combining other cutting-edge technologies with satellite, we implemented the use of a polling device that was installed at every monitor of every virtual university site for academic programs, a very expensive technology at the time. Unfortunately, the devices were not sufficiently useful to justify such a costly investment. In hindsight, I realize that the technology was not the problem, although we probably would not make the same choice today even under different circumstances; the problem was that the technology was not appropriate for the learning-distribution model we were using. The learning-distribution model was based heavily on asynchronous interaction and, therefore, depended primarily on technology that facilitated this type of interaction. However, the polling device could only be used for synchronous interaction and, as such, was applied very sparingly.

This was an expensive but valuable lesson. We learned that each technology is a different tool for providing educational programs. Each tool may have very specific applications that may not be appropriate for many distance-learning programs. In the example above, the technology we chose was wrong for the learning-distribution model that was being followed at the time. The rule that should flow from this lesson is to first define and firmly establish the learning-distribution model for the program and then select the technology that best suits this model.

Where the VU has been very successful is in the integration of technologies, which is important in providing a highly enriching experience for students. Most of our programs combine technologies that range from the effective use of satellite to the use of Web pages, computer software, and networked systems to facilitate virtual work groups. As a result of this, anonymous surveys answered by our students have consistently indicated the following three positive responses: (1) a high level of satisfaction with the exposure to sophisticated technology, (2) a high level of satisfaction with the opportunity to work and interact on an international scale with bright and interesting people, and (3) a high level of satisfaction in having developed the discipline and skills to work and learn individually.

The objective of universities is to increase human talent and promote in-depth learning. For this, it is necessary to determine the ideal equation as a function of the existing study models—instruction, self-study, and collaborative work—the technology available to the recipient, their learning style, the course content, and the professor's vision. If the formula is correct, it will be possible to foster optimum learning levels and allow students to apply their knowledge to tangible situations that contribute significantly to the progress of their communities.

In summary, we have found that technological development and the educational model work like cogs in a gearbox, where technology is the key. It is the vehicle that allows more and more people to travel at high speed in the spheres of knowledge, where the professor continues to be the principal guide for a group of increasingly committed students.

Quality: A Fundamental Reason

Some reasons for introducing innovative formulas within education may be to increase productivity, to make access easier for larger groups of the population or to enhance quality. However, the fundamental reason for introducing new models or technologies should be quality itself.

Quality does not necessarily mean we need to create complex or even sophisticated systems. It depends on the objectives of each particular program. Sometimes quality can be very basic in terms of content as well as technology. This has generally been the case for our teacher training program, which is tailored to meet the current training needs of a massive group of K-12 teachers. On the other hand, quality can also mean the use of highly sophisticated computer networks and software to accommodate collaborative work in small groups. Hence, quality comes in both large and small packages, often depending on the objectives and learning model of an individual program.

When implementing changes, process quality can assure the quality of the results. For example, if productivity is stressed as the reason for change, there is a temptation to eliminate indispensable elements such as interactivity and feedback because the initial cost of technology-driven models is higher than in traditional models. This would necessarily produce deficiencies in the learning system. Therefore, it is essential for any distance-learning system to establish mechanisms for evaluating its programs and for supporting its students' administrative as well as academic interests.

The same situation would occur if we were to heighten access without maintaining the quality of our student selection processes Assuring a high level of preparation in candidates to the distance-learning program guarantees that their contributions will truly enhance the learning of those who interact with them on a daily basis. Thus, the significance of knowledge increases exponentially. One example of how this is achieved at the Virtual University is by requiring the same admission exam of our students as that of the traditional ITESM students. Notwithstanding this requirement, we have enjoyed a very high 30% annual growth rate for our academic programs.

Interactivity—Asynchronous and Synchronous

The new educational models need to consider interaction as a critical element. All learning–teaching processes have to rank asynchronous communication as a top priority. This communication should be among the students themselves, and between them and their teachers, supported by information technology. Such activities generate a great deal of participation and lead to the enrichment of ideas. This probably represents one of the most significant breakthroughs in learning of recent times. The 21st century executive will need the ability to learn, work, discuss, and make decisions in distributed time and space.

This asynchronous process generally takes more time than in a traditional group meeting. However, it is also likely that the decisions made will be more intelligent, because the decisions made in a one- or two-hour meeting may be rushed. We usually meet to listen, analyze, and propose, without further action. On the other hand, in an asynchronous environment, by reading, analyzing, commenting on, and calmly reviewing the ideas of everyone involved, and then making our own contribution, our responses are necessarily more informed and better grounded. This leads to active learning processes, the development of innovative proposals, and greater commitment to the agreements that are reached. Additionally, it promotes the participation of all players, regardless of their geographic location.

There is not a single educational philosophy that advocates learning without interaction, as far as I know. Interaction is an indispensable component of quality educational programs. Just last year, in our business administration and engineering graduate programs alone, 190,000 messages were asynchronously exchanged as a result of work activity in collaborative groups. This figure does not include students' correspondence via e-mail.

Furthermore, synchronous interaction is an important component of the live class sessions. In addition to the satellite transmission of professors' presentations, including visual materials (computer-generated slides, video, etc.), we offer both an Internet-based interactive system and videoconference facilities. The combination of these technologies lends warmth and meaning to the sessions.

At the Virtual University, we have acquired a great deal of experience in mastering the communication aspects of distance learning. However, we still face enormous challenges, particularly in overcoming variations in available technology from one site to the next. We administer the telecommunications and computer networking among sites in over 100 Mexican cities as well as in cities in nine other Latin American countries. Still, we feel that we have generally done well in the midst of the challenges. Students tend to comment quite favorably with respect to the value and importance of the interaction they have experienced with students from other cities and countries, with their tutors, and with their professors. Notwithstanding the successes, there is always room for improvement. For example, compliance has been inconsistent with respect to our "7–24" policy, which gives professors seven days to report exam and project grades and 24 hours to respond to individuals' questions and concerns about their academic programs. Therefore, we are continuously striving to better ourselves.

Selecting the Technology

Just as the combination of existing educational models allows us to satisfy different learning–teaching needs, the mix of technological tools allows us to cover different process demands. The advantages and shortcomings of each technology should be considered before determining how intensive their use will be in a particular program.

Video—via satellite or fiber-optic broadcast—has unique qualities with regard to synchronous content. When they have a teacher in front of them, students tend to feel protected and secure. To a certain extent, video puts them close to the traditional learning mechanisms that guided them in the past and allows them to keep up to date on the contents of a course. In addition, video affords the opportunity to expose many people to the wisdom and experience of great thinkers in person. Despite the many advantages, however, video is a tool with very low interactivity. In contrast, the greatest value of the Internet is its enabling of interaction without the need to coincide in time and space. It is a wonderful tool for collaborative learning.

Furthermore, it is important to consider the professor's point of view, because one may like video and feel that the Internet is boring. For another, video is a necessary evil and the Internet is great. I believe that the right strategy is to select combinations of video and Internet (and other technologies) that give students and professors the best of both worlds.

Considering for a moment the selection of technology to meet different process demands, I cannot emphasize enough the importance of selecting technology only after giving painstakingly careful thought to the learning-distribution model in which it will be used. I am reminded of a situation where we had been very successful at applying a technological platform in the traditional classroom. ITESM professors went through a training program at the Virtual University to redesign their courses, improving teaching-learning methods in the traditional classroom. The technological platform that they have learned to apply in their courses has been a manageable and useful tool for their purposes. However, when we attempted to apply the same technology in our virtual courses, we discovered it was not compatible with our distance-learning based system.

Of course, only so much can be known before making a decision. There will always be some risks when pushing the envelope to offer the best distance-learning products and services possible. Just be sure that you take only the worthwhile risks in selecting technology, because the expense of making a mistake here can be considerable.

Another important factor in selecting the technology mix is the variety of economic situations and technological infrastructures among countries, particularly in Latin America. For instance, the most common and economical conduit to the Internet is telephone. However, a country with greater economic resources may be able to provide Internet via cable, or even satellite, which allows for more versatile interaction among individual users. This approach also gives teachers more room to be creative and to personalize the teaching–learning experience, making the experience more engaging and interesting for both teachers and their pupils.

Customized Learning

Not all of the VU programs use the same technological combination. For example, the virtual business classroom, the program for updating faculty skills, and the Senior Municipal Administration Seminar use mostly video conferencing technology. These courses are offered at sites that usually do not have Internet access. The master's degree programs and undergraduate courses make more intensive use of both Internet and video. We are customizing different educational-technology models for different market segments.

Determining the technological combination and the teaching–learning model most suitable for each course depends on the type of program to be taught and the market it is targeting. Three fundamental variables must be analyzed: the technology available to the recipient, the type of information that must be processed, and its demand for time and space synchronicity.

The first issue deals with the availability and cost of using the existing technology at a given university. Related considerations deal with reliability and bandwidth. All of these are determinants of delivery capabilities.

The kind of information a course deals with is located at a point on a continuum. This ranges from structural information such as data, figures, and structured value relations, to conversational information where the context is paramount to understanding meaning. Therefore, hard courses (exact sciences) need an infinitely lesser degree of synchronicity than soft courses (the humanities).

Additionally, people with marked left-brain preference usually have a greater capacity for abstraction and analysis, and therefore have less need for the support of a teacher-guide. The Anglo-Saxon culture, for instance, works very well in an asynchronous individual world. The majority of Latinos, however, have a right-brain dominance, so we need more mingling and interactions with our fellows and the facilitation of a professor. Our culture is social, we like to be with our buddies, to talk with friends and see people. Because of these tendencies, a certain level of synchronicity in time has its advantages for the Latin American culture. In general, we need external elements to help us achieve our goals. Synchronous video events serve to keep the student on-course and moving ahead on the assignments required to pass a course.

Video has the most value when used synchronously because a student, even if lacking a telephone to interact with a professor, has the experience of having him or her there. Students tend to like live television, and so they like live video too. It is possible that in the future, video will reach the level of asynchronicity in time and space that Internet has today. Then we will be able to send video through Internet2 to students computers, and students would not have to visit the receiving classrooms. However, although this possibility exists today, we should not forget that live video can be very useful. It reminds students every week of where they are (or where they should be). This allows them to have greater control of their own progress.

In contrast with video, we gain the most value from the Internet when we use it asynchronously. We live in a world that has 24 time zones where geographic distances are measured in thousands of miles. Work in our global economy requires people to work effectively with others in different geographical locations and time zones. Students, therefore, have to develop the skills to learn, work, discuss, and make decisions in an asynchronous manner. When this process is interwoven with daily life, the resulting decisions have proven to be richer and more effective. Time has been used effectively.

Thus, one of the most important aspects that should be considered in planning higher education processes is the selection of the suitable technology mix to drive the learning style and the conditions of the receiving audience. Computer-based technologies will facilitate self-learning and electronic teaching, which in turn will allow education to adapt to the changing needs of the next millennium.

In order to achieve this objective at the Virtual University, we want to stop having a single product to which everyone must adapt. Rather, we want to have a versatile product that can satisfy different needs. This example can be seen very clearly in the automotive industry. The same car can have modified versions that take into account the particular needs of a market segment. The same thing happens with education: We are going to have hybrid academic programs aimed at satisfying the demands of different recipients.

The VU has programs applied at two different levels of synchronicity. For example, the MBA program has two parallel frameworks. One is a totally asynchronous, online approach, aimed at individuals with a left-brained thinking preference, a structured mentality, and an engineering mind. The other is a less asynchronous, satellite-broadcast modality aimed at populations with learning styles where the right hemisphere of the brain predominates.

This constitutes an important competitive advantage because some universities have a single technology, a single educational model, for only one kind of market.

Motivating and Supporting Professors

Once again, history repeats itself, and professors are facing a situation that produces accelerated change in their function within the educational process. Today, as in the past, some are enthused with the idea of promoting this new trend, while others are resistant to change. Then there are those who are at the junction of deciding whether they should be a part of this proposal or not.

This resistance to change is quite understandable. People instituting change often describe the unwillingness to change as a sign of low motivation or irrationality. Actually, people who are less willing to adopt new learning models are being quite rational. They initially are facing potential losses. There are losses in competence (I do not know how to use or build multimedia systems), power (before I controlled the classroom, but not under the new system), and rewards (the esteem I receive will not be as dominant in the new system). In this context, the challenge is to minimize the losses and support new forms of competence, power, and rewards.

In order to facilitate the faculty adjustment process, higher education institutions should provide flexible spaces, foster voluntary participation, and provide unlimited support to the most enthusiastic professors. A key element is having a solid training program for distance-learning that provides instruction on the redesign of courses and draws upon the knowledge of experts on instructional design to guide and assist teachers in this new educational environment. Also, by paying for professors' training and possibly providing some additional monetary incentive, the institution demonstrates the importance of the transition and its appreciation of the effort made by professors to adapt their teaching methods.

Professors participating in those programs essentially need additional time to prepare and teach their courses. They also need the support of their assistants, who in turn require institutional support to prepare courses, to model collaborative learning and perform evaluations jointly with the lead professor. Preparing a virtual course may require twice the time needed to prepare a traditional one and require a great deal of technological expertise. This can be a frustrating experience, at least in the beginning. That is why we find it necessary to have a design and technology team behind every professor, which assists with the design of Web pages, design of materials, design of visual aids, esthetic enhancements, production (including pre and postproduction needs), and the technological platforms used for interaction.

Student Culture

It is essential to help students leave behind their dependency on teachers. This is particularly difficult in cultures such as ours, where a matriarchal society is evidenced in behavior patterns. These reflect the previous pattern of teaching–learning: "I pay for the teacher to teach me, and explain things to me ... not to learn things by myself."

This is a greater problem that also has to do with students' lack of self-confidence and certainty. A large number of students have been led by the hand under a traditional scheme in which they are mere spectators. As a result, when they are placed on the stage, they do not know how to perform. Procrastination and laziness are the worst enemies of those who have been traditionally led along the pathway of teaching and very little self-learning. However, this pattern is gradually changing. One of the philosophies we share at the Virtual University is that of the movie *Field of Dreams*, which is, "if you build it, they will come." So we try to do everything first-rate from our teaching–learning models to our interactive technology, in the belief that our students will begin warming up to this new learning culture. We believe that our students' ability to identify quality causes them to be more demanding of the Virtual University's programs. That forces us to constantly provide course activities that are relevant, practical, and dynamic in nature. Once they are motivated, the challenge is to keep the ball rolling. A high level of difficulty does not seem to be an obstacle. The important thing is to continue to provide relevant topics and dynamic learning activities, which means that we are constantly reinventing ourselves.

Technological development and educational needs put us in a unique position to provide knowledge, but one has to come aboard. If during the 12th century the illiterates were those who did not have an opportunity to attend and listen, and in the 15th century the illiterates were those who did not know how to read, then the illiterates of the 21st century will be those who do not develop the skills to participate in discussion groups, learn actively, and communicate asynchronously on a global scale.

Institutional Leadership

An aggressive distance-learning project is a progressive concept that will probably stir up controversy and, therefore, come up against opposition. The university or institution providing this type of education must have strong, convincing, reliable leadership. Projects of this nature will make mistakes. Therefore, it is indispensable that there be strong technical, financial, and political support.

Similar projects have been launched at other institutions and later folded, not because they were bad or poorly administered projects, but due to a lack of institutional leadership for the project. The VU has been fortunate to have the best possible leadership behind it—leadership that does not back down and that sticks its neck out, daring the opposition to come forward. For example, the Virtual University is known institutionally and publicly as one of ITESM's six strategies for achieving its mission for the year 2005. That demonstrates extreme confidence in our project and its level of importance to the institution. Time, money, and patience are also very important to have from the institution's leadership. The Virtual University would not be where it is today without these resources.

Finally, another crucial aspect of ITESM's leadership, which has been instrumental in our success, is its high expectations of the Virtual University. As an institution, ITESM has always been its own greatest competitor and, as such, is very demanding of itself. Consequently, the same academic rigor that is applied to the traditional programs is also applied to the Virtual University's programs.

Academic Regulations

Given that we are in the midst of an educational revolution, it is necessary to adopt regulations and legislation that are flexible enough to facilitate the transition to a distance-learning environment. In a traditional educational setting, the students, faculty, and administration are united in one place, as are the administrative processes. As we know, this is not the case in this new environment, which is why it is very important to know where flexibility is needed.

For example, if you as an institution are equally strict with registration for distance-learning classes, as with traditional classes, knowing that the new process requires more time and room for adaptation, then many people will not get registered, will become disenchanted with the process, and possibly will drop the program altogether. This would be a serious problem for any distance-learning institution, considering the effort that goes into gaining the trust, interest, and commitment of these potential students in the first place. Therefore, academic calendars should perhaps use tolerance ranges in order to facilitate registration.

Evaluations, for example, should center more on processes and less on content, and should predominantly consider collaboration. However, this is not to be construed to mean that the academic programs should be any less rigorous than those of traditional classrooms. To the contrary, the academic standards should be every bit as rigorous. Students from distance-learning programs will be competing for jobs and business with those from traditional academic programs. In fact, we conducted a comparative study of our graduates and those of the traditional programs at ITESM. Results indicated that the VU graduates have been just as successful in the workplace.

Global Technology

We should take advantage of technology to give our students a global vision of the world, in accordance with current trends. In the future, students from different regions of the world will take our courses, regardless of the university in which they are enrolled. This is a sign that cultural and linguistic barriers will disappear to foster the development of what is currently known as citizens of the world.

Technology does not respect national borders. This is evident in the growth of the Virtual University, which began in 1989 with courses at various ITESM campuses in Mexico, and has grown since then to operate throughout the continent with sites and associations in nine other Latin American countries, the United States, and Canada. This expansion happened because VU chose to use the technology available to it. With recent advances in Internet technology, future possibilities to expand and compete globally are endless.

Education should promote understanding among nations and foster respect and collaboration among peoples. The new educational models being developed will allow future generations to stay abreast of breakthroughs in science, to get close to the arts, and, fundamentally speaking, to be more capable of learning, creating, and knowing. They will have a curiosity that is only achieved when one's own perspective is transformed and one moves on from being a mere spectator to being a builder in this original, mysterious world that we have inherited.

REFERENCE

Kahn, J. (1999, December 20). The global greats. *Fortune*, 222.

APPENDIX: PRODUCT LINES OF THE VIRTUAL UNIVERSITY

Currently, the Virtual University at Monterrey Tech has four product lines: academic programs, teaching skills enhancement programs, programs for business, and programs for public servants.

Academic Programs

Among the academic programs there are 16 master's programs in the areas of education, administration, engineering, and technology. All meet the quality standards that characterize the Monterrey Tech. Currently, there are approximately 9,800 students taking active part in these courses, while about 5,000 are registered at the undergraduate level.

Programs for Enhancing Teaching Skills

More than 9,000 professors have graduated from the ITESM Programs for Enhancing Teaching Skills each year. The growing number of participants from institutions other than the ITESM—especially grade school teachers —reflects the high level of interest in these programs and their impact on the educational community of Mexico and Latin America.

During the first year, 394 professors from two countries graduated. The second year, the figure grew to 3,200 teachers from four countries and by the third year, 9,555 professors from 10 countries participated in these programs. This is a very significant contribution of the Virtual University because it has a decisive impact on the quality of elementary education, where the most important educational problems in Mexico and Latin America reside.

Company Programs

Company programs of the Virtual University are offered in the Virtual Company Classroom and in company-based programs.

Universidad Virtual Empresarial is the first virtual interactive training satellite system designed to turn any meeting room into a Tech Classroom. The purpose is to raise the competitiveness of Mexican and Latin American companies through the educational services of ITESM, at their own facilities.

Currently there are 956 UVEs where seminars, special diploma courses, lectures, conferences, special programs and language courses are taught to 30,000 participants per year. The goal is 2,000 UVEs by the end of the Year 2000.

In company programs, as the name implies, are designed based on the specific competencies of a particular organization. To give an example, Bancomer was given a 14-hour program on organizational culture for 31,000 employees. Courses have been designed for Aeropuertos y Servicios Auxiliares, Gates Rubber de México, and Coca-Cola, among other organizations.

Training Programs for Public Officials

The changes undergone by Mexico in recent years have given rise to the need for training government officials so they can face the challenges of new competitive markets. With the purpose of bolstering the efficiency of people in government positions and supporting their commitment to the nation's well-being, the Virtual University facilitates concepts and techniques to help public servants plan their administration and use resources efficiently and productively. It also develops their managerial skills through the application of the principles of quality management.

The idea is to provide training at the different government levels—municipal, state, and federal—and in the different branches of government—legislative, executive, and judiciary.

The beginning is at the municipal executive level with a program called *Seminario de Alta Administración Municipal* (SAAM) [Senior Municipal Administration Seminar], which has successfully trained more than 3,000 public officials in nine countries, but this is only the beginning. The SAAM is predominantly a satellite model.

Chapter 8

The FAST Program: A Computer-based Training Environment

Sanjay Srivastava
Carnegie Mellon University

T he FAST program is a technology-based teaching and learning system for investment finance. FAST stands for Financial Analysis and Security Trading. The FAST teaching method is experiential in nature and has four main objectives:

- To provide a practical understanding of problems that commonly occur in financial markets.
- To teach the tools or theories that have been advanced to help solve these problems.
- To understand how these theories are put into practice and the tools applied
- To gain an understanding of how well these applications work.

This teaching method is implemented using Financial Trading System (FTS) software. The software lets students participate in two types of activities: interactive markets, in which students react to each others' decisions in real time, and simulated markets, in which students react to real-world prices and information. Detailed descriptions of the software, tutorials, and method of teaching are given later in this chapter.

CREATION AND EVOLUTION

The Origins

In 1988, John O'Brien, also a professor at Carnegie Mellon University, and I started adapting methods from experimental economics to financial markets. Our motivation was to build tools to conduct research in financial markets. Some 12 years later, more than 50 universities use the FAST learning environment.

Originally called *Simulab* (for simulation laboratory), the tools were developed to study behavior in successively more complex financial markets. The area of study was market efficiency, and we were particularly interested in studying how the efficient markets hypothesis performed when we confronted experimental subjects with more complexity in the nature of assets they were trading. This work is summarized in O'Brien and Srivastava (1991).

An efficient market is one in which the prices of financial assets reflect all available information. Some previous experimental studies had provided support for market efficiency, but these conclusions were obtained in very simple settings where not much sophistication was needed on the part of the subjects to reach efficiency. Because of this, a detailed analysis of the relationship between complexity and market efficiency was warranted.

We started with stock markets, making the relationship between information about a company and the value of the company more and more complicated in different experiments. The idea was to provide experimental subjects with some information about the prospects of different firms and then would trade the stocks of the firms with each other. We would then study whether the prices at which they traded were consistent with market efficiency.

In principle, the trading could have been conducted manually, i.e., with oral negotiation of prices, as in previous experiments of this type. But since we wanted to study complex environments, we quickly found manual trading to be difficult. This led us to develop the interactive market software that formed the basis of the FAST lab.

The FTS (Financial Trading System) is basically networked software that allows people to trade with each other. This means that they can set the prices at which they are willing to trade, agree to trades, and also keep track of their positions in the various securities. In 1988, network technology was not as developed as it is now, so we created a portable network—essentially a set of cables that allowed us to connect the computers together and transfer data. This network proved to be quite valuable in that it allowed us to carry the cables and set up connections anywhere.

Another problem was that we needed a pool of experienced subjects. When running an experiment, the subjects first learn how the environment works (including the mechanics of the software, the nature of the problem facing them, how they win, etc.). The solution was to conduct the experiments as part of a course, where we would have a dedicated pool of students whom we could train in different ways.[1] And so we offered a course with the unlikely name Simulab.

The first course was marked by technical difficulties. John O'Brien and I designed and wrote all of the software, and software fixes frequently were being made right up to the start of class. The computers were housed in a trailer, and the wiring for our portable network would often disconnect from the computers. Despite these difficulties, the course itself was very successful. The students greatly enjoyed learning by doing, and the course provided them with insights into several aspects of market interaction that they had not really thought about before. These included the relationship between the market mechanism[2] and market efficiency, and also the role of derivative securities (such as options) in disseminating information. This relationship is explored in O'Brien and Srivastava (1993). One comment from the students that stood out was that the course helped them understand the relatively abstract notion of market efficiency, because it is difficult to quantify exactly what it means for prices to reflect information.

In the subsequent two years, the course continued to enjoy success, and we completed our initial research agenda. The software was refined and made much more reliable, though the focus remained on market efficiency. The teaching method also evolved. Principally, we discovered that it was difficult to predict the outcome of the market trading sessions. While the theoretical solution was known, it frequently did not emerge from the trading. The role of the instructor therefore evolved into one of an interpreter of theories and concepts in light of market activity as opposed to simply an expositor of the theory. This is discussed in more detail below, in the detailed description of the learning environment.

Mexico, 1991

The next major development occurred in 1991, when we received visitors from Instituto Tecnologico y de Estudios Superiores de Monterrey (ITESM) in Mexico, including the Deans of two campuses. We were asked to demonstrate the system, after which we were asked if they could adopt it. This led

---

[1] Using proper controls and independent groups to retain experimental validity.

[2] That is, the rules by which trading is conducted.

to a trip to Mexico City the following week to test whether the FTS software worked on the computers in their labs. After a successful test, the system was adopted at three ITESM campuses: Mexico City, State of Mexico (just outside the city), and Monterrey. Over the next year, O'Brien and I commuted from Pittsburgh to Monterrey and Mexico City to teach classes on Fridays and Saturdays. This culminated in December 1992 with a special one-week class for about 20 instructors from the various ITESM campuses on using the system.

The experience with Mexico led to three major developments. The first was the preparation of an instructor's manual. It was a necessary part of being able to transfer the system to instructors at the ITESM campuses. The manual summarized the technical details of running the system, a course outline, lecture notes, questions the students may ask, and likely outcomes from a trading session.

The second development was an expansion of the system in terms of what could be taught using it. Recall that our initial focus was on stock markets. But at ITESM, the Simulab course had to serve as a general course in investment finance, and so it had to include material (including trading sessions) on other financial assets, such as bonds, options, and futures.

The final development was the emergence of linked sessions across ITESM campuses, where students at different campuses could trade with each other in real time. At that time, we exploited the capability of the satellite system that linked ITESM campuses to transmit real-time market information to the different campuses. Later, the system was extended so that different sites could be connected via a modem, and now, it can connect sites via the Internet.

Tokyo, 1992

In 1992, the School of International Politics, Economics, and Business (SIPEB) at Aoyama Gakuin University adopted the Financial Trading System. The adoption followed a similar pattern to Mexico: an initial visit to test the system, followed by courses taught in Tokyo as part of their MBA program, by John O'Brien and myself. The link with Tokyo led to the development of material on foreign exchange rates and in financial risk management, both areas of much interest to the participants there.

Due to the distance involved, we stayed in Tokyo for about three weeks at a time to teach the first few courses. Later, SIPEB created a global classroom that allowed us to teach by interactive video. The video-based courses were taught in conjunction with Aoyama Gakuin faculty, providing us with a way to transfer the teaching experience to their faculty over time. To this day, we continue to teach one course in this way. One of the purposes of the global classroom was to link students at different campuses. For several years, we held joint trading sessions between students at Carnegie Mellon and in Tokyo. Especially interesting were sessions where the students could see each other on the video as well.

The FAST Program and Live Market Data

In 1992, the FAST program was created to replace Simulab. FAST represented a major expansion of the ideas behind Simulab and the interactive markets it utilized. Through a partnership with Reuters, we obtained access to market data from all over the world, and the FTS software was extended to allow students to trade real-world securities at real-world prices. This led to the creation of the first educational trading room at a university, and simultaneously led to dramatic changes both in what was taught and could be taught using the system, and also in the demands placed on students and instructors.

The interactive markets have several important features. First, they are relatively simple and can be designed to focus on a small problem, or piece of a problem, at a time. Second, they are true markets in that one person can buy one only if another is willing to sell. Third, they last for a short time, allowing students to quickly experience a variety of situations.

Real-world markets, on the other hand, are not controllable in the same way. They are complex and interlinked, and it is usually difficult to isolate the impact of a particular event on market outcomes. From the point of view of trading, they also have the unrealistic feature that real-world prices do not react to student trading activity. The successful merger of the interactive markets and the real-world data took quite a while to achieve. Ironically, the main issue was complexity, the problem we started with in 1988 and was not solved effectively until 1993, when we developed the tutors, described below.

The Tutors

By early 1993, it was becoming clear that while the interactive markets were very successful in teaching financial concepts, the jump from them to the real-world markets was quite large. Three major problems were institutional details, market jargon, and computational complexity. The institutional details (for example, the way in which securities are quoted) meant that it was not easy to transfer knowledge acquired in the interactive markets to real-world data. The sheer quantity of jargon further impeded this transfer, and the types of computations required to apply concepts to real-world markets were not only beyond the capabilities of most of the students but also outside the scope of the courses we taught. Further, most instructors were not familiar enough with either the institutional details or the jargon to overcome these obstacles.

In an attempt to solve these problems, we created the tutors: CAPM Tutor for stocks, Bond Tutor, and Option Tutor. Each tutor comes in three parts. One part is analytical software that performs the calculations necessary to apply concepts to practice. The second is an online, hyperlinked textbook that contains the relevant theoretical material.[3] The third is the applications guide, also online with hyperlinks, which consists of step-by-step instructions, including explanations of the institutional details and jargon that allow the successful translation of theory into practice. (The applications guides and textbooks can be viewed at http://www.ftsweb.com and one example of a tutorial is given in Appendix C.)

Diffusion, Consolidation, Recognition

Starting in 1994, an increasing number of universities began to adopt the FTS software.[4, 5] Except for adapting the system to new network technology and operating systems, much of our effort in the next three years was devoted to revising, updating, and extending the support material. The applications guides that accompany the three tutors were completed, and this material was also published on the Internet.

We have spent considerable effort adapting the system to a large variety of countries and developing new cases that are relevant to changing market conditions. Because financial markets are so dynamic, we face constant pressure to adapt the system to new markets and instruments. This ongoing effort is greatly helped by the community of users, who typically spur system modifications. For example, both the Mexican devaluation in 1994 and the Asian currency crisis led to the creation of currency risk cases. The emergence of the Russian government bond market led to a series of cases on

---

[3]In 1993 and 1994, the textbooks accompanying the tutors, together with the early versions of the software, were published by Southwestern Publishing Company. The recent versions are only available online, mainly because of the frequency with which they are updated.

[4]Since the system requires an instructor, universities are the primary users of the interactive and simulated markets. Financial institutions interested in using the system for training typically work through a university. The tutors, on the other hand, are also used by traders at financial institutions and by individual investors.

[5]The current list of users can be found at www.ftsweb.com.

emerging market debt. The evolution of financial engineering techniques led to cases of risk management. The public disclosures on the two-tiered pricing system at the NASDAQ led to an adaptation of the system to allow dealers to trade at different prices than investors.

In 1996, the FAST lab won the Smithsonian-Computerworld Award for innovative uses of information technology and became a part of the permanent archives of the Museum of American History at the Smithsonian.

DETAILED DESCRIPTION OF THE LEARNING ENVIRONMENT

The Financial Trading System has three components:

- Interactive markets, where the students trade with each other.
- Real-time markets, where they trade at real-world prices.
- Tutors that combine analytical software, how-to tutorials, and also online texts.

Table 8.1 summarizes some basic dimensions of these three components.

Interactive Markets

In the interactive markets, students try to implement solutions to a variety of problems in a competitive, real-time setting. Students act as traders in the markets, react to market activity, and learn how their responses affect the market. The problem they face is summarized in a trading case that resembles the cases that are normally taught in investment courses at the undergraduate or MBA level.

TABLE 8.1   Basic Dimensions of FAST Components

Interactive Markets	Students trade and try to implement solutions to pre-designed problems. Requires real-time decision-making and adaptation to behavior of others and their response to your behavior.
Real Time Markets	Students manage portfolios but at prices taken from real-world exchanges. Requires reaction and adaptation to real-world events, but real world does not react to student actions.
Tutors	Calculators and graphical analytical tools to help understand real-world complexities and to aid in decision-making.

The best way to illustrate the teaching and learning process is to describe actual examples.[6] I will use two cases, case B04 and case RE1, summarized in Appendices A and B. The first case provides an example of using FAST to teach something that is usually taught in a traditional course. The second is an illustration of something that is easy to teach using the FAST program and quite difficult to teach otherwise. In fact, the latter was one of the cases for which the system was developed.

Case B04 (the bond risk case) deals with managing the risk of a portfolio of interest-rate-sensitive assets and liabilities, a problem faced by many banks, pension funds, and insurance companies. To further motivate the case, consider a pension fund, which has some defined liabilities (e.g., a series of payments that have to be made to retirees). Against these liabilities, the plan has assets (e.g., contributions that have been invested). Over time, as interest rates change, both the assets and liabilities will change in value. The problem is to ensure that the value of the assets does not fall below the value of the liabilities (which would mean that the pension fund is underfunded).

A classical technique to manage this type of problem is given by the bond immunization theorem. The theorem rests on calculating two values, the *duration* and *convexity* of the liabilities, and then choosing an asset portfolio so that the same values computed for the assets relate to those calculated for the liabilities.

We now have the problem that is faced and a proposed technique for solving it. This part is no different from typical classroom instruction. Where FAST differs is in the next step, where students are placed in the position of being asset-liability managers. In the case, they start with the defined liability and must acquire an appropriate asset portfolio. The case has been designed to match the assumptions of the bond immunization theorem, and so in principle, the proposed solution should work. Equipped with this knowledge and having performed their calculations, the students enter the market to execute their trades. Note that at this point, having analyzed the case and prepared a strategy, the students have already solved a problem set on this approach to asset liability management.

Our experience is that the theoretical solution typically does not come about, for several reasons. I will describe two. First, the theory assumes that you can always trade at the theoretically correct prices; in a typical market, this only happens if there is a lot of liquidity (i.e., lots of buyers and sellers

---

[6]While I will use a case involving bonds to illustrate the operation of the system, note that the FAST cases cover stocks, bonds, currencies, and derivatives such as options and futures, without any particular bias. Further, it is relatively easy to modify the existing cases to match conditions in different countries and also possible for users of the system to create their own cases.

willing to trade), resulting in the ability to execute trades at fair prices. In the interactive markets, however, it is not unusual to find that the prices at which others are willing to trade with you makes implementing of the theoretical solution a bad strategy. In fact, as soon as others know that you are trying to buy a particular security, the price of that security is quickly bid up. This means that to be successful, you must be able to react in real time to the actions of others and develop strategies, either in terms of the assets to be purchased or in the timing of the purchases, based on what is happening in the current market session.

A second reason that the expected result does not occur is that it is difficult to predict why others are trading. Although the case is phrased in terms of controlling risk, provides incentives to do so, and is presented in the context of a specific technique, some participants inevitably take on more risk for the possibility of obtaining higher returns.[7] Who will behave in what way is difficult to predict *a priori*, and can have a substantial effect on the nature of the market. In fact, the prices of the securities being traded soon reflect this behavior, sometimes making the original solution even worse!

Class discussion follows several repetitions of the session, at which time the general market activity is replayed and individual strategies discussed. This discussion typically focuses on various alternative strategies that could be employed and their relationship to the original theoretical strategy. In a course, subsequent cases would explore extensions of the basic environment, including real-world complications that will probably cause the theoretical result not to work as expected.

To summarize, the primary difference between teaching using the trading case and teaching using traditional methods is that rather than simply learning a technique, students are forced to think about the application of that technique. They learn very quickly that there is a big difference between the theory and the practice. This in itself raises some interesting challenges for the instructor; for example, having little control over the outcome, the instructor can be placed in the position of having to explain how an unexpected outcome arose. Another interesting experience of many instructors has been that the concepts and techniques typically have to be taught repeatedly, because students absorb them slowly as they begin to understand the application. We have also found enormous variations in how people learn; some are able to quickly move from theory to practice while others seem unable to comprehend the problem until forced to work through the application.

---

[7]There are well-documented cases of pension funds that have invested in risky securities for the extra return they offer.

The second case, RE1 (the market efficiency case) illustrates the ability of FAST to teach something that is quite difficult to teach in a traditional way. This case will illustrate how FAST can help make concrete concepts that are less straightforward in the traditional classroom.

Case RE1 is concerned with market efficiency, a concept that underlies much of modern finance. One definition of an efficiency is that the prices of financial assets should reflect all available information that affects the values of the assets. This is more abstract than the bond immunization theorem because it is difficult to quantify exactly what information affects asset values and what it means for prices to reflect that information.

The market efficiency case helps make these limitations concrete. In the case, there are two publicly traded firms. The future values of the stocks are determined according to a prespecified probability distribution. The students in the interactive markets have to determine how much they think the stocks are worth. In a typical trading session, each student is given private information about the prospects of the firms. The students are not allowed to see each other's information. In a simple form of the case, if anyone knew the information available collectively to the market, they could calculate the true value of each stock. So the market efficiency question can be framed simply: Is the price that emerges from the interactive markets consistent with the information collectively available to the market? This makes precise not only the information that is available but also what it means for prices to reflect this information.

The class discussion following the market session can now focus on matters such as whether the market was efficient or not, what factors contribute to efficiency, and how the trading process reveals information. More complex issues can also be addressed. For example, the FTS software allows changes in the market structure, from specialist markets to dealer markets, and we can study the effect of market structure on market efficiency. Another topic may be to introduce derivatives such as options, and see if markets with derivatives have different efficiency properties than those without. This flexible, experiential learning environment provides a powerful way to understand complex, abstract concepts.

Real-Time or Simulated Markets

The experience gained in the interactive markets is easily extended to real-world markets. These simulations incorporate data from international financial markets, providing a transition mechanism that allows participants to apply the knowledge they have gained from the controlled settings to the real world. Consider our bond risk case, B04. Here, the extension consists of a portfolio management exercise in which students are again given a liability stream but have to choose as their assets a set of bonds that exist in the real world. The asset portfolio and the liability stream are managed going forward in time, with portfolio values changing as real-world prices change. Various different strategies can be attempted, the aim again being to understand how well the theories work when actually implemented.

In the simulated markets, the students trade at prices taken from real world exchanges. This has one important drawback: Unlike prices in the interactive markets, these prices do not react to student behavior. However, they offer the benefit of providing exposure to and an understanding of real-world financial markets.

The simulated markets allow students to apply their knowledge to a wide variety of markets, including stocks, bonds, and derivatives. Unlike the interactive markets, the real-time systems need external market data. The FAST lab at Carnegie Mellon has relied on the Reuters data feed to obtain quotes on different securities from different exchanges, while other universities have used other systems, such as Bridge. Recent versions of the simulated trading system let students interact using data available on the Internet. This also has the advantage of letting students work on the exercises away from the lab and at their convenience.

It is important to understand that in these exercises, it is rarely the case that beating the market is important. In fact, we are careful to base our assessments mainly on how a concept was applied and how well the student understands the strengths and weaknesses of that concept. The latter becomes clear when students explain their performance relative to what was expected and in light of market events that occurred during the simulation.

The Tutors

The tutors are analytic tools that help students perform some of the more complex calculations required to apply portfolio management techniques in the simulated real-time markets. One complication introduced by the simulated markets is that the types of calculations students have to perform become much more complex. Returning to the bond risk case, there are typically thousands of combinations of bonds that can be chosen as assets to immunize a given liability. For example, on October 15, 1999, there were more than 300 U.S. Treasury securities with maturities ranging from two weeks to 30 years. So the first problem we face is: How do we make all the necessary computations for each bond? Once we have done this, how do we select a portfolio of assets out of all the possible combinations?

The first problem is mainly a computational one, whereas the second requires the development of additional concepts that let us apply the theory to practice. A third problem is to teach the institutional features that surround markets, such as the types of securities that are traded, how prices are quoted, how to obtain data, and so on. To solve these problems, the tutors for stocks, bonds, and derivatives allow students to quickly perform necessary calculations. Figure 8.1 illustrates calculations relevant for the bond immunization problem using Bond Tutor[8] and U.S. Treasury data.

Typically, the tutors are used in conjunction with the simulated markets.[9] In Fig. 8.2, the real-time position management system (which students employ to buy and sell securities) is illustrated with the same bonds. So we think of the tutors as providing analytical support to the students, whereas the simulated market system allows them to trade alongside real-world markets.

Over time, the tutors have been extended to include a wide-ranging set of tutorials that are comprehensive guides to the concepts of investment finance and their practical implementation. This includes information on how to obtain and analyze current and historical data and also includes the ability to "backtest" concepts, i.e., to see how the techniques being applied to the current market would have worked historically. Table 8.2 summarizes some of the learning features of the FAST environment.

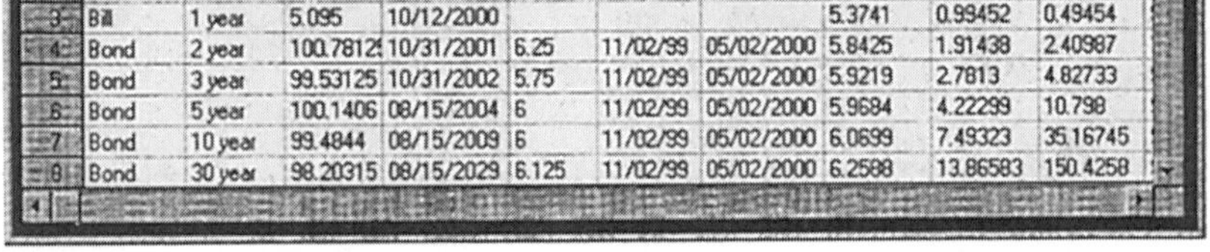

	Type [B/Z/N]	Name	Quote	Maturity	Coupon	Last Coupon	Next Coupon	Yield to Maturity	Duration	Convexity
1	Bill	3 month	4.35	11/04/99				4.4650	0.05479	0.0015
2	Bill	6 month	5.005	05/25/2000				5.2219	0.61096	0.18664
3	Bill	1 year	5.095	10/12/2000				5.3741	0.99452	0.49454
4	Bond	2 year	100.78125	10/31/2001	6.25	11/02/99	05/02/2000	5.8425	1.91438	2.40987
5	Bond	3 year	99.53125	10/31/2002	5.75	11/02/99	05/02/2000	5.9219	2.7813	4.82733
6	Bond	5 year	100.1406	08/15/2004	6	11/02/99	05/02/2000	5.9684	4.22299	10.798
7	Bond	10 year	99.4844	08/15/2009	6	11/02/99	05/02/2000	6.0699	7.49323	35.16745
8	Bond	30 year	98.20315	08/15/2029	6.125	11/02/99	05/02/2000	6.2588	13.86583	150.4258

FIG. 8.1. Sample Bond Tutor calculations.

[8]The title Spreadsheet Link relates to the part of Bond Tutor that links to data in a spreadsheet. Other examples of the tutors can be found at http://www.ftsweb.com.

[9]They are sometimes also used to support the trading cases in the interactive markets.

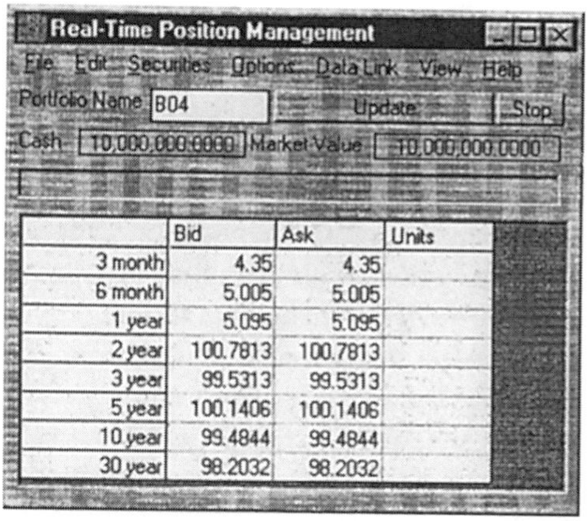

FIG. 8.2. The simulated market.

TABLE 8.2 Learning Features in the FAST Environment

- Active learning through trading.
- Experiential learning about differences between theory and practice.
- Opportunity to learn about complex concepts not easily taught in the traditional classroom (e.g., market efficiency case).
- Opportunity to learn in simulated real-time environments.
- Use of tutors to help students operate in complicated markets.
- Ability to learn at one's own rate.

SUCCESSES AND FAILURES

In the decade or so since we started, more than 50 universities in about 20 countries have used our software with varying degrees of success. There have been notable successes and also notable failures in the effective use of the system. Below, I will describe some of the results of various implementations and potential lessons.

In my view, faculty involvement is the most important factor in determining success or failure. Teaching with FAST requires the instructor to understand not only conceptual material but also how to translate it into practice. This can be difficult, especially in the fast-moving world of investment finance, but the successful use of the system demands it.

As a result, we have seen success whenever an individual faculty member has been the driving force—the faculty-champion—behind the system.

About 90% of the current users fall into this category. Although these instructors receive some support from their universities, they appear to be primarily self-motivated to explore innovative ways of teaching finance. The faculty tend to be comfortable with technology, a key element since the FAST learning environment is based on a technology infrastructure that requires flexibility and the capacity to adapt to unexpected outcomes. Teaching in this environment also requires instructors to deal with the uncertainties that characterize the constantly changing financial markets, the unpredictable nature of the simulations, and the uncertainty that comes with using technology-based learning tools. As opposed to a traditional form of teaching finance where an instructor can block out the activities for a given class in a fairly predictable way, the instructor in a FAST environment needs to be able to react to the new and unexpected events that occur in a simulation and use these as opportunities for learning. Another aspect of longer-run success has been an ability to attract faculty-champions into core teaching groups to support this form of learning.

The less successful cases have been those where an institution acquired the system and then asked its instructors to integrate it into their courses. There was little initial effort to assist faculty members in learning about FAST. Since this learning environment is so different from traditional methods of teaching finance, the selection, training, and motivation of the faculty-champion is critical.

Another factor in the less successful cases has been the failure to provide resources such as time off from other duties so faculty members could successfully implement the learning system.

A critical issue at the institutional level is to provide resources for both the implementation and sustainability of this learning environment and also for its evolution. In some of our earlier experiences, preoccupation with the technical aspects of FAST precluded some institutions from focusing on preparing the faculty, students, and organization to implement and accept the change. It is the level of integration of the technical and social aspects of this learning environment that are critical for its success or failure.

There are also cases in the middle, where success has come over a protracted period of time, involving a lot of effort on our part. Success at such institutions has typically come about as a result of the institution hiring instructors specifically to teach using the system.

Let me provide some specific examples of successes. A shining example of success is the experience of the Academy of the National Economy in Moscow,[10] which licensed the FTS software in 1993. This was a new direction for

---

[10]In the Soviet era, the academy was a training school for managers of state enterprises.

the Academy, which was using one of the first market-based training systems in Russia, and for us as well, since the Academy did not have an MBA program in which our courses could be easily intermingled. Olga Menshikova, an economist, and Ivan Menshikov, a mathematician, run the program, and, through great personal effort, created a very successful executive education market in investment finance.[11] All the material in the instructor's manual was translated into Russian, and our involvement with them led to the development of bond trading cases in emerging markets.

The success of the Academy's FAST experience stemmed directly from the determination of the instructors and managers of the program to succeed and their willingness to put in the effort required. What is remarkable is that they succeeded in a very difficult environment, where they created a market to teach investment finance in a country that at that time had virtually no financial markets.

Another example of success is at the University of Reading in Reading, England, where professor Brian Scott-Quinn started the International Security Markets Association (ISMA) Center. In just five years, the center grew to become one of the largest educational centers for investment finance in the world, and technology-based education forms the core of its educational mission.

Our efforts in Japan and at ITESM in Mexico have taken longer to succeed. This is partly because they were early adopters of the system, and our ability to diffuse the system was less than perfect. The fact that instructors were not already in place, with the appropriate buy-in to teaching with the system, has also delayed success. Both institutions now have faculty who were hired and trained specifically to use FAST resources, and both have firmly established their programs. In contrast, another university in Mexico City, ITAM (Instituto Tecnologico Autonomo de Mexico), adopted the system at the behest of a faculty member, and has been using it successfully from the beginning.

In terms of the learning environment itself, the content and supporting technology have changed in many ways. Many of these changes have been stimulated by an international partnership, others have been in response to changes in financial markets, and some have come about because of our own learning. The ability to evolve this learning system in response to changing demands is another component of its success.

---

[11]I had known Ivan previously because he and I had similar research interests in the mathematical modeling of voting systems.

RECENT DEVELOPMENTS

Without a doubt, the most important recent changes have occurred because of the Internet. One effect is financial, and comes from the widespread availability of free financial information. This means that the cost of setting up an educational trading room, like the FAST lab, has dropped dramatically. In the past, such an endeavor required considerable resources to pay for data, separate networks to maintain privacy of data, and personnel to manage the systems. Now, any computer lab has essentially the same capabilities and does not need to rely on proprietary data providers.

A second, related, implication has come from the changing demand for educational services. Before 1997, adoption of the system was driven either by individual faculty members or university administrators. Now, we find that students and individuals outside universities are increasingly using parts of the system on their own. Some of this is driven by the fact that computer technology has evolved considerably since we started, and some is driven by the widespread availability of data.

A software-related implication of data availability on the Internet is that we now face increasing pressure to automatically access and interpret data, including the merger of information from different sources to help analyze an investment problem. Much of our recent effort has gone in this direction. An example of this is in Appendix C, where a tutorial demonstrates the steps from accessing data to analyzing it.

Finally, perhaps the most significant future development I see is the much wider applicability of the double auction markets that form the basis of the interactive markets.[12] When we started, the dominant auction markets were stock markets and currency markets. Recently, however, we have seen wide-ranging applications of auction markets. These include financial activities such as auction markets for bond trading as well as applications in manufacturing and product distribution. The interactive markets provide a natural framework for extending the learning environment to this wider class of applications.

REFERENCES

O'Brien, J., & Srivastava, S. (1991). Dynamic stock markets with multiple assets: An experimental analysis. *Journal of Finance*. XLVI, 1811–1838.

O'Brien, J., & Srivastava, S. (1993). Liquidity and persistence of arbitrage in experimental option markets. In Friedman, D. & Rust, J. (Eds.), *The Double Auction Market* (Sante Fe Institute Studies in the Sciences of Complexity Proceedings, Vol. XIV) (pp. 397–419) Reading, MA: Addison–Wesley.

---

[12]A double auction market is one in which there are multiple buyers and sellers for the same objects, and in which prices at which traders are willing to buy and prices at which they are willing to sell are quoted.

APPENDIX A: SUMMARY OF TRADING CASE B04

Case Objective

To understand the concepts of duration and convexity; to learn how the bond immunization theorem is applied in managing the risk of bond portfolios.

Key Concepts

Duration; convexity; yield to maturity; interest rate risk; bond immunization theorem.

Case Description

There are four fixed-income securities. You only trade for one period, though the securities have cash flows up to four periods in the future. The cash flow from each security at the end of each period is shown below. You start with a negative (short) position in either the first or the second security, and can only trade the last two securities.

The yield curve is initially flat at 10%. After one period, it shifts either up or down, in a parallel fashion. Your position at the end of the period is marked to market at the new yield curve, and this determines your performance.

Prices in this case are determined by the traders, so all trades will take place at bids and asks that either you or another trader in the system enter.

Case Data

The cash flows from the securities are shown in Fig. A8.1.

	Payout at end of Period 1	Payout at end of Period 2	Payout at end of Period 3	Payout at end of Period 4
Sec 1	0	160	200	250
Sec 2	30	100	47	0
2YrZer	0	100	0	0
3YrZer	0	0	100	0

FIG. A8.1. Cash flows from securities.

Trading Objective

Your aim is to hedge the risk of your position to parallel shifts in the yield curve. Your compensation is the following:

Final Portfolio Value	Points
Less than 5000	0
Between 5000 and 10000	Equal the value divided by 1000
More than 10000	10

A trading screen sample is shown in Fig. A8.2

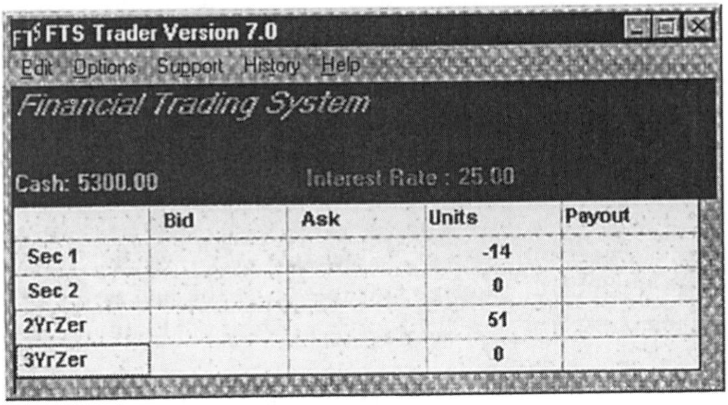

FIG. A8.2.   Sample trading screen.

APPENDIX B: TRADING CASE RE1

Case Objective

To understand market efficiency and the role of prices in disseminating information.

Key Concepts

Market efficiency; rational expectations

Case Description

There are two stocks, traded over two periods. The dividends paid by these stocks at the end of period 1 and the values of the stocks at the end of period 2 depend on what happens to each firm's local economy in general and to each firm in particular. The interest rate each period is set at 0%, so the time value of money plays no role in this case. You can borrow at this rate and also short sell the stocks.

The events that affect the values of the firms are given below. The firms compete in different markets, so the events affecting the firms are not correlated. In this case, the events affecting a firm are also independent across time. You may receive information about these events. This information is displayed in the input window and in the information window.

Case Data

Figure B8.1 describes the (independent) events facing each firm, and the dividends paid at the end of period 1.

The value of each firm at the end of period 2 depends on both the period 1 event and the period 2 event. See Fig. B8.2.

Firm ABC		Dividend
Event x	Poor economic conditions, labor strife	0
Event y	Poor economic conditions, no strife	12
Event z	Fair economic conditions, good labor relations	24
Firm CRA		Dividend
Event w	Poor economic conditions, labor strife	0
Event x	Poor economic conditions, no strife	12
Event y	Fair economic conditions, no strife	12
Event z	Fair economic conditions, good labor relations	24

FIG. B8.1.   Independent events and paid dividends—Period 1.

Firm ABC

Period 1 Event	Period 2 Event		
	x	y	z
X	0	0	12
Y	0	12	24
Z	12	12	24

Firm CRA

Period 1 Event	Period 2 Event			
	w	x	y	z
w	8	8	12	18
X	8	8	12	18
Y	8	8	12	18
Z	8	8	12	18

FIG. B8.2.   Details of Case RE1.

Trading Objective

Your aim is to make as much money as you can. See Fig. B8.3 for a trading screen sample.

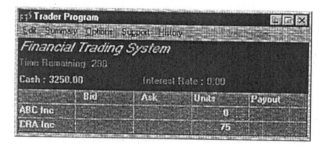

FIG. B8.3.   Sample trading screen.

APPENDIX C: SAMPLE TUTORIAL

In this tutorial, you will learn:

- How to get historical stock price data from the Internet.
- To study statistical properties of the data.
- How to select portfolios using mean-variance efficiency.

[Note: For this appendix, I have removed the technical details about interpreting and analyzing the data, and have provided links to the on-line applications guide where these details can be found.]

In the first step, we will use the Internet data capability of CAPM Tutor to collect historical data on eight technology stocks. We will store the data we download in an Excel spreadsheet, so we can use it repeatedly without having to download it every time.

We have typed in the stock names into an Excel spreadsheet, shown in Fig. C8.1.

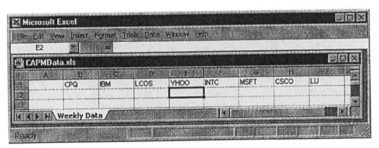

FIG. C8.1.   **Excel spreadsheet.**

Note that the tickers start in column B, which is the second column. The first column is reserved for dates.

Make sure this spreadsheet is running, run CAPM Tutor, and click on **Historical Data from the Internet**, as shown in Fig. C8.2.

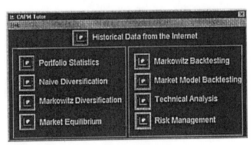

FIG. C8.2.   **CAPM Tutor contents screen.**

The screen shown in Fig. C8.3 will appear.

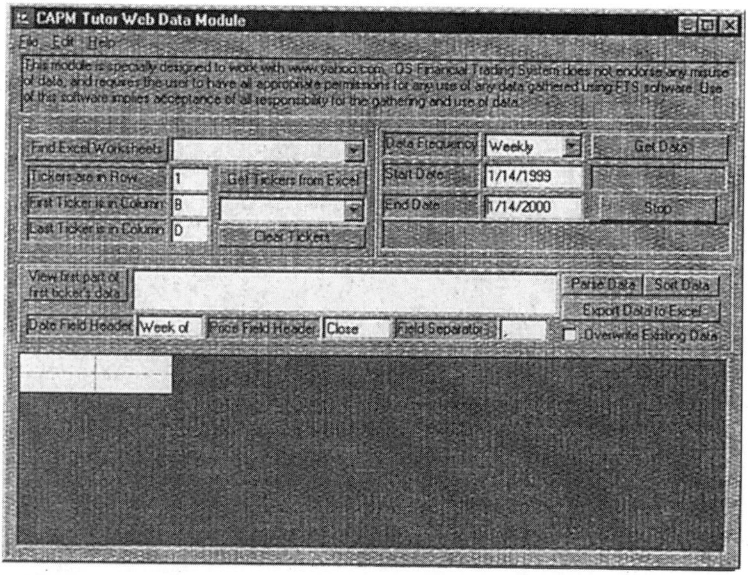

FIG. C8.3. Historical data module interface.

Reading in the tickers from our Excel spreadsheet

We can either type in the tickers or read them in from the spreadsheet; the latter is clearly more convenient.

- Click **Find Excel Worksheets** and select the worksheet **Weekly Data**. The tickers are columns B through I of row 1 (we reserve the first column for dates).
- Type in this information and then click **Get Tickers from Excel**. The program will now read in the tickers and allocate space for the data.
- Let us get daily data for one year. Set the data frequency and type in the relevant dates.
- Click **Get Data**. (The program retrieves the data from Yahoo.)
- Click **Parse Data**.

Your display now should look like Fig. C8.4.

- CAPM Tutor requires the data to be in historical order, while Yahoo provides it in reverse order. So click **Sort Data** and then **Export Data to Excel** to put it all in the spreadsheet. *Note:* the program writes the data starting in row 2. If you already have existing data, do not export the data to the same spreadsheet. Instead, copy the data and paste it in to where you want to store it.

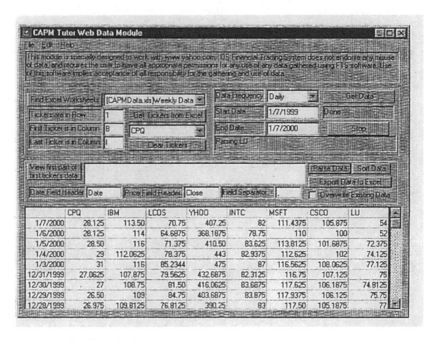

FIG. C8.4. Historical data module interface.

Once you have sorted and exported the data, your spreadsheet should look like Fig. C8.5.

	A	B	C	D	E	F	G	H	I
		CPQ	IBM	LCOS	YHOO	INTC	MSFT	CSCO	LU
2	1/7/1999	44.4134	94.8419	35.75	160	64.5132	75.25	51.8125	58.1743
3	1/8/1999	45.2231	93.3356	45.875	171.812	64.7316	74.9375	53.3438	57.5501
4	1/11/1999	48.2131	94.1753	65.5	207.688	69.7542	73.75	52.3438	56.3954
5	1/12/1999	46.4689	92.0915	52.25	201	67.684	71.0938	49.0625	53.8674
6	1/13/1999	45.7215	92.3092	48.4688	184	69.3798	71.9062	47.9375	52.0573
7	1/14/1999	44.4134	89.8833	42.875	171.969	66.7594	70.875	48.1875	52.8999
8	1/15/1999	46.4689	92.0293	43.9375	158.5	67.5704	74.875	50.8438	55.0534
9	1/19/1999	48.7114	95.6682	56.4688	161.5	69.567	77.8125	53.1875	56.9572
10	1/20/1999	48.0885	96.7879	52.4062	143.594	69.0055	81.3125	53.0625	57.675
11	1/21/1999	47.5279	98.0319	58.5	132.5	66.6346	79.1562	50.6562	53.3993
12	1/22/1999	46.0329	89.4479	55.0625	143	64.3261	78.125	51.4062	51.5891
13	1/25/1999	46.5312	90.5676	52.5938	156	65.1996	80.9375	51.7188	50.965
14	1/26/1999	49.0852	92.3715	55.1875	175.625	68.3503	85.7812	53.5625	54.9285
15	1/27/1999	47.341	88.7326	55.75	167.938	66.2602	84.3125	51.7188	55.6899
16	1/28/1999	47.0296	88.9192	61.5625	183.875	68.4751	87	54.4375	56.6657
17	1/29/1999	47.4858	91.1896	68.5	177.125	70.3469	87.5	55.7812	56.2286

FIG. C8.5. Sample historical data.

We are now ready to analyze the data. Close the CAPM Tutor Web Data Module, and select Portfolio Statistics from the main screen. Three windows will pop up, including the Excel Data Link. Our data are in columns B through I of the spreadsheet, and are in rows 2 to 255.

- Click **Find Excel Worksheets** and select **Weekly Data.**
- Type in the row and column information.
- Click **Initialize Excel Link.**
- Double click over CPQ to select all stocks. (See Fig. C8.6.)
- Click **Create CAPM Tutor Data Set.**
- The Excel Link window disappears, and the data have been successfully transferred.

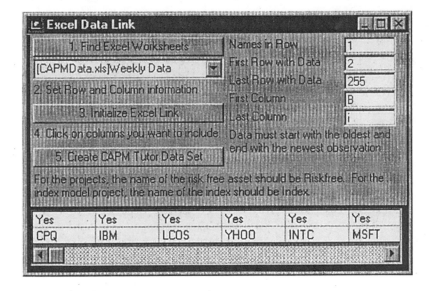

FIG. C8.6.   Excel data link example.

Figure C8.7 shows the Portfolio Statistics display now.

- Type in 1 next to Weights under CPQ. This means that the weight of CPQ in your portfolio is 1 or 100%, so that all your money is invested in CPQ.
- Click **Return Histogram.**

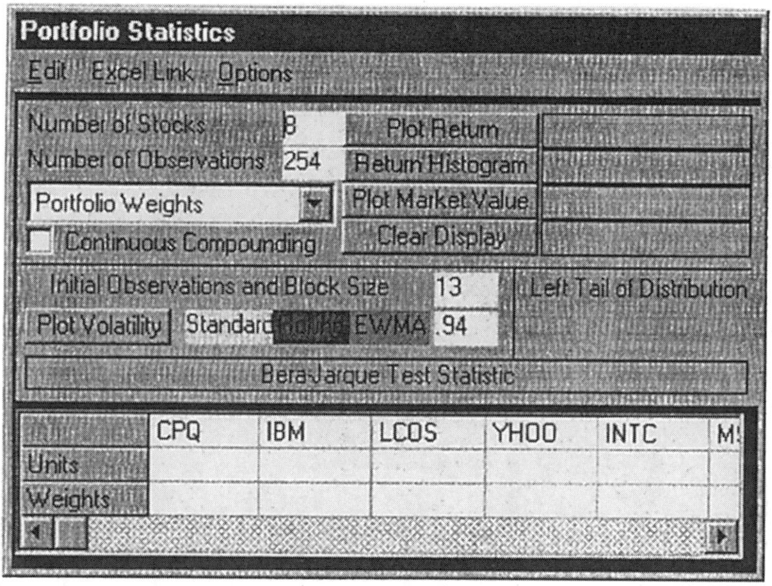

FIG. C8.7.   CAPM Tutor data analysis interface.

Figure C8.8 shows the displays.

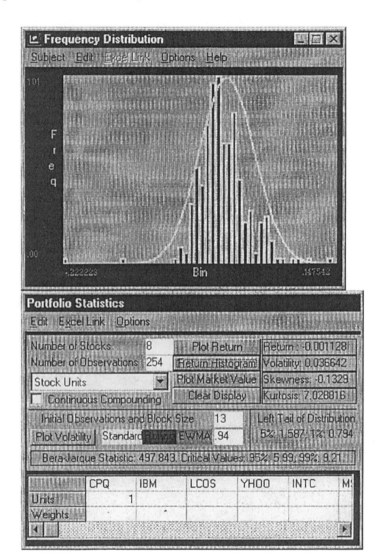

FIG. C8.8.   CAPM Tutor display: Portfolio return histogram.

You can see that the average return from CPQ over this period has been negative, with a lot of kurtosis. The histogram indicates that the returns have been concentrated in the middle with a few extreme losses. The smooth line shows you how the historical return distribution compares with the normal distribution. The Bera–Jarque statistic indicates a failure to pass that normality test.

Details on the statistics and their interpretation can be found in the CAPM Tutor Applications Guide at http://www.ftsweb.com.

- Type in 50 for **Initial Observations and Block Size** and Click **Plot Volatility** to see how the volatility of the stock return, calculated in three different ways, has performed. The display in Fig. C8.9 will show you the sharp changes in volatility that have occurred, ranging from about 2% a day to over 6% a day.

- You should study the properties of the different stocks as well of portfolio returns. For portfolios, simply type in either the quantity (or Units) of each stock held or the portfolio weight. It is important to understand these properties, specially deviations

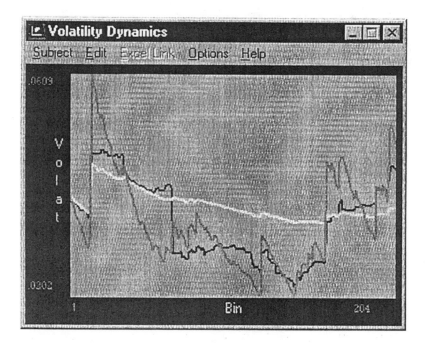

FIG. C8.9. CAPM Tutor display: Volatility analysis.

from normality, since many theories of portfolio selection are based on normally distributed returns.

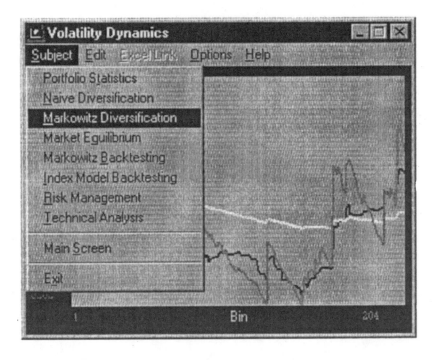

FIG. C8.10.   CAPM Tutor: Contents menu.

DIVERSIFIED PORTFOLIOS

From the Subject menu, select Markowitz Diversification (Fig. C8.10).

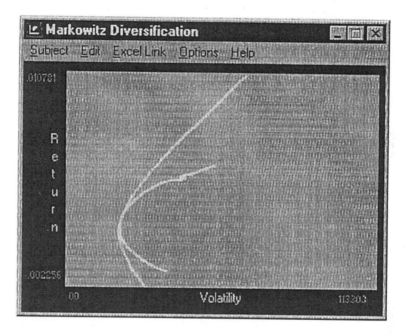

FIG. C8.11.   CAPM Tutor display: Efficient portfolios.

Reinitialize the data by clicking **Create CAPM Tutor Data Set** and say **Yes** if you are asked to rescale the display.

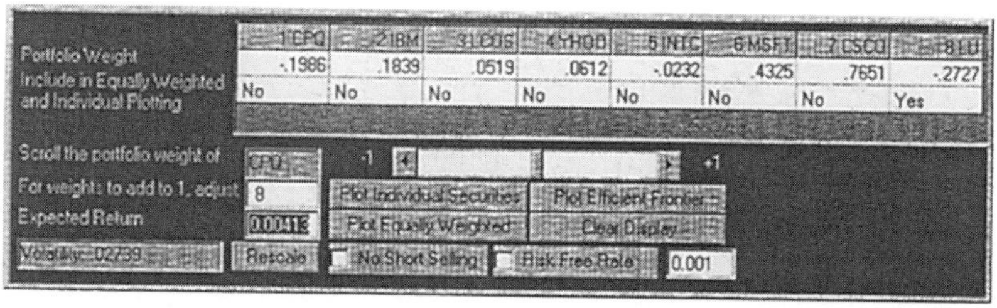

FIG. C8.12.   CAPM Tutor display: Portfolio selection.

Plot the Efficient Frontier with and without short selling. (See Fig. C8.11.) With short selling, type in the return 0.00413 and press enter. You will see

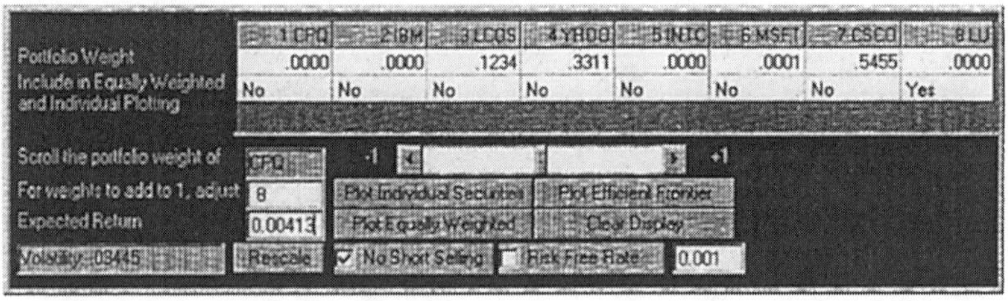

	1 CPQ	2 IBM	3 LCOS	4 YHOO	5 INTC	6 MSFT	7 CSCO	8 LU
Portfolio Weight	.0000	.0000	.1234	.3311	.0000	.0001	.5455	.0000
Include in Equally Weighted and Individual Plotting	No	No	No	No	No	No	No	Yes

Scroll the portfolio weight of	CPQ	-1 ◄ ► +1	
For weights to add to 1, adjust	8	Plot Individual Securities	Plot Efficient Frontier
Expected Return	0.00413	Plot Equally Weighted	Clear Display
Volatility .08445	Rescale	☑ No Short Selling ☐ Risk Free Rate	0.001

FIG. C8.13. CAPM Tutor display: Portfolio selection.

the portfolio weights corresponding to the return shown in Fig. C8.12. Now, switch on no short selling and press enter again. The portfolio without short selling is shown in Fig. C8.13.

The first portfolio short-sold CPQ while the second set its weight at zero. You can see that the volatility is higher with no short selling.

- Details on how to use CAPM Tutor for portfolio selection can be found at http://www.ftsweb.com.

Chapter 9

Cognitive Tutors: From the Research Classroom to All Classrooms

Albert T. Corbett
Kenneth R. Koedinger
William Hadley
Carnegie Mellon University

*I*n the late 1970s several researchers had the insight that artificial intelligence might be productively grafted into computer-based instructional environments. Reports of these now-classic projects in the book *Intelligent Tutoring Systems* (Sleeman & Brown, 1982) inspired our research team to begin developing a type of intelligent learning environment called "Cognitive Tutors™." Cognitive tutors are rich problem-solving environments constructed around a cognitive model of the learner. They are designed to facilitate learning by doing, to make thinking visible, and to support complex problem analysis, solution and communication. Our primary motivation 15 years ago was to develop authentic learning environments in which to test the evolving ACT-R cognitive theory (Anderson & Lebiere, 1998), but it quickly became clear that the cognitive tutors are very effective learning environments (Anderson, Corbett, Koedinger, & Pelletier, 1995). Students working with our early programming and geometry proof tutors outperformed comparable students in conventional learning environments by one standard deviation. This is about half the effect that human tutors can achieve (Bloom, 1984), but two or three times larger than the average effect of conventional computer-assisted instruction (e.g., Cohen, Kulik & Kulik, 1982; Kulik, 1994; Niemjec & Walberg, 1987).

In 1990, our team added an educational goal to our research agenda—to develop a cognitive tutor that could make the transition from our research labs and closely monitored classroom pilot projects to widespread dissemination. The resulting research project, funded by the National Science Foundation (NSF), produced the Cognitive Tutor Algebra I course and that course is in use in about 150 public and private U.S. schools during the 1999–2000 academic year, including urban, suburban, and rural high schools and middle schools in 14 states ranging from the east coast to the west coast, as well as a handful of postsecondary institutions and Department of Defense Education Administration schools in the United States and Europe. So far as we know this is the first intelligent learning environment to successfully make the transition into widespread use, and we expect the number of partner schools to continue increasing dramatically.

Our chapter describes this successful design research project through which we accomplished three major goals:

- Targeting a recognized educational challenge,
- Developing a comprehensive solution that is demonstrably effective, and
- Addressing the social context of the implementation of that solution.

In the following sections we briefly describe cognitive tutor technology, review its early hothouse successes, describe the challenges and successes of the Cognitive Tutor Algebra I project, describe the path forward, and conclude with a discussion of lessons learned.

COGNITIVE TUTORS—THE APPROACH

Individual human tutoring is perhaps the oldest form of instruction. Countless millennia since its introduction, it remains the most effective—and most expensive—form of instruction. In late 1970s and early 1980s there was a surge of interest in the potential of artificial intelligence to capture some of the benefits of human tutors in computer-based tutoring systems (Sleeman & Brown, 1982; Wenger, 1987). Intelligent tutoring systems (ITSs) are problem-solving environments that variously employ expert systems to (a) reason about the problem-solving domain and analyze student activity, (b) make decisions about instructional interventions, and (c) reason about the student's knowledge state. Early support for ITSs arose largely among artificial intelligence researchers who recognized them as rich environments in which to develop artificial intelligence algorithms. The principal measure of success was the proportion of student behaviors that an ITS could interpret and respond to meaningfully.

In the mid 1980s, our research lab began to develop a type of intelligent tutoring system called a *cognitive tutor*. Cognitive tutors are distinguished from the larger class of intelligent tutoring systems by their grounding in cognitive psychology. Each cognitive tutor is developed around a cognitive model of the problem-solving knowledge students are acquiring. A cognitive model is a type of rule-based expert system that is intended to solve problems in the same ways students solve them (e.g., Brownston, Farrell, Kant, & Martin, 1985). The initial motivation was to evaluate and develop Anderson's (1983) ACT* theory, a unified theory of the nature, acquisition, and use of human knowledge. As a result, cognitive tutors are grounded in empirical evaluations and empirically driven cognitive theory. Our tutor evaluation criteria have been educational effectiveness (Anderson, Corbett, Koedinger, & Pelletier, 1995; Koedinger, Anderson, Hadley, & Mark, 1997) and success in predicting student performance (Corbett & Anderson, 1995). Cognitive tutor research has served to validate ACT*'s fundamental assumption that problem-solving knowledge can be represented as a set of independent if-then production rules (Anderson, Conrad & Corbett, 1989) and has served to refine the learning assumptions in the more recent ACT-R theory (Anderson, 1993; Anderson & Lebiere, 1998).

Students working with a cognitive tutor interact with computer interfaces that support them in complex problem-solving activities. Under the surface, the Cognitive Tutor is tracking student problem solving actions using its cognitive model of the knowledge students are acquiring. Through a process we call *model tracing*, cognitive tutors can follow different students working through a problem in different ways and provide student-centered learning support that is adapted to each individual's approach and needs.

Completing a Problem

Figure 9.1 displays the problem-solving interface of our Algebra I Cognitive Tutor near the end of a problem. The problem statement in the upper left corner of the screen presents a situation and asks several questions. Students answer the questions by filling in the worksheet in the lower left corner. The worksheet starts out as an unlabeled table of empty cells. Students first identify relevant quantities in the problem and label columns accordingly, then enter appropriate units in the first row of the worksheet, enter a symbolic formula for each quantity in the second row, and answer the questions in successive rows of the table. Students also graph corresponding functions with the graphing tool in the upper right corner. Again, the

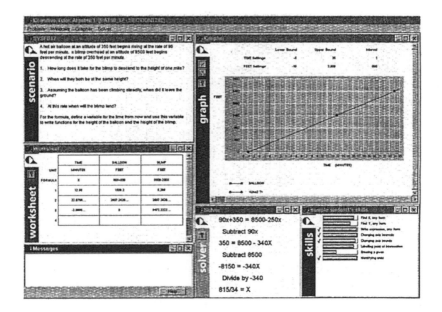

FIG. 9.1. The Algebra I Cognitive Tutor screen near the end of a problem.

grapher tool is an unlabeled grid at the beginning of the problem. Students label the axes, adjust the bounds and scale for each axis, plot the points from the worksheet, plot the linear functions, and compute the intersection. A symbol manipulation tool (middle bottom window) is available for students to use in answering the questions and finding the intersection of the functions. In this figure, the student has completed three of the questions in the worksheet, used the symbol manipulation tool to solve an equation in answering one question, and graphed one of the two linear functions.

Note that at any point in time, the student may pursue a variety of problem solving goals. For example, this problem describes a hot air balloon that is ascending and a blimp that is descending, and the fourth question asks: "At this rate, when will the blimp land?" The student might plausibly take four different problem-solving actions to begin tackling this question. She might:

1. Recognize that landing translates to a height of 0 and enter the given value 0 in the blimp column of row 4 in the worksheet;
2. Graph the blimp descent function to read off the elapsed minutes associated with a height of 0.

3.   Use the equation solver to find the elapsed minutes associated with a height of 0 by solving $0 = 8500 - 250X$.

4.   Unwind the equation $0 = 8500 - 250X$ in her head to find the elapsed time and type the arithmetic expression $-8500/250$ in the Time column of row 4.

In model tracing, the cognitive model can be used to trace the student's solution path no matter which of these options she pursues. The cognitive model runs in step-by-step synchrony with the student. At each step, the student's action (e.g., typing in a worksheet cell) is compared to all the actions the model is capable of generating at the time. As with effective human tutors, cognitive tutor feedback is brief and focused on the students' problem solving context. If the student action is correct it is simply accepted by the tutor. If the student action is incorrect, it is rejected and flagged (either in red or bold font). If the incorrect action matches a common misconception, the tutor also displays a brief just-in-time error message in the messages window (the lower left window of Fig. 9.1). The tutor does not automatically provide detailed advice, but instead offers students the opportunity to reflect on and correct their own mistakes. However, the cognitive model provides problem solving advice if the student asks. There are generally three levels of advice available for each problem-solving goal. The first level reminds or advises the student of an appropriate goal to accomplish. The second level provides general advice on solving the goal. Finally, the third level provides concrete advice on solving the goal in the current context.

Figure 9.2 displays some snapshots of characteristic student–tutor interactions. In the left panel of Fig. 9.2.1 the student has read the problem description and correctly typed "Time" at the top of the first column to label one of the relevant quantities. The student proceeded to label the second column, but typed a unit of measure—feet—instead of typing in the quantity that is being measured in feet. The tutor presents a just-in-time error message displayed in the right panel: "Feet is a unit to measure something in this problem. Try using a more descriptive phrase. What is measured in feet?" In the left panel of Fig. 9.2.2 the student has filled in the problem headers and requested help on the given value of the first question: "How long does it take for the blimp to descend to the height of one mile?" The right panel displays the three help messages that are displayed successively if the student asks for one, two, or three levels of help. When the second and third messages are presented, the words "blimp" and "height of one mile" are highlighted in question 1 of the problem statement window. In the left panel of Fig. 9.2.3 the student has entered the given value 0 for question 3: "Assuming the balloon has been climbing steadily, when did it leave the ground?" The student inad-

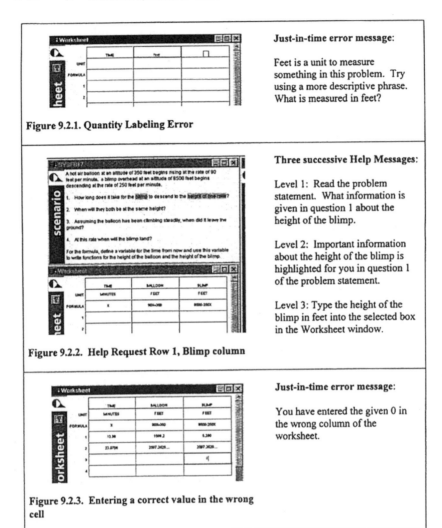

Figure 9.2.1. Quantity Labeling Error

Just-in-time error message:

Feet is a unit to measure something in this problem. Try using a more descriptive phrase. What is measured in feet?

Figure 9.2.2. Help Request Row 1, Blimp column

Three successive Help Messages:

Level 1: Read the problem statement. What information is given in question 1 about the height of the blimp.

Level 2: Important information about the height of the blimp is highlighted for you in question 1 of the problem statement.

Level 3: Type the height of the blimp in feet into the selected box in the Worksheet window.

Figure 9.2.3. Entering a correct value in the wrong cell

Just-in-time error message:

You have entered the given 0 in the wrong column of the worksheet.

FIG. 9.2.   Example student-tutor interactions.

vertently entered the value in the blimp column instead of the balloon column and the tutor provides the just-in-time error message: "You have entered the given 0 in the wrong column of the worksheet."

The cognitive model also is employed to monitor the student's growing knowledge during learning, in a process we call *knowledge tracing*. The tutor infers the student's knowledge of component problem-solving rules in the cognitive model from the student's performance and uses these estimates to individualize the problem-solving sequence. This student model is displayed on the screen in the "skillmeter" in the bottom right corner of Fig. 9.1. Each histogram represents a problem-solving rule in the model, and the shading represents the probability that the student knows the rule. Check marks indicate that the student has mastered the rule. Knowledge tracing is employed to individualize the problem sequence and help the student achieve mastery of the component problem-solving rules. Within each curriculum section, successive problems are selected to provide students the greatest opportunity to apply rules they have not yet mastered.

Cognitive Tutors in Context

Cognitive tutors are not intended to stand alone in education, but to serve as one tool in a full course curriculum. They do not provide declarative instruction, which is typically provided through class activities and reading. In our Cognitive Tutor Algebra and Geometry courses, 60% of class periods are organized around disposable looseleaf text materials. These class periods primarily consist of small-group problem-solving activities that are in turn reported to the full class. In the remaining 40% of class periods, students develop their individual problem-solving skills working with the cognitive tutor, which provides some of the benefits of an individual human tutor. Because help is available as needed on a step-by-step basis, students are able to advance at their own rate in the cognitive tutor lab and reach a successful conclusion to each task.

Cognitive tutors are not intended to replace the classroom teacher, but cognitive tutor courses offer most teachers new challenges and opportunities. While whole-group lecturing is the norm in American classrooms, learning is student-centered in our cognitive tutor courses and students learn by doing, rather than solely by listening and watching—both in the classroom and in the cognitive tutor lab. In the classroom, the teacher facilitates small-group problem-solving and whole-class discussions. In the computer lab, the tutors act as a set of classroom assistants that enable students to progress through the most common difficulties and free the teacher for more extensive individual interactions with students than are typically possible in a classroom setting. Perhaps the most common concerns that teachers express in preservice training are their own unfamiliarity with the cognitive tutor technology and classroom management issues that may arise with students moving at their own pace in the cognitive tutor laboratory. In practice, however, these concerns do not materialize. Students easily become familiar with the technology, and the tutors provide just the support students need to move successfully at their own pace. When we hold in-service training sessions after the courses have started, teachers have more questions about managing small-group problem-solving than about managing the cognitive tutor lab.

LABORATORY AND HOTHOUSE CLASSROOM SUCCESS

The first two cognitive tutors we developed in the mid 1980s were a Lisp Programming Tutor and a Geometry Proof Tutor. Each of these tutors is a problem-solving environment analogous to the Algebra I Cognitive Tutor displayed in Fig. 9.1. The Lisp Tutor, which is closely integrated with a Lisp programming text (Anderson, Corbett, & Reiser, 1987), has been in continuous use in a self-paced programming course at Carnegie Mellon University since 1984. Students read through the text and complete corresponding programming tasks with the help of the Lisp Tutor. The Lisp Tutor has proven to be an extremely productive research environment (Anderson, Conrad, & Corbett, 1989; Corbett & Anderson, 1995; Corbett & Trask, 2000) as well as a highly efficient learning environment. Students working with the Lisp Tutor completed programming problems in as little as one-third the time required by comparable students working in a conventional programming environment, as displayed in Fig. 9.3, while scoring 25% higher on subsequent tests (Corbett & Anderson, 1991).

The Geometry Proof Tutor (GPT), which was developed to support students in completing Euclidean proofs, was piloted in a Pittsburgh high school from 1985 to1987. This project served as an early prototype for our current high school math tutor project. Students used the tutor in their regularly scheduled geometry classes and with the geometry teacher in the room. GPT also proved to be a highly effective learning environment. Students in the GPT classes scored a letter grade higher on a subsequent paper-and-pencil geometry proof test than comparable students in control classes, who spent the same amount of time in conventional classroom problem-solving activities, paper-and-pencil seatwork, and boardwork.

During this pilot, Janet Schofield, a social psychologist at the University of Pittsburgh, completed an important observational study of GPT's impact on the classroom as part of a larger study of the impact of computer technology in a Pittsburgh high school (Schofield, 1995). She noted that the cognitive tutor transformed the classroom in two general ways, as summarized in Fig. 9.4.

Schofield observed that cognitive tutors transformed the teacher–student relationship. Teachers spent more time interacting with students who needed the most help, in contrast with whole-class instruction in which teachers tend to interact with the more successful students. The teachers

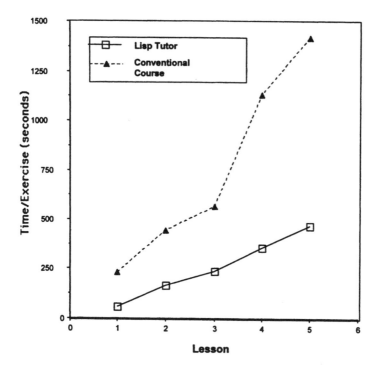

FIG. 9.3. Average Lisp programming problem completion times across five lessons for students using the Lisp Tutor and students working in a conventional programming environment.

spent the most time in extended interactions with individual students in the act of problem-solving and learning by doing. Schofield also documented that students found cognitive tutors motivating. She noted increased time spent on tasks, greater involvement, and increased effort. She noted that students in the comparison classes spent as much as 15 minutes chatting about nonacademic topics. In contrast, during the tutor sessions, it was common for students to begin working before the starting bell and to continue working after the closing bell. In one anecdote, she noted that a fist-fight almost broke out between a student who arrived early to work on geometry proofs and another student who was working late on the same workstation.

Both the Lisp Tutor and Geometry Proof Tutor represent hothouse successes. The self-paced course that employs the Lisp Tutor (and subsequent Prolog and Pascal tutors) has been taught exclusively by its developers. When GPT was piloted a member of the university research team was al-

---

Cognitive Tutor Technology Transforms the Classroom

1. Cognitive tutors transform the teacher-student relationship.

    • Teachers serve as collaborators in learning.

    • Teachers shift attention to students who are struggling.

    • Teachers provide more extensive individualized help.

2. Cognitive tutors motivate students to spend more time on tasks.

    • Students view the environment as a personal challenge/competition.

    • Students enjoy using the tutor.

    • Students feel free to express negative affect.

    • Students feel less embarrassed when they make mistakes.

(Schofield, 1995)

FIG. 9.4.   Impact of cognitive tutor technology on the classroom (Schofield 1995).

ways present in the classroom. To take the next step, these two projects were followed by the ANGLE Geometry Tutor Project, which marked a transitional phase in moving from the research lab to the classroom (Koedinger & Anderson, 1993). Like GPT, ANGLE is a problem-solving environment in which students construct graphical representations of Euclidean proofs, as shown in Fig. 9.5.

In each problem-solving step, the students select premises, post a conclusion, and identify the theorem justifying the conclusion. As with the earlier tutors, ANGLE proved to be a highly effective learning environment, but even more importantly the ANGLE project provided two lessons that helped guide the subsequent Algebra I project. For the first time, we encountered a curriculum compatibility problem. By the time ANGLE was piloted, the city high schools had adopted a new geometry text that de-emphasized proofs (in response to the 1989 National Council of Teachers of Mathematics curriculum standards), and it was difficult to integrate the tutor into the course. Second, the ANGLE evaluation study revealed a significant teacher interaction effect. The project teacher who had helped develop the tutor and was inti-

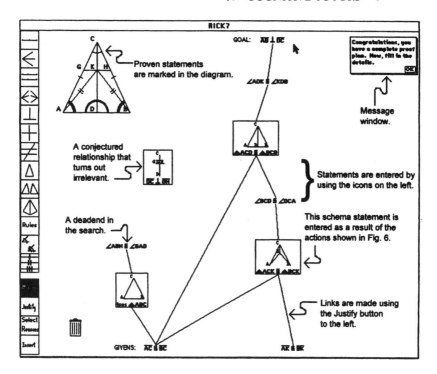

FIG. 9.5. The ANGLE Geometry Tutor. Reprinted from A. Corbett, K. Koedinger, and J. Anderson, *Intelligent Tutoring Systems*, copyright © 1997, p. 862., with permission from Elsevier Science.

mately familiar with the integration strategy achieved greater learning effects than other teachers who were much less familiar with the integration strategy. This result underscores the critical role of addressing the context surrounding educational technology use. Without careful attention to curriculum integration and sufficient training for teachers, an otherwise good solution may not reach its potential.

WIDESPREAD DISSEMINATION

In 1990, we embarked on an NSF-funded project to develop a cognitive tutor application that would not only be an effective research and teaching tool but that could make the transition from hothouse success to widespread use. We set the following goals to achieve this outcome:

- Target an important educational need,
- Develop a comprehensive educational solution,
- Demonstrate the educational effectiveness of the solution, and
- Support adoption and successful use by addressing the social context of implementation.

Our efforts to satisfy these goals are described in the following sections.

Need: The Crisis in U.S. Mathematics Education.

In 1990, a crisis in mathematics education was recognized across the United States. This realization dates back to the 1983 report by the National Commission on Excellence in Education entitled *A Nation at Risk: The Imperative for Educational Reform*. This report sounded alarms concerning mathematics, language arts, and science education. It offered a dozen indicators that K-16 education was failing students across these domains. A key indicator of failure in mathematics education was the dramatic increase in college courses that review high school math content. In public four-year colleges between 1975 and 1980, developmental mathematics courses that remediate algebra and geometry increased by 72%, growing to represent one-quarter of all mathematics courses taught. Developmental mathematics continued to be the fastest-growing component of postsecondary mathematics instruction throughout the 1990s.

Successive administrations of the National Assessment of Educational Progress proficiency tests in 1982, 1986, and 1990 offered some small encouragement, as mathematics achievement levels gradually crept upward, a trend that continued throughout the 1990s. The 1996 National Assessment of Educational Progress (1997) found that while mathematics achievement levels across the 4th, 8th and 12th grades increased an average of 10 percentage points since 1990, 80% of students performed at a less than proficient level. Also, American high school students were reliably outperformed in mathematics achievement by students in 14 of 20 comparison countries in the Third International Mathematics and Science Study (U.S. Department of Education, 1998).

Algebra and Geometry for All Students. In an early response to this mathematics education crisis, the National Council of Teachers of Mathematics (NCTM) produced a series of reports beginning in 1989 with recommendations for curriculum, teaching and assessment reform. One key recommendation of the first NCTM report was that all students should take algebra and geometry. This recommendation reflected both the perceived importance of mathematics in the emerging high-tech economy and empirical findings on the importance of algebra and geometry. For instance, a study by Pelavin & Kane (1990) investigated numerous potential factors contributing to students' college performance and found that the best predictor of college success was taking and passing algebra and geometry in high school. While the NCTM recommended algebra and geometry for all students, it did not recommend the traditional algebra and geometry content and style. Instead, the group recommended an emphasis on problem-solving, reasoning among multiple representations (e.g., natural language, tables, graphs, symbolic expressions) and communication. This emphasis was consistent with the recommendations of mathematics education researchers (e.g., Janvier, 1987; Kaput, 1989).

Developing a Comprehensive Solution: Cognitive Tutor Algebra I

In 1991, the Carnegie Mellon research team first partnered with the third author, Pittsburgh public schoolteacher Bill Hadley, who served as the curriculum expert on the Algebra I project. The Carnegie Mellon team had also partnered with highly talented teachers in the previous geometry projects, but in the Algebra I project we entered without preconceived notions of the curriculum content. An important difference from the geometry projects is that we set out to develop a full one-year course into which the cognitive tutor would be integrated. Curriculum content decisions were guided by Hadley, who had independently begun developing a new curriculum consistent with the NCTM reform standards. The course that was developed addresses both basic foundational skills and the higher-order reasoning skills advocated by the NCTM. Students are asked to model authentic problem situations with tables, graphs, and symbolic expressions; solve the problems; and express their solutions in writing using complete sentences. Figure 9.6 displays a sample final exam question that exemplifies the course objectives. These objectives guided the development of the cognitive tutor problem-solving interface displayed earlier in Fig. 9.1. The design of the cognitive model and the text materials were guided by cognitive principles based on the ACT-R theory and by empirical studies of algebra student thinking and learning.

The principal ACT-R assumption guiding design of the cognitive tutor and cognitive model is the distinction between declarative and procedural knowledge.

Declarative knowledge is the factual or experiential knowledge that is absorbed (or encoded) through observation or instruction. In contrast, pro-

---

Cellular Telephone Problem (Day 1)

You are told that tomorrow you are to order cellular phone service for the officers in your company. Your boss will provide you with information about the amount of "airtime" (number of minutes of phone time) per month that each officer needs. She will have this information for you about an hour before you must present your report to the president of the company.

The local cellular phone company provides this information about their three services.

Economy Service: Costs $19.95 per month and $0.31 per minute of airtime.
Silver Service: Costs $40.95 per month and $0.16 per minute of airtime.
Gold Service: Costs $80.95 per month with no charge for airtime.

To prepare for tomorrow you must do a mathematical analysis of these three different plans. This analysis should include defining variables, writing equations, making tables, constructing graphs, finding slopes and intercepts, and finding points of intersection. Your boss suggests you look at these plans over a range of airtime from 0 to 500 minutes per month, and how much airtime that you can get per month with each of these plans for a total cost of $100. She also makes it very clear that you must include the range of airtime for which each plan is the cheapest.

PRODUCE THIS ANALYSIS! Work you do today will be collected and can be used tomorrow.

Cellular Telephone Problem (Day 2)

One hour before the meeting where you will present your recommendation for cellular service, your boss provides the following data on the company's employees projected cellular phone use.

President and Vice-President (2 people): Both of these officers project that they will need on average 600 minutes of airtime per month.

Other Executive Board Members (10 people): These employees project their average airtime to be about 180 minutes per month.

Managers (20 people): The managers project their airtime to be on average about 50 minutes per month.

Use this information and the analysis you made yesterday to write a report recommending which of the three plans your company should use for their employees. You may recommend one plan or different plans for different employees, but you must support your recommendations with mathematical information from your analysis. Your boss has also directed you to include in your report reasons why you believe that the solution that you have recommended is the best for each group of employees and the company. (Your boss reminds you to make sure to include the range of airtime minutes per month when each of the plans would be cheapest!!)

FIG. 9.6. Algebra I final exam question.

cedural knowledge is goal-oriented and mediates problem solving. The ACT-R theory assumes that students initially encode declarative knowledge or facts (e.g., adding the same quantity to both sides of an equation preserves the equality). Early in problem-solving, students employ analogy and very general problem-solving skills to relate the declarative knowledge they have gathered to relevant problem-solving goals. Subsequently, domain-specific procedural knowledge is encoded as a set of independent if-then production rules that reference the problem-solving goal, the current problem state, and what actions to take (e.g., if the goal is to solve an equation of the form ax + b = c for x, add –b to both sides and solve the resulting equation). Both declarative and procedural knowledge are strengthened with repeated applications.

The use of inductive support in the algebra tutor is an example of empirically driven tutor design. We hypothesized that initial algebra learning would be more effective if we provided inductive support, that is, if we helped students generalize abstract algebraic symbol patterns from their existing concrete knowledge of arithmetic procedures (cf., Bednarz, Kieran, & Lee, 1996). When presenting word problems—for example, "A rock climber is on the side of a cliff 67 feet off the ground and climbing at a rate of 2.5 feet per minute"—U.S. algebra textbooks (e.g., Forester, 1984), typically ask students to start by representing the situation in an algebraic expression (e.g., 67 + 2.5x), and then to solve for a particular concrete instance of that expression (e.g., x = 2). In the inductive support strategy, students first are asked to solve the word problem for a concrete instance, like 2 minutes. Only then are they asked to write the abstract algebraic expression, which they can now do more easily than in the traditional approach because they can generalize from the arithmetic steps they performed (e.g, 2*2.5 + 67). In a laboratory study comparing alternative versions of the initial Algebra I Cognitive Tutor, we demonstrated that students learned significantly more using an inductive support version of the tutor than with a version based on an existing textbook approach (Koedinger & Anderson, 1998). It is interesting to note that the introduction to writing expressions in a text from Singapore (Singapore Ministry of Education, 1999), the top-performing country in the international study of 8th grade level-math performance (U.S. Department of Education, 1998), has students first solve for a concrete instance before abstracting to the algebraic expression.

Demonstrating Educational Effectiveness

We began piloting the Algebra I course in Pittsburgh's Langley High School in 1992–1993. Students worked with the cognitive tutor two days a week and participated in other classroom activities the other three days. These other activities included some whole-class instruction and extensive small-group problem-solving activities with the paper curriculum. The pilot project was extended to two other city schools in 1993–1994, and a year-end assessment of the course was completed that year (Koedinger, Anderson, Hadley, & Mark, 1997) and then replicated in 1994–1995. Because our Algebra I curriculum and cognitive tutor address both basic foundational skills and higher-order problem-solving skills, the evaluations were designed to test achievement in both categories. Table 9.1 displays the results of these assessments. *Standardized Assessments* in the table include questions excerpted from the Iowa Algebra Readiness Test and a subset of Math SAT questions. The NCTM *Standards Assessments* include a problem situation test that assesses students' success in applying an algebraic analysis to authentic problem situations and a representation test that assesses students' success in pairwise translations among symbolic, graphical, tabular, and verbal representations. These tests were designed to be challenging for students and avoid ceiling effects that would reduce the sensitivity of comparisons.

To summarize the results, the Cognitive Tutor Algebra I course led to large and consistent gains on the NCTM standards oriented assessments (approximately 100% improvement over the control subjects) and moderate and statistically reliable gains on the standardized assessments (about 10% improvement over controls).

Another form of effectiveness validation comes from the U.S. Department of Education, which recently completed a review of 61 K-12 mathematics curricula submitted by developers-vendors. The programs were reviewed on three criteria: quality, usefulness to others, and educational significance. Cognitive Tutor Algebra I was one of five curricula receiving the highest, "exemplary" designation.

TABLE 9.1 Year-End Assessments of Cognitive Tutor Algebra I

1993–1994 Year-End Assessment: Three Pittsburgh High Schools		
	Assessment Measure	
	NCTM Standards proportion correct	*Standardized Assessments proportion correct*
Cognitive Tutor Algebra I	0.38	0.42
Traditional Algebra I	0.19	0.37
1994–1995 Year-End Assessment: Three Pittsburgh High Schools		
	Assessment Measure	
	NCTM Standards proportion correct	*Standardized Assessments proportion correct*
Cognitive Tutor Algebra I	0.21	0.35
Traditional Algebra I	0.11	0.33

Addressing the social context of educational technology implementation

As we learned from the ANGLE field studies described above, successful educational technology implementation requires more than just a good technology. Attention must be paid to the social context of the school, training center, or company in which the technology is being used. From the beginning of the Cognitive Tutor Algebra 1 project, we paid close attention to integrating the technology with existing curriculum objectives, textbooks, and teaching processes. As we began disseminating the course, we continued to address issues of social context. In 1995–1996, our research team began disseminating the tutors more widely beyond the three alpha research sites. We issued a request for proposals, made subsequent presentations to teachers and administrators, and recruited three Pittsburgh-area suburban school districts that year. Our goal was to enter into an ongoing educational partnership with client school districts in which the technology served to empower rather than replace the classroom teachers. As documented by Schofield (1995), our technology enables teachers to engage in extended interactions with individual students while the other students are engaged and making effective progress with the cognitive tutor.

Our contributions to the partnership included a number of efforts that went beyond technology research and development *per se* to address various elements of the context of technology use. These contributions included:

- A loose-leaf paper curriculum that currently contains five volumes: a 400-page text, assignments, assessments, a teacher's edition, and a cognitive tutor users' guide.
- Installation of the cognitive tutor in a workstation lab.
- Required preservice training for all teachers.
- Site visits during the academic year for additional in-service training.
- E-mail and telephone hotline support for technical and curriculum questions.
- E-mail users group.
- Teacher focus group feedback meetings.

Dissemination Progress

In addition to our three alpha research sites in Pittsburgh and three new suburban sites, two colleges began piloting the Algebra I Cognitive Tutor in developmental mathematics courses in 1995–1996 bringing the total number of sites to eight. In 1996–1997 we offered the cognitive tutor to high schools outside the Pittsburgh area for the first time and the course was piloted in eight Milwaukee, Wis., schools and in one Pensacola Fla., high school. The Milwaukee project has now grown to 13 schools and the school district has designated a half-time lead teacher to serve as coordinator and liaison. Two Pittsburgh-area schools also joined the project that year, along with four Department of Defense Education Administration (DoDEA) schools in Europe and a third college, bringing the total sites to 24. Nationwide dissemination has continued to grow at a steady rate; in 1998–1999 Cognitive Tutor Algebra I was being used in 75 schools, including such locations as Norwalk Conn., New York City; Buffalo, N.Y.; Charlottesville, Va.; Knox County, Ken.; San Diego, Calif.; and Reynolds, Ore (Fig. 9.7). In July 1998, Carnegie Mellon University founded Carnegie Learning, Inc. to assume responsibility for dissemination and support of the Cognitive Tutor Algebra I along with the Cognitive Tutor Geometry and Algebra II courses that were subsequently developed at the university. In the current academic year (1999–2000), about 150 schools are employing one or more cognitive tutor mathematics courses and more than 300 sites are projected for the 2000–2001 academic year.

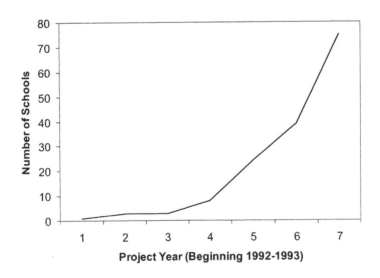

Dissemination of Cognitive Tutor Algebra I

FIG. 9.7.   Dissemination of the Cognitive Tutor Algebra I course.

An important point to make is that with the exception of the three initial alpha sites, three colleges, and DoDEA schools, this dissemination was entirely self-funded by participating schools. The site-license fees have changed over the years, particularly as dissemination activities moved beyond the Pittsburgh area, but for the past few years, the fee for a single-school site license has been $25,000. Schools have variously paid these fees with textbook funds, discretionary funds, and both public and private grants.

PATH FORWARD AND CURRENT CHALLENGES

We have built on the success of the Algebra I Cognitive Tutor project in three related directions. First, we established the Pittsburgh Advanced Cognitive Tutor Center at Carnegie Mellon in 1995 to continue basic research and practical development of cognitive tutors. Second, as described earlier, Carnegie Mellon University established Carnegie Learning, Inc. in 1998 to assume market-driven research, development, and dissemination activities. Third, in 1999, in a joint effort with the University of Pittsburgh, we received a major grant from the National Science Foundation to form a research center to study human tutoring and to develop dramatically more effective third generation computer-based tutors.

The PACT Center

The Pittsburgh Advanced Cognitive Tutor (PACT) Center was established at Carnegie Mellon to continue research, development, and piloting of cognitive tutor technology and courses. Our team has just concluded a project in which we developed Cognitive Tutor Geometry and Algebra II courses. This project was funded by five Pittsburgh-area foundations (the Howard Heinz Endowment, the Buhl Foundation, the Grable Foundation, the Richard King Mellon Foundation, and the Pittsburgh Foundation) to improve mathematics achievement both locally and nationwide. We have just embarked on a middle-level mathematics project in which we are developing a three-year sequence of courses leading up to algebra. In this project, we will continue the research and development practices we believe were critical to the success of Cognitive Tutor Algebra I. These practices include "participant design" (cf. Beyer and Holtzablatt, 1998), whereby practicing teachers work half-time on our development team and half-time in the classroom piloting evolving versions of the tutor and text materials, and "principled design" in which we bring to bear cognitive theory and empirical methods to better understand and address student learning needs.

Carnegie Learning, Inc.

In parallel with our university-based dissemination of Cognitive Tutor Algebra I, the Carnegie Mellon Technology Transfer Office engaged in licensing negotiations with several textbook publishers, educational software companies and computer companies. As our dissemination activities progressed, we realized that our educational partnership dissemination model varied from the models of these well-established outlets. As a result, Carnegie Mellon spun off a new company, Carnegie Learning, Inc., to assume the market-driven development and dissemination activities piloted in the PACT Center. Carnegie Learning has already more than doubled the number of schools around the country that are committed to the Cognitive Tutor Mathematics courses and expects more than 300 sites in the 2000–2001 school year. Carnegie Learning, Inc. is building on this success to fund the PACT Center's middle-school mathematics project mentioned in the prior section. The company will begin assuming broader research and development activities over the coming years and is simultaneously identifying other examples of successful educational technology guided by cognitive science principles that can broaden its offerings of educational solutions.

The CIRCLE Center

Fifteen years after the inception of intelligent tutoring systems, human tutors remain the most effective and most expensive learning environments. As a consequence, the National Science Foundation has funded a joint Center for Interdisciplinary Research on Constructive Learning Environments (CIRCLE) at the University of Pittsburgh and Carnegie Mellon to study the effectiveness of both human tutors and computer tutors. The end result is intended to be a third generation of computer-based tutors that make more effective use of natural-language dialog and problem-solving scaffolding that more nearly approximate those used by human tutors.

LESSONS LEARNED: KEYS TO DISSEMINATION SUCCESS

We end with some general observations about the dissemination of educational technology. The decision to adopt Cognitive Tutor Algebra I is not an easy one. When a school adopts the program it is not adopting supplemental software that can be added to existing practice. Instead, the school and its mathematics faculty are adopting a new course curriculum whose problem-solving emphasis differs both in content and form from traditional algebra texts. They are also adopting a teaching style that is more student-centered than current practice for most teachers, both in the computer lab and in small-group problem-solving activities. In accounting for the success of the dissemination efforts, we need to acknowledge both the opportunity that exists in mathematics education along with the design factors that contributed both to initial adoption decisions and to sustained use of Cognitive Tutor Algebra I.

Opportunity

As implied earlier, the 1990s were an opportune decade in which to offer a novel approach to high school mathematics education in the United States for two broad reasons. First, a number of comprehensive national and international assessments raised awareness of the need to improve our mathematics education. This awareness was magnified by two related trends: the call for mathematics education reform as embodied in the NCTM reports and the call for greater accountability. Second, the cost of educational technology continued to drop throughout the decade.

Growing Expectations and Accountability.   In response to the mathematics education crisis and recognition that all students need to master academic mathematics courses, many school districts and state departments of education in the United States are raising the bar for mathematics achievement. Algebra and geometry are increasingly being required for high-school graduation. Statewide assessments increasingly have consequences for students and school districts. At least 48 states have or are defining statewide standards and assessments that increasingly are employed to evaluate schools and govern student graduation. To cite two examples:

- The state of Kentucky has charged its school districts with demonstrating consistent achievement gains on statewide assessments over the years, or, in the extreme case, risk yielding control of their schools to expert teachers designated by the state.
- The state of New York is changing the role of its Board of Regents exams. In the past, approximately 15% of students passed the exams and earned the distinguished regents diploma. Beginning in 1999–2000, students must pass a revised Board of Regents exam to graduate.

The NCTM reform recommendations further magnified this opportunity by arguing that traditional mathematics education is not adequately serving students. Among other recommendations, the NCTM advocated open-ended assessments and student-centered classrooms focused on learning by doing. Of necessity, these recommendations provided only a framework for reform and created a curriculum and assessment vacuum that our project (and other curriculum projects) could fill. A noteworthy observation is that all schools are looking for new solutions and improved outcomes, not just low-performing schools. Even the most successful school districts are not satisfied with how well they are serving their students. Of the first six suburban school districts that adopted the Cognitive Tutor Algebra I course, three rank among the top eight districts in Allegheny County (out of 42 districts) on the Pennsylvania System of School Assessments, and one is top-ranked in nearby Beaver County.

Technology. The computing power necessary to support cognitive tutors has become more widely available in schools over the past decade. The original Geometry Tutor was implemented on Xerox workstations that cost approximately $20,000 each. ANGLE, in turn, was developed on a Macintosh workstation at a time when most schools still had Apple IIes. Now, the typical workstation being purchased by schools is sufficiently powerful to run cognitive tutors and the cost of an entire lab for 25 to 30 students is less than $50,000. When we began disseminating the Algebra I tutor, schools typically acquired a new workstation lab to run the software. Now it is far more common that schools already have the necessary technology. Workstations are typically acquired as productivity tools to support Internet access and document production, but schools are actively seeking demonstrably effective educational software—like the tutors—to further increase workstation utility.

Adoption and Sustained Use

We believe many factors contribute both to the decision to adopt Cognitive Tutor Algebra I and to its sustained use in schools once it is adopted. Of the many sites that have adopted the program over the past five years, only three sites have since abandoned it. This total abandonment rate over five years of approximately 4% is far less than the textbook industry's annual "churn" rate of about 15%.

Match to NCTM Standards. Cognitive tutor mathematics courses have gained acceptance not just because they employ educational technology to achieve substantial learning gains, but because they are among the first courses that are designed to match NCTM curriculum, teaching, and assessment standards. In these courses, algebraic and geometric topics are introduced in the context of authentic problem-solving activities, and the informal problem-solving knowledge students bring with them serves as the foundation for developing formal algebra and geometry knowledge. This approach is embodied in the Algebra I Cognitive Tutor interface displayed in Fig. 9.1 as well as in the paper-based activities. The courses are designed to foster learning by doing. Small-group problem-solving activities enable students to be active learners outside the cognitive tutor laboratory, and the cognitive tutors provide just the help students need to develop individual problem-solving skills. As shown in Fig. 9.6, course assessments, like the curriculum itself, emphasize the application of algebra and geometry knowledge to solve problems, reason among multiple representations, and communicate mathematical conclusions.

Fully Integrated Technology. The cognitive tutor technology is fully integrated with the algebra course and plays a necessary role in the course structure. The paper text, assignment and assessment materials, and cognitive tutor activities were jointly designed to target the same educational goals, with similar, student-centered problem-solving activities. The small-group classroom activities are designed to introduce topics, while the text is designed to immediately engage students in problem-solving activities that build on their existing knowledge. The small-group activities provide students the opportunity to explore topics together and refine each other's ideas. In the cognitive tutor lab, students apply these mutually developed constructs to develop their individual problem-solving knowledge.

Empirical Evaluations and Achievement Gains. We are able to provide empirical evidence that Cognitive Tutor Algebra I yields increased achievement gains. Achievement gains are of growing importance and schools, teachers and students are increasingly held accountable for outcomes. For example, when the Kentucky Department of Education organized a statewide Results-Based Practices Showcase, curriculum vendors were required to demonstrate minimum achievement gains over a three-year period. Of the 450 vendors contacted across all curriculum areas, only 61 could demonstrate the results. Perhaps not coincidentally, most of the mathematics projects that could offer the empirical evidence were other National Science Foundation-funded projects.

Of course, achievement gains in each local school district will be important in sustained use in the long run. So far, we have essentially replicated the pattern of achievement gains reported in Table 9.1 in Milwaukee. In this assessment, Cognitive Tutor Algebra I students performed 25% better on standardized test questions than comparable students in traditional Algebra I and 50% better on problem solving and reasoning among multiple representations.

It should be noted that these successful year-end summations are the culmination of a sustained empirical evaluation process that is interwoven with cognitive tutor development. The cognitive tutor design, development, and piloting process is accompanied by (a) basic research in mathematics learning (e.g., the research on inductive support cited earlier), (b) detailed assessments of student problem-solving performance in the tutor environment, which serve to refine the cognitive model, and (c) pretesting and post-testing that is also designed to refine the model. Project staffing reflects these ongoing assessment activities. Cognitive tutor development is typically supervised by a cognitive psychologist, whose time on the project is divided fairly evenly between design and assessment. In addition, for each person-year of tutor development time by research programmers, we allocate a half-year of research assistant time to carry out assessments.

Professional Development. We originally provided five days of preservice professional development as part of the Cognitive Tutor Algebra I package. About half of this time was devoted to the cognitive tutor technology and teacher interactions in the computer lab. The other half was devoted to the curriculum and teacher interactions in the classroom. We have noticed over the years, though, that teachers tend to focus on the technology in preservice training, because it is both novel and tangible. However, this comes at the expense of the curriculum and classroom issues. Once the school year begins, students have little difficulty with the technology, and teachers then call the hotline with curriculum and teaching questions and focus the site visits on these issues. As a result, in 1998–1999 we shifted to three days of preservice training, followed by in-service professional development days during the year.

Classroom Impact. The impact of cognitive tutor technology on the classroom—primarily on student motivation, but also on the teacher–student relationship—has been an important factor in both the adoption and sustained use of Cognitive Tutor Algebra I. Students are actively learning by doing in the cognitive tutor classroom and the tutor is helping them solve problems successfully. As Schofield (1995) documents, students find this environment highly motivating; they are actively engaged in doing mathematics and spend more time on task than in traditional classrooms.

Palpable student engagement in mathematics problem-solving activity plays at least two roles in our dissemination success. First, it helps schools decide whether to adopt the model, because it adds credibility to our reported achievement gains. Second, it fosters sustained use, because it makes teaching more rewarding and more fun. When students are actively engaged in problem solving, most teacher-student interactions are about mathematics, not classroom management. As Schofield notes, teachers can shift their attention to students who are struggling, and since interactions are typically student-initiated, students are ready and willing to learn. The teacher can take advantage of these "teachable moments" by engaging in extended interactions with individual students while the rest of the class is making measurable progress.

Our challenge has been to effectively convey the high level of student engagement. In 1995–1996, we asked each of our project schools to write letters describing the classroom. Figure 9.8 provides excerpts from the six letters. In addition, anecdotes continue to come in from other sites around the country. Two examples follow:

Teacher Comments

- The use of the computer tutor, or PAT, has created an environment where students are actually excited about mathematics and, more so, they are excited about algebraic concepts.
  - Lisa Simms, Beaver Area High School

- The room is quiet, the decibel level is low. Some students talk to the machine, others to the person next door, but all are reading, thinking, and doing math.
  - Mary Ellen Hamrock, Brashear High School

- Students seem to be less intimidated by problem-solving situations and are more willing to attempt solutions to new problems.
  - Bob Janosko, Fox Chapel High School

- Students now love coming to class. They also spend time during their study halls, lunch, before and after school working on the computers. Self-confidence in mathematics is at an all-time high.
  - Kathy Dickensheets and Ray Peters, Hampton High School

- Parents have often said, "If they had this when I was in school, not only would I have passed algebra, but I would have understood why I was doing it."
  - Jackie Snyder, Langley High School

- The kids had an unwritten respect for the machine and its capabilities. Gone are the phrases "this is too hard -- I can't do this." Instead I hear, "how do you do this -- why is this wrong."
  - Maxine Malloy, Carrick High School

FIG. 9.8. Excerpts from letters describing the Cognitive Tutor Algebra I Classroom.

- A Milwaukee high school has a 30-minute activity period over lunchtime in which students may engage in any activity they choose, including conversation and recreation. Teachers report that during this free period the cognitive tutor lab is full of students working on algebra problems, with more students waiting for a computer to open up.
- A New York City high school teacher reported a student was in tears while working in the cognitive tutor lab one class period this semester. When he asked what was wrong, the student said nothing was wrong—she had just never understood mathematics before!

Note that the second anecdote suggests that cognitive tutors are motivating not only because they are challenging and fun (as Schofield hypothesizes), but because students may be experiencing an unfamiliar—and exhilarating—level of success in problem solving.

Technical Support. Technical support, both software installation and the hotline, are an important part of the site-support package. While workstation LANs are becoming common in schools, the level of technical support varies widely across sites.

Community of Users. Teachers face a variety of challenges when introducing new curricula, technology, teaching styles, and assessment styles. In a variety of ways we have tried to create a community of users to provide support in tackling these challenges. We require a commitment from both administrators and teachers when Cognitive Tutor Algebra I is adopted and strongly recommend that at least two teachers participate. Indeed, among the sites that have dropped the program, support was limited either to a single administrator or to two teachers; in each case, the program ended when those personnel left the sites. We encourage schools to hold family algebra nights, often in conjunction with our site visits. We hold teacher meetings in the Pittsburgh region and hope to propagate this model to other regions of the country. Finally, we sponsor a national e-mail users group.

It is difficult to rank the importance of each of these factors in adoption and sustained use. Certainly, achievement gains and classroom impact are critical, but curriculum structure and support are also important. While the Kentucky Results-Based Showcase required demonstrable achievement gains for admission, it also developed a consumers guide rating the curricula offerings on many of the other dimensions discussed here: On-site support, complete curriculum, professional development and demanding school commitment. Cognitive Tutor Algebra I received the highest rating on all four dimensions.

CONCLUSION

Although educational software has been available in classrooms since the 1960s, we believe that this is the first widespread dissemination of software that employs artificial intelligence to support learning and problem solving. To a large extent this is because much of the early work in this area was focused on issues in artificial intelligence with less emphasis on educational effectiveness. Today, however, there is a thriving artificial intelligence and education community that is placing more emphasis on educational effectiveness, and we hope to see other successful software emerge. While we demonstrated the educational effectiveness of cognitive tutor technology early on, we only achieved widespread dissemination when we stepped outside our roles as cognitive psychologists and computer scientists to tackle the challenges of making the software user-friendly and useful for teachers in the classroom. Even though this project demonstrates that artificial intelligence is not just for research anymore, many challenges remain in understanding and enhancing cognitive tutors. One is to better understand human tutor effectiveness and incorporate more effective tutorial dialogues in our cognitive tutors. A second challenge is to learn to develop cognitive tutors more rapidly; a third is to better understand effective teacher performance in the cognitive tutor classroom and provide even more effective professional development.

Whereas some lessons from our experience relate specifically to the development of intelligent tutoring systems, others are more generally relevant to other educational technology efforts. The role of cognitive psychology theory and deep analysis of student knowledge is particularly important for cognitive tutor development. However, cognitive analysis can have a broader impact on other forms of educational technology and educational material development more generally (Bransford, Brown, & Cocking, 1999; Bruer, 1993). If a widespread impact is to be achieved, this inward investigation must be accompanied by an outward investigation of the broader context of technology use. We have emphasized a three-part strategy. First, target a clear educational problem that is well-recognized as such by the relevant stakeholders. Second, use a development process that engages in formative and summative evaluation to ensure that the technology that is developed is better than existing alternatives. Third, address the social context of the implementation of this technology. Pay attention to how the technology integrates with other components of the educational solution, such as text materials and teachers or trainers. Finally, provide initial training and on-going support for the individuals adopting the technology.

REFERENCES

Anderson, J. R. (1983). *The architecture of cognition.* Cambridge, MA: Harvard University Press.

Anderson, J. R. (1993). *Rules of the mind.* Mahwah, NJ: Lawrence Erlbaum.

Anderson, J. R., & Lebiere, C. (1998). *The atomic components of thought.* Mahwah, NJ: Lawrence Erlbaum Associates.

Anderson, J. R., Conrad, F. G., & Corbett, A. T. (1989). Skill acquisition and the LISP Tutor. *Cognitive Science, 13,* 467–505.

Anderson, J. R., Corbett, A. T., Koedinger, K. R., & Pelletier, R. (1995). Cognitive tutors: Lessons learned. *The Journal of the Learning Sciences, 4,* 167–207.

Anderson, J. R., Corbett, A. T., & Reiser, B. J. (1987). *Essential Lisp.* Reading, MA: Addison Wesley.

Bednarz, N., Kieran, C., & Lee, L. (1996). *Approaches to algebra.* Boston, MA: Kluwer Academic Publishers.

Beyer, H., & Holtzblatt, K. (1998). *Contextual design: Defining customer-centered systems.* San Francisco, CA: Morgan Kaufman.

Bloom, B. S. (1984). The 2 sigma problem: The search for methods of group instruction as effective as one-to-one tutoring. *Educational Researcher, 13,* 4–15.

Bransford, J. D., Brown, A. L., & Cocking, R. R. (1999). *How people learn: Brain, mind, experience and school.* Washington, DC: National Academy Press.

Brownston, L., Farrell, R., Kant, E., & Martin, N. (1985). *Programming expert systems in OPS5: An introduction to rule-based programming.* Reading, MA: Addison–Wesley Publishing Company, Inc.

Bruer, J. T. (1993). *Schools for thought: A science of learning in the classroom.* Cambridge, MA: MIT Press.

Cohen, P. A., Kulik, J. A., & Kulik, C. C. (1982). Educational outcomes of tutoring: A meta analysis of findings. *American Educational Research Journal, 19,* 237–248.

Corbett, A. T., & Anderson, J. R. (1995). Knowledge tracing: Modeling the acquisition of procedural knowledge. *User Modeling and User-Adapted Interaction, 4,* 253–278.

Corbett, A. T., & Anderson, J. R. (1991). Feedback control and learning to program with the CMU Lisp Tutor. Paper presented at the annual meeting of the American Educational Research Association, Chicago, IL.

Corbett, A. T., Koedinger, K. R., & Anderson, J. R. (1997). Intelligent tutoring systems. In M. Helander, T. K. Landauer, & P. Prabhu (Eds.), *Handbook of human-computer interaction, second, completely revised edition.* New York: Elsevier Science, pp. 849–874.

Corbett, A. T., & Trask, H. (2000). Instructional interventions in computer-based tutoring: Differential impact on learning time and accuracy. *Proceedings of ACM CHI'2000 Conference on Human Factors in Computing Systems* (pp. 97–104). New York: ACM Press.

Forester, P. A. (1984). *Algebra I: Expressions, equations, and applications.* Menlo Park, CA: Addison–Wesley.

Janvier, C. (1987). *Problems of representation in the teaching and learning of mathematics.* Hillsdale, NJ: Lawrence Erlbaum Associates.

Kaput, J. J. (1989). Linking representations in the symbol systems of algebra. In S. Wagner & C. Kieran (Eds.), *Research issues in the learning and teaching of algebra* (pp.167–181). Reston, VA: National Council of Teachers of Mathematics.

Koedinger, K. R., & Anderson, J. R. (1993). Effective use of intelligent software in high school math classrooms. In P. Brna, S. Ohlsson, & H. Pain (Eds.), *Proceedings of AIED 93 World Conference on Artificial Intelligence in Education* (pp. 241–248). Charlottesville, VA: Association for the Advancement of Computing in Education.

Koedinger, K. R., & Anderson, J. R. (1998). Illustrating principled design: The early evolution of a cognitive tutor for algebra symbolization. *Interactive Learning Environments, 5,* 161–180.

Koedinger, K. R., Anderson, J. R., Hadley, W. H., & Mark, M. A. (1997). Intelligent tutoring goes to school in the big city. *International Journal of Artificial Intelligence in Education, 8,* 30–43.

Kulik, J. A. (1994). Meta-analytic studies of findings on computer-based instruction. In E. Baker & H. O'Neil (Eds.), *Technology assessment in education and training* (pp. 9–33). Hillsdale, NJ: Lawrence Erlbaum.

National Center for Education Statistics (1997). *The nation's report card, the National Assessment of Educational Progress (NAEP).*

National Commission on Excellence in Education (1983). *A nation at risk: The imperative for educational reform.*

National Council of Teachers of Mathematics (1989). *Curriculum and evaluation standards for school mathematics.* Reston, VA: The Council.

Niemiec, R., & Walberg, H. J. (1987). Comparative effects of computer-assisted instruction: A synthesis of reviews. *Journal of Educational Computing Research, 3,* 19–37.

Pelavin, S. H., & Kane, M. (1990). *Changing the odds: Factors increasing access to college.* Report #003969. New York: College Board Publications.

Schofield, J. W. (1995). *Computers and classroom culture.* Cambridge, England: Cambridge University Press.

Singapore Ministry of Education (1999). *Primary mathematics 6A third edition.* Curriculum Planning and Development Division.

Sleeman, D. H., & Brown, J. S. (1982). *Intelligent tutoring systems.* New York, NY: Academic Press.

U.S. Department of Education (1998). *National Center for Education Statistics, pursuing excellence: A study of U.S. twelfth-grade mathematics and science achievement in international context, NCES 98–049.* Washington, DC: U.S. Government Printing Office.

Wenger, E. (1987). *Artificial intelligence and tutoring systems: Computational and cognitive approaches to the communication of knowledge.* Los Altos, CA: Morgan Kaufmann Publishers.

Chapter 10

The Development of the Studio Classroom

Jack M. Wilson
Rensselaer Polytechnic Institute

INTRODUCTION

*T*he roots of the Studio Course model at Rensselaer can be found in the research in physics education and the calculus reform movement of the 1980s. Instructors became convinced that there had to be a better way to teach than the various lecture models that dominated the education systems, especially at the large universities. The pressures of advances in computing, communication, and cognitive science both mandated change and enabled it. Computing tools were advancing such that the power was doubling every 18 months, but little had been done to use that power in education. New forms of communication through networks, e-mail, and the World Wide Web were revolutionizing communication and could do the same for education. Instructors were learning more and more about how students learn, obstacles to learning, and techniques to improve learning from the research in the cognitive sciences, particularly as it applied to physics teaching.

BACKGROUND

New learning environments needed to be designed to allow students to be-come far more engaged with one another, with the instructor, and with newly created technology-based materials. In the 1980s, my colleagues and I were involved in reanalyzing the introductory physics curriculum to deter-mine how it needed to change to prepare students for the information world. In the M.U.P.P.E.T. project, Redish and I called for an entirely new, technology-based approach to physics (MacDonald, Redish, & Wilson, 1988). As we developed the M.U.P.P.E.T. curriculum, we became more and more familiar with the research in physics education and its implications for course design. At the same time, an active community was becoming inter-ested in the application of technology to physics education and in the devel-oping understanding of student learning. Some worked on the creation of microcomputer-based laboratories, some on video disks and digital video, others were interested in physics simulations, and still others focused on modeling and numerical approaches to problem solving.

Driven by the conviction that a host of excellent ideas were being devel-oped, but that the overall implementation of those ideas suffered from a lack of integration, Redish and I formed the CUPLE consortium, short for the Comprehensive Unified Physics Learning Environment (Wilson & Redish, 1992a, 1992b). It was comprehensive because it made an effort to include many of the teaching approaches that had been developed inde-pendently. It was unified because it was designed around a set of standards for collecting materials and having them work together with a common user interface on a common hardware and software platform. The CUPLE pro-ject received its initial funding from the Annenberg CPB project, quickly followed by an IBM corporate grant. Later funding from the National Sci-ence Foundation allowed the completion of the project. Many of the fin-ished modules were deployed in the traditional physics course at Rensselaer as laboratory modules, homework, or class activities.

At the same time as this ferment in physics, the mathematics community was undergoing its own reexamination. Their projects were driven by two is-sues: the incorporation of technology into the curriculum and the creation of a better introductory course in calculus. The Calculus for a New Century conference pulled this all together into a clear call for reform in calculus. William Boyce of Rensselaer attended that conference and returned to campus convinced that Rensselaer should help spearhead the change. Boyce had authored one of the most popular calculus texts at that time and was an ideal person to lead the charge. He began the Rensselaer Computer

Calculus project in 1988. By 1991, the project results had been deployed to all 1,100 calculus students in the freshman class.

Very soon thereafter, Joe Ecker, then Chairman of Mathematics at Rensselaer, and I began to feel that the revised physics and calculus courses were exciting, but not yet right. Technology had been grafted onto traditional courses. Problems had been changed and curricula revised, but the courses had not really been fundamentally redesigned. To address this concern, we decided to redesign the courses from the group up, taking a "zero-based budgeting" approach. In doing this we decided not to be bound by past practice, existing facilities, or present personnel. Instead, we asked ourselves what an ideal physics or mathematics course might look like. We had always been envious of our brethren at liberal arts colleges who could experiment with smaller class sizes. We particularly liked ideas such as the Workshop Physics approach of Priscilla Laws (Laws, 1991). We also knew that we wished to incorporate cooperative learning techniques (Treisman, 1990; Treisman & Fullilove, 1990) throughout the courses. We asked ourselves if we could design an interactive learning course that took advantage of these techniques and yet operated economically in the context of a large research university educating more than 1,000 students in calculus and 600 students in physics each semester.

Thus was born the studio classroom. The name and some aspects of the pedagogy were borrowed from architects and artists, who are known for their studio programs. The classroom climate was modeled on interactive courses, often in humanities, found at the liberal arts colleges. This all had to be done while meeting our technological research university's need for rigor and complete coverage.

WHAT MAKES A STUDIO CLASSROOM?

I am often asked: what makes a studio classroom? Is it a prescriptive approach? Are all studios the same? The answers to the last two questions are certainly no, but the answer to the first is more difficult. Putting yourself in the place of a student can help you see the key difference. If a student goes to a lecture course, what does he or she expect to do? Many say they would listen, take notes, or read the blackboard. Those who may not have been as diligent in their studies might read the paper, talk to friends, or study for another course. A few will give what is perhaps the most correct answer, given the notoriously poor attendance in large lectures at major universities: they would cut class altogether. Attendance in introductory lecture classes is notoriously poor in the major universities.

However, if the same people are asked what they would do in a studio, they might answer "draw," "sculpt," "paint," or "design." Indeed, artists and architects have used the studio for years as an essential part of training.

The difference between the two types of classes lies in who the actor is in each class. In the lecture, the lecturer is the actor and the students are merely an audience. In the studio, the student is the active one and the professor becomes the audience.

Of course, it is never quite that simple. Sometimes I try to explain the difference with a joke: "If you walk into a classroom and find the professor working hard while the students rest or sleep, you must be in a traditional class. If you find the students working while the professor rests, it must be a studio class!" Any faculty member who has taught in a studio environment knows that to be a joke, because their continued activity is critical to the success of the studio classroom. Still, this statement does serve to highlight the importance of students becoming active and engaged rather than a passive audience.

The studio classroom demands more of its students than traditional lectures, a fact that is not lost on the students. One student noted on his class evaluation form, "For years students have been able to sign up for this class, cut the lectures, read the text, study the back tests in the files, and get a passing grade. You forced me to learn this material. I'll never forgive you for that."

RECOGNITION

The Studio Course has been recognized as a significant breakthrough in providing high-quality cost-effective courses in articles in Newsweek (April 29, 1996), the New York Times (January 8, 1995), the Wall Street Journal (November 13, 1995) and the ASEE Prism. The RSVP Distance Learning Program at Rensselaer won the 1993 U.S. Distance Learning Association award for best university distance learning program and the association's 1996 award for its cooperative engineering and management distance learning program with General Motors. The Studio Course model won the 1995 Theodore Hesburgh Award from TIAA/CREF, presented at the 1995 annual meeting of the American Council on Education. Richard Riley participated in the presentation of the award at the meeting, which was keynoted by President Clinton. Rensselaer was the recipient of the first annual Boeing Outstanding Educator of the Year Award. From 37 nominees, Rensselaer was selected to honor its achievements in undergraduate education in the engineering, manufacturing, computing, mathematics, physics, and chemistry disciplines. In 1996, Rensselaer was honored with the Pew Charitable Trust Prize. Rensselaer is the only university to have been awarded this "triple crown" of higher education awards.

Perhaps more notable, our idea is now being replicated. In the spring of 1999, the Pew Charitable Trust formed a program to invest $8.8 million in universities that wish to restructure along lines similar to those discussed here. The program is located at Rensselaer as the Center for Academic Transformation.[1]

DETAILED DESIGN OF THE STUDIO CLASSROOM

Pedagogical Considerations[2]

As noted earlier, the design of the studio course draws heavily on research in science education and, particularly, physics education. The introductory science and mathematics courses at many of our large universities around the world can be an intimidating experience for new students. It is not only the difficulty of the material, but also the experience of sitting in large noninteractive classes with lecturers who are mathematically unapproachable even when they may be personally approachable.

Sheila Tobias provides one of the best chronicles of student reactions in the typical introductory course (Tobias, 1990). This format of large lecture, smaller recitation, and separate laboratory continues to be the dominant method of instruction at the larger universities. The faculty usually conduct lectures while the laboratories are taught by teaching assistants. Often, the recitations are taught by mixtures of teaching assistants and faculty, with that mix varying widely from university to university.

Most physics, chemistry, or calculus learning takes place in recitation or problem sessions, in spite of their uneven quality. Most laboratories are not well taught and not well integrated with the courses. Taught by teaching assistants with minimal training, the laboratories are universally panned by students. Because of this perception of low quality and the resources required to run laboratories, several larger universities have abandoned them altogether.

Faculty and staff at major universities, aware of the shortcomings of this system, have undertaken many reform efforts. The American Association of Physics Teachers has devoted decades of meetings to the discussion of how to improve lecture courses. One recurring theme is the use of lecture

---

[1]Center for Academic Transformation: http://www.center.rpi.edu.

[2]The following section has been adapted from Wilson, 1994.

demonstrations that range from spectacular to humorous. Faculty, students, and even the general public love and remember the best demonstrations and the best demonstrators. Books have been written on how best to do demonstrations and which demonstrations might be done. Educators have also tried audio, video, and now computers to make lectures more interesting and instructive. Unfortunately, later interviews with students often reveal that their memories of the demonstration are not often accompanied by an understanding of the physics that took place.

Many efforts to improve introductory courses start with an assumption that there are good lecturers and bad lecturers, and students can learn more from the good lecturers. The strategy, then, is to improve the bad or replace it with the good. Even many applications of technology are efforts to improve or replace human lecturers with electronic ones. Many institutions have used videotaped materials to replace the traditional prelaboratory lecture with videotapes of good lecturers who can articulate in clear English the goals and procedures for the laboratories. Others (including myself) have created computer-based pre-laboratories toward the same ends (Wilson, 1980). With the creation of the "Mechanical Universe" this approach of using technology to replace the lecturer may have reached its highest form. Each video opens with a scene of students filing into a large lecture hall and then listening attentively to the opening remarks of a truly outstanding lecturer. Today, we are seeing the same kind of approach on the Web, where lectures are videotaped, digitized, and made available as streaming video. The lecture notes are converted into PowerPoint slides and sometimes made available over the network.

These are all worthy efforts toward noble goals, but a more serious reexamination of our assumptions and approaches was required. Evidence has been pouring in from those doing research in science education, but it seems to have had little effect on physics or the other sciences in most of our largest universities. Hestenes' "Force Concept Inventory" and later tests have been applied across the country in a variety of institutions with equivalent results (Halloun & Hestenes, 1985). Harvard's Eric Mazur felt that his students were really learning in his lectures until he gave them Hestenes' test. The disappointing result inspired him to develop innovative interactive techniques for use with large enrollment courses (Mazur, 1997).

There are, of course, some notable exceptions. Ron Thornton's (Tufts) article, "Learning Motion Concepts Using Real-time Microcomputer-based Laboratory Tools," is particularly interesting, because it compares traditional lecture approaches with interactive methods using microcomputer-based laboratories and shows that the interactive methods can reduce student error rates spectacularly (Thornton, 1990).

Eric Mazur's article provides an honest personal anecdote illustrating the statistical evidence amassed by Halloun and Hestenes (1985), Laws (1991), Thornton and Sokoloff (1998), and Thornton (1990) that even a good "lecturer" does not directly improve student learning. Certainly, there are significant differences in the affective domain showing that students enjoy the course more, appreciate the subject, and come away with improved attitudes to the discipline. This can probably be linked to student retention and recruitment of majors, and perhaps even to increased learning through other course work such as reading, problem solving, and laboratories. Providing good lectures is obviously superior to providing poor lectures, but still does not lead directly to increased learning.

A standard counter argument is that "lectures must work, because students have been learning that way for centuries." The problem with this approach is that it neglects to take into account the many other ways that students learn, such as reading, problem solving, discussion with other students, discussion in the recitations, performing laboratories, and so on. Frequently, this attitude is based upon a generalization from the speaker's own experiences, which are (by definition) atypical.

Ultimately, we decided to de-emphasize (but not eliminate) the lecture, increase the number of hands-on activities, keep problem solving at about the usual level, and use more collaborative learning and team approaches in our redesigned courses.

Development

At one critical point in 1993, my colleagues and I convened a panel of nationally prominent educators, architects, and industry representatives to review the status of our programs and plan for future programs. We expected such a diverse group to provide a diverse perspective, but never expected to reach any kind of a consensus. We were surprised, then, at the participants' strong consensus to reduce the emphasis on the lectures, to improve the relationship between courses and laboratories, to increase the amount of student activity while scaling back the amount of time spent watching a teacher, to expand the number of team and cooperative learning experiences, to integrate rather than overlay technology into all of the courses, and—above all—to do all of this while reducing costs!

Our goal for the studio courses was to bring the interactivity often found in small-enrollment courses into courses with large enrollments. We combined lecture, recitation, and laboratory into integrated sessions hosted in one studio facility. A team composed of a faculty member, graduate student, and, in some cases, an undergraduate student, taught the classes. The goal was to design a course that cost no more than the alternatives.

Facilities

Over the years there have been a number of variations on the facilities design. Some have used clusters and others have used a theater in the round configuration. In physics, the theater in the round configuration features two-meter-long worktables, each designed for two students, with open workspace and a computer workstation. The tables often contain equipment for the day's hands-on laboratory. The tables form three concentric partial ovals with an opening at the front of the room for the teacher's worktable and a projection system. The workstations are arranged so that when students are working together on an assigned problem, they turn away from the center of the room and focus their attention on their own group workspace. The instructor is able to see all workstation screens from the center of the oval, thereby receiving direct feedback on how things are going for the students.

In any course, when the teacher wants to conduct a discussion or give a minilecture, they ask the students to turn toward the center of the room. This removes the distraction of a functioning workstation directly in front of the student during the discussion or lecture period, yielding a classroom in which multiple foci are possible. Students can work together as teams of two, or two teams may work together to form a small group of four. Discussion as a whole is facilitated by the semicircular arrangement of student chairs, in which most students can see one another with a minimum of swiveling. This is particularly important since only 20 to 40% of classroom time is spent using the computers; the remainder is devoted to group activities, hands-on laboratories, and discussion.

This type of classroom is friendly even to instructors who favor the traditional classroom in which most of the activities are teacher-centered rather than student-centered. Projection is easily accomplished, and all students have a clear view of both the instructor and any projected materials. As a facility in which the instructor acts more as a mentor-guide-advisor, the theater-style classroom is unequaled. Rather than separating the functions of lecture, recitation and laboratory, the instructor can move freely from lecture mode into discussion and can assign a computer activity, ask the students to discuss their results with their neighbors, and then ask them to describe the result to the class. Laboratory simply becomes another classroom activity that is mixed in with everything else. The studio course uses the latest in computing tools and incorporates use of cooperative learning approaches. We have created a powerful link between lecture materials and problem-solving and hands-on laboratories.

Equipment

The first of our studios was equipped with networked desktop computers shared by two to four students. A 64-student classroom might have 32 desktop systems installed with a typical price of $2,000 to $3,000 per desktop. This classroom could host 10 to 12 sections of a course per week, serving 640 students per semester. Although we would have liked to change them more frequently, we used the original computers for five years before replacing them. Amortizing the cost of the computer over 10 semesters (a conservative choice, since we also used them in summer) yields a cost of $20 to $30 per student. This cost—tiny in comparison to the cost of personnel—was the smallest cost of the course.

In the middle of the decade, we began a pilot project to convert from university-owned desktops to student-owned laptops. A faculty committee led by Mark Holmes, Chair of Mathematics, and John Kolb, Dean of Computing and Information Services, led a four-year pilot program to develop the courses, support the faculty, and create a plan for full implementation (Holmes & Porter, 1996). The last obstacle to overcome was to have the overall cost be lower using the laptop models and to provide the financial aid that many of our students needed. We are now one year into the full implementation phase of the project, and are delighted with the results.

Cost Considerations

The traditional physics course met in three different kinds of facilities: a modern 500-seat lecture hall, a typical 30-seat recitation or discussion room, and a 25-seat laboratory. The introductory calculus course used a similar lecture hall, the same 30-seat discussion rooms, and a 30-seat computer laboratory. Scheduling 600 to 1,000 students in these facilities was an art in itself. In physics there were two lecture sections, 25 to 30 recitation sections, and 30 to 40 laboratories to be scheduled each week. These events were staffed by faculty and graduate students and required support staff for both the lecture demonstration and laboratory. In contrast, if the studios were sized from 48 to 64 students each, the same number of students per week could be accommodated in 12 to 15 sections. It was thus possible to meet the cost constraints (Zemsky & Massy, 1995).

Many of the traditional courses had met for four to six hours per week, with approximately two hours devoted to lecture, two to recitation, and two to laboratory. In the studio, we collapsed all of this into four hours. The reduction from six to four contact hours is an important aspect of stewardship of both student and faculty time and resources. In spite of the one-third reduction in contact hours, evaluations demonstrate that students learn the material faster and as well as or better than in the traditional courses (Wilson, 1994). Zemsky and Massy (1995) cited the Rensselaer Studio Courses for their focus on constraining costs while enhancing quality.

Calculus, physics, and chemistry were the three largest introductory courses at Rensselaer in the early 1990s. Each had a model that educated 600 to 1,100 students in lecture, recitation, and laboratory. The laboratories were quite different, with chemistry requiring wet labs with the usual safety equipment, physics using laboratories with much less stringent requirements, and mathematics using computer laboratories. The courses also differed in their use of faculty. Chemistry used all faculty in its recitations, mathematics used nearly all graduate students, and physics was a mix. We were able to redesign each of these courses in a way that was economically competitive with other alternatives.

Studio courses developed later, particularly in electrical engineering replaced primarily lecture-based classes with studios. These required additional resources to add laboratory experiences that were not present in the traditional course, and thus tended to be more expensive than the original approach.

Whether the studio courses are more or less expensive than the alternatives depends upon the alternative model. If one is willing to put 500 students in a lecture hall and dispense with both discussion sections and laboratories, there might be no savings from switching to a studio, but the quality of such teaching would be unacceptable to most institutions. There are always "cheaper" alternatives, but the cheaper alternative may not actually be the least expensive when all costs are taken into account. As a number of universities prepared their proposals to the Pew Charitable Trust program administered through the Center for Academic Transformation at Rensselaer, they discovered that alternatives that did not look immediately cost effective became so when "rework" was considered. "Rework" occurs when there is a large failure rate in an initial course and students must repeat the course at least once. This has the effect of increasing the number of students who take a particular course. If one-third of the students fail to complete a course and then take that course over, it has the effect of increasing the enrollment by 50% in the steady state. This increase of 50% in enrollment requires more faculty, facilities, and support staff and can increase cost up to 50% for those models that are linear in cost.

Deployment

In the fall semester of 1993, Professor Joe Ecker taught the first full studio course in calculus. In the spring of 1994, Professors Wayne Roberge and Jack Wilson followed with the first physics studio. At about the same time, Professor Frank DiCesare designed a new engineering lab that featured many characteristics of the studio courses.[3] During the fall 1994 semester, the CUPLE Physics Studio was expanded to full deployment in all Physics I sections and Physics III sections and a pilot deployment in Physics II. In 1995, the physics department voted unanimously to end the traditional course in favor of the full deployment of the studio.

The studio quickly spread into other disciplines, and each model adapted the studio philosophy to the faculty teaching that discipline. For example, the first studio chemistry courses at Rensselaer used very little technology but adopted most of the logistical and pedagogical innovations of the other studios. Professors R. Spilker and J. Brunski created a freshman engineering studio, and the concept was used in writing, genetics, economics, and many other courses.

The Electrical, Computer, and Systems Engineering (ECSE) department has developed five of the most advanced Studio classrooms on campus. The facilities are currently being used for the following courses:

- Electric Circuits
- Electronic Instrumentation
- Analog Electronics
- Digital Electronics
- Fields and Waves
- Microelectronics Technology
- Computer Components and Operation
- Computer Architecture, Networks, and Operating Systems
- Laboratory Introduction to Embedded Control
- Control Systems Engineering

This represents all of the introductory level courses in electrical and computer engineering and has created an entirely new learning experience for our students. The studio facilities are being used to integrate the learning of fundamental concepts and the professional practice skills that are so important to an engineering education. Combining all of these learning activities into the new studio courses has eliminated separate theory and lab courses.

---

[3]M. R. Muller & L. E. Ostrander, "A Multimedia Lab Course in Embedded Control," http://litec.rpi.edu/.

The ECSE Studios use computer video projection, high-speed networked computers, and the equipment normally found in electrical-computer engineering laboratories such as scopes, logic analyzers, multimeters, power supplies, and prototyping materials. A key ingredient in these studios is the creative use of lighting and audio to stimulate student-student and student-instructor interactivity.

Corporations such as Hewlett Packard, IBM, Intel, and Sun have been significant contributors to the creation of these studios. In 1996, a number of campuswide process teams were created to look at our programs. The campuswide team on the introductory curriculum recommended that all introductory courses move into these interactive formats over the next few years. The Curriculum Reform Implementation Team, chaired by then Dean of Engineering Richard Lahey, ratified that recommendation and prepared the implementation plans. Although implementation is not yet complete (and likely never will be), the result was pervasive use of the studio model.

A TYPICAL COURSE DAY

It is difficult to describe a typical studio course, since there is quite a bit of variation from discipline to discipline, campus to campus, and professor to professor. Although the details differ, there are enough common characteristics to make such an effort worthwhile. Here I will describe a specific studio, Physics I, that I have taught on several occasions and that shares most of its features with the studios taught throughout the physics department. In an effort to achieve some uniformity, the Physics I and II sections have a course manager and the syllabus and activities are jointly decided by a committee of faculty.

In most classes, students come with a homework assignment of three to six problems to turn in. The first portion of the class is devoted to a discussion of these problems and is much like a recitation. The problems are quite similar to those used in the traditional class except that more of the problems use symbolic mathematics software (Maple, Matlab, or Mathematica), a spreadsheet, or even an object-oriented modeling tool. As I go over questions that they have about the problems, I often call on the students to present the solutions. Other students then comment on the problems. I try to complete the problem discussion within 20 minutes.

The students then move into some kind of laboratory or group problem-solving activity. In the first class of the semester that activity is adapted from the well-known work of Ron Thornton and Priscilla Laws using the motion detector to measure and graph the motion of students (Thornton, 1990; Laws, 1991).

Next we present a topic with a five-minute discussion followed by a laboratory on that topic. For example, we once set up a video camera and filmed a student throwing a ball. The video was directly digitized into the computer and made available over the network to each work area. Students then analyzed the motion using the CUPLE digital video tool, and created a spreadsheet containing the position versus time data. The analysis proceeded in the usual fashion, resulting in graphs of position versus time, velocity versus time, and acceleration versus time for each component. The final laboratory report remains in electronic format, although we often have the students record observations on a written worksheet. The laboratories (22 per semester in this specific case) are performed entirely at each work area. When we introduced Newton's Second Law, for example, we had the students calibrate a force probe and then hang a spring and mass from the probe with an ultrasonic range finder under the mass to measure the position. From this, the students can calculate acceleration versus time and compare to the force divided by the mass.

You may notice that this experiment foreshadows the introduction of Hookes' Law and the topic of oscillations, both of which come later in the course. There are questions on the worksheet that ask the students to observe and comment upon each of these phenomena, but I do not attempt to name them or introduce theory at this time. I try to introduce and explore the concept prior to naming it.

In both examples given above, the computer-based laboratory data acquisition and analysis tools are embedded into a hypermedia text that introduces the topics, links the students to related materials, and poses questions for the students to answer using these tools. A consortium of schools led by Rensselaer and the University of Maryland created these hypermedia activities through the CUPLE project. Funding has come from the Annenberg/Corporation for Public Broadcasting, the IBM Corporation, and the National Science Foundation. Teams of faculty and students working together created most of the materials. The student involvement has added a fresh approach to much of the material, which is appreciated by the students taking the course. Today, many of the original CUPLE materials have been supplanted by more recent developments or by commercially available materials.

Hands-on activities are an integral part of the physics studio. In fact, the number of hands-on laboratories is more than twice as large as the traditional course. Each activity is shorter than the traditional laboratory, but is tightly integrated with both the homework and class discussion. The laboratory portion of the class ranges from 20 to 40 minutes and is often combined with a computational activity.

Lab activities fall into three major categories: microcomputer-based laboratories (MBL) as described above, video laboratories, and modeling and simulation projects. The video laboratories allow the students to film an event, feed the video directly into their computers and then play that event back as video on each computer screen. They bring up a graphical overlay on the screen and place points on the graph directly over the object as it moves.

Those of us old enough to have done this with spark marks on waxed tape or with a Polaroid camera will recognize that the activities are conceptually quite similar and lead to the same kinds of data analysis. On the other hand, the relationship between the marks and the moving object is far more obvious to the student than it was in the earlier cases. Since the class uses the same equipment each week, set up for this lab is limited to bringing in the video camera and plugging it into the network. This is also far less cumbersome and less expensive than the specialized equipment that was used to do the spark tapes or strobed Polaroid pictures.

Each session ends with a discussion of the material assigned for the next class. At this time, I often call attention to the fore-shadowing that has occurred in the problem-solving and laboratories, pulling it together to introduce the next topic. This part of the class is often referred to as the minilecture. I prefer to introduce the formalism after the phenomenon rather than before. Table 10.1 summarizes some of the features of a studio and a traditional course.

RESULTS

We focused on a variety of metrics for success. Some of the metrics that we looked at included:

- Student performance on traditional tests
- Student attendance
- Student performance on cognitive tests
- Student performance on problem solving
- Student attitudes toward the courses
- Student retention
- Faculty attitude toward the courses
- Student success in later classes

My experiences with the studio courses have been very encouraging. Student response is particularly satisfying. They have been quite enthusiastic about the courses, as measured by responses on end-of-semester surveys. In the calculus studio, nearly twice as many students agree that they en-

TABLE 10.1 Some Features of the Studio and Traditional Courses

Studio	Traditional
Physical Setting	
Studio space designed for	Lecture hall
Discussion	Recitation room
Mini lectures	Laboratory room
Group work	
Teaching Process	
Students center of discussions and solving	Professor gives lecture
Emphasis on group work	Assistant runs recitation
	Students work in laboratory
Learning	
More active learning	More passive learning
High levels of interaction	Lower interaction
High integration of homework, class discussions, presentations	Less integration of homework, class discussions, presentations

joyed the studio course as compared to the traditional lecture-recitation-lab format.

One question on an external survey conducted last semester by the Dean of the Undergraduate School stirred quite a bit of interest in the administration and faculty. When students were asked whether they would cite a particular studio course as "a positive reason to attend Rensselaer," over 90% of the students agreed! This compares to 63% who agreed with this proposition in the mathematics courses that had been downsized but retained the traditional lecture approach. When student responses were controlled for popularity of the teacher and course, there were significant (actually spectacular) gains in students' satisfaction.

Our experiences indicate that instructors are rated far higher in teaching evaluations in the studio courses. The one exception was a brilliant lecturer who was comfortable with his slightly lower evaluations because he believed so deeply in what he was doing. This is a significant issue at institutions like Rensselaer where student evaluations and research results play equally major roles in salary, promotion, and tenure decisions. More and more of the research universities are revamping these criteria to reemphasize the teaching aspects of the professor's role.

Student performance has been more difficult to measure. We saw a variety of results in the various studios. Some showed no significant difference, while others showed significant improvement. For example, students in the physics studio performed as well as or better than students in the traditional courses in spite of the one-third reduction in class contact time. This was demonstrated by student performance on tests matched in difficulty, length, and content to tests from previous years and tests given in the same year in the traditional course. In both mathematics and physics, more topics were covered in the studio courses than in the lecture courses. Further, with the support of an anonymous donor, we have undertaken a longitudinal study of student performance and attitude that is following the students through their undergraduate career.

Maintaining the improvements does take some vigilance. Later studies of the physics studio under different instructors showed that gains on a focused test of mechanics learning were not improved over traditional alternatives and that the average size of the sections had dropped to just over 30 students. The size of the sections was increased back toward the design goal of 48 to restore the economic efficiency, and interactive learning techniques based upon educational research have since lead to further learning gains (Cummings & Marx, 1999).

Once most departments introduced studio classes, they retained those models. The department of mathematics is a notable exception to that. Mathematics involved far fewer of their faculty in the introductory course than did chemistry, physics, or biology. The conversion to the studio did require more faculty involvement and less graduate student involvement, and as a result, the mathematics models evolved in a slightly different direction.

Professor Harry Roy has done some comparison of recitation and computer-assisted learning techniques in his studio genetics classes. Although students received each model favorably, neither by itself improved performance compared with the other. However, student satisfaction improved dramatically when lecture, laboratory simulations, and problem solving were combined. Roy also reported increased satisfaction as an instructor.

THE STUDIO AT OTHER UNIVERSITIES

The studio classroom has been deployed at a variety of universities and in a variety of disciplines. I am often asked if studios can only work in large universities, technological universities, or technical classes. Nothing could be further from the truth. The primary challenge was to make the studio model work within the confines of the large technological universities. These kinds of pedagogical models have been far more prevalent in the arts and humanities and at liberal arts colleges. Making them work in the environment of a technological university took great care in both design and implementation.

When other universities deploy the studio classroom, they invariably put their own spin on the model. Some will acknowledge the relationship to the Rensselaer studio classroom and others will not, but that is not important. What is important is that creative faculty are developing and deploying learning environments that are better for students and better for faculty.

Some of the other Universities that have deployed studio style classrooms include:

- Penn State University (http://www.science.psu.edu/facaffairs/strategic.htm) (http://www.psu.edu/ur/archives/news/ GE.html) (http://dps.phys.psu.edu/about.htm)
- Arizona State University (http://www4.eas.asu.edu/phy132/)
- Indiana State University (http://physicsstudio.indstate.edu/)
- Cal Poly San Luis Obispo (http://www.cob.calpoly.edu/Evan/polyplan/polyplan.htm) (http://chemweb.calpoly.edu/ phys/)
- Ohio State University (http://www.physics.ohio-state.edu/~ntg/26x/2064_pictures.html)
- The University of Amsterdam (http://www.wins.uva.nl/research/amstel/)
- The University of New Hampshire (http://einstein.unh.edu/academics/courses/)
- The Curtin University of Technology (Australia) (http://www.physics.curtin.edu.au/teaching/studio/)
- The University of Massachusetts—Dartmouth (http://www.aps.org/meet/CENT99/BAPS/abs/S3455002.html)
- The Colorado School of Mines (http://einstein.mines.edu/physics100/frontend/main.htm)
- Acadia University. (Canada) (http://ace.acadiau.ca/math/boutilie/)
- Santa Barbara City College (http://www.cs.sbcc.net/physics/redesign/final_report/reportb.html)

The breadth of these efforts makes it impossible to describe each of the programs here, and the scale of the dissemination is even more impressive when one considers the many descendants of the workshop courses developed by Priscilla Laws and collaborators. In many respects the workshop and studio models share the same intellectual roots.

GOING THE DISTANCE:
THE VIRTUAL STUDIO CLASSROOM[4]

Distance learning is no longer the province of the "correspondence schools" or "diploma mills." It has become the focus of nearly every great university. Schools like Rensselaer and Stanford have been heavily involved for over a decade through their large programs in engineering education.

In 1999, MIT signed a cooperation agreement with Cambridge University that created a joint venture in technological university education and research. The British government agreed to provide $109 million and to raise $26 million from private sources to create a new center based in Britain (Chronicle of Higher Education, 1999a CNET News.com, 1999). MIT has also arranged to provide Singapore with higher education services (Chronicle of Higher Education, 1997) and received a $25 million gift from Microsoft to enable the distance-learning portion of the relationship (Chronicle of Higher Education, 1999b).

New York University has gone so far as to spin off its distance learning program as a for-profit venture called "NYU On-line." Their plan is to augment the $1.5 million investment from NYU with capital raised from private venture capital sources (Chronicle of Higher Education, 1998).

In addition, the Wharton School of Business at the University of Pennsylvania, Johns Hopkins University and Teachers College at Columbia University created a joint venture with Caliber, which is itself a joint venture of MCI and Sylvan Learning Systems, to offer their programs at a distance. These are all top-ranked programs. Although these programs did not evolve in the way expected by their proponents, they remain clear evidence that distance learning has entered the top-tier mainstream.

In the rush to enter the distance learning market, universities have not always been careful to take into account the lessons learned from centuries of higher education. Many of these programs are driven by technology and not pedagogy. Technology is a powerful driving force that must be reckoned with, but centuries of history and the recent research coming out of the cognitive sciences on how human beings learn will have much to say about where this technology will take us.

For the virtual university to be successful, it will have to replace the traditional modes of distance learning, such as satellite video, tele-training keypad response systems, and interactive video conferencing, with a much more robust educational model. Our goal is to provide the distant learner with as much of the studio experience as possible. In this model of interac-

---

[4]This section is adapted from Wilson and Jennings (2000) and Wilson (in press).

tive multimedia distance learning, one creates a virtual studio with students connected together over a network that carries data, voice, and video to the students' computers. Each student has access to multimedia materials created for the course and delivered from CD-ROM or across the network. In short, we plan to take the studio classroom to the distance!

Part of any virtual classroom will be activities in which the students and instructors interact through live voice and video while working together with a synchronous collaborative software package. By the same token, part of any virtual classroom will be asynchronous activity, or activities done at the students' own time and pace. The actual mix of synchronous and asynchronous activity will be adjusted to suit each course and audience. As more of a course is conducted asynchronously, the more flexible the course can become.

What is to prevent the course from becoming fully asynchronous? If we are to fulfill the desire for anytime-anyplace education, a fully asynchronous course sounds quite desirable. Why should students be bound to a particular time, if not a particular place? Many efforts are underway to do just that. The Sloan Foundation is funding universities to develop Web or Lotus Notes-based courses that are taken at the students' convenience. Interactivity is included through asynchronous use of e-mail, news groups, or other electronic discussion modalities.

Once again, however, history and experience provide a cautionary note here. There is a rather long record of efforts to break the constraints of place and time. Some of these were based upon text delivery and others on computing. The completion rate for students in these self-paced courses is often less than can be tolerated. If the education experience is not critical to the student's progress or if the student is well motivated, this may not be a problem. If there are alternative approaches available, then the self-paced models will work very well for the highly motivated. Michigan State has long offered its students a modularized, self-paced physics program, called PhysNet, that was designed along the lines of a Keller Plan course. When the students are not highly motivated or when there is a desire to move large percentages of a group through certain educational experiences, an asynchronous approach might not work. A Ford Motor Company vice president concerned with education and training tells the story of creating a CD-ROM to introduce a new technique to certain Ford employees. The CD-ROM was designed to support about 15 hours of instruction, but the users only averaged 1.5 hours, with disappointing results.

In the tradeoff between synchronous and asynchronous time, we will have to strike a careful balance. Certainly there is a place for asynchronous techniques, but there will also be a need to incorporate a structure of continuous feedback and interaction that ensures a satisfactory success rate. The more we are able to move instruction in the asynchronous direction, the more flexible the environment will be and the greater the gains in economic efficiency. When the balance is struck it is unlikely to be fully asynchronous or synchronous.

Our work indicates that a course in which most of the activity is asynchronous but which includes regular synchronous meetings might be effective, flexible, and efficient. Perhaps 10 to 20% of the course activity could be synchronous. The synchronous activity also allows one to incorporate the discussion, small group projects, and role playing that are so important to student learning. This model is often referred to as the 80/20 Model.

In our experience, an effective interactive multimedia distance learning environment will have the following characteristics:

- Delivery on standards-based multimedia PCs equipped for live video-audio interactions and connected to a robust ip multi-casting network.
- A mix of synchronous and asynchronous activity.
- Use of Web and CD-ROM-based multimedia materials.
- Use of professional-quality software tools for CAD, symbolic math, spreadsheets, word processing, etc.
- Live audio and video interactions among the students and with faculty.
- E-mail interactions among the students and faculty.
- Small group discussions.
- Collaborative software for application sharing over the network.
- Access to rich resources on the network.
- Ability to "pass the floor" to students to allow them to lead the class through an activity.
- Course administration software to track student progress.
- Classes with a mix of students in traditional and workplace settings.
- Classes with a global perspective and global audience.

In partnership with AT&T, we created a prototype of such a system, which was tested in the AT&T University of Sales Excellence. A follow-on architecture was spun off as the ILINC LearnLinc system (which uses ip multicasting, and agents to reduce bandwidth scaling from n^2 to nearly flat as n (the number of interacting sites) increases.[5] Each year since 1995, LearnLinc has been put into use in an NSF Chautauqua Program that linked Rensselaer Polytechnic Institute and the School of Engineering at

---

[5]ILINC LearnLinc: http://www.ilinc.com.

the University of Pittsburgh into linked virtual classrooms. Faculty from around the nation, as well as Asia and Europe attend the three-day workshop on the use of multimedia tools in science, mathematics, and engineering education. Although the instructor often alternates teaching from Pitt and Rensselaer, students reported that they felt the instructors were in the room with them no matter where they were actually located. Observers noted that the students at a local site were often better able to communicate while making eye contact through the system than across the room!

In spring 1997, Professor Chun Leung used these techniques to teach a graduate course in astrophysics that teamed a classroom at Rensselaer with a classroom at Hong Kong City University. The course was taught in the early morning in New York and in the early evening in Hong Kong. Students met each day (often enjoying different meals together!) in the paired classrooms. Students made presentations from each site and came to know and work with counterparts that they had never met in person.

Kent State University has deployed this system to teach nursing, business, and English to branch campuses across the state of Ohio. Our Center for Integrated Electronics and Manufacturing has delivered a short course in chemical mechanical planarization to semiconductor fabricators like Intel, Matsushita, and Applied Materials. One of the sites reached was in Osaka, Japan.

Professor Bradford Lister, Director of the Rensselaer Anderson Center for Innovation in Undergraduate Education, has developed two innovative distance learning courses for the National Technological University.[6] *Hands-On Multimedia* and *Hands-On World Wide Web* combine satellite broadcasts with synchronous web-based tutoring sessions and asynchronous hands-on exercises conducted via the Internet. Hands-On Multimedia was restricted to 100 students at six sites, while Hands-On World Wide Web attracted over 8,000 participants at 500 sites in the United States and Asia. These virtual studio courses used WebCT, ILINC LearnLinc, Citrix Winframe server, and MS Internet Information Server.

CONCLUSION

The studio model has been adopted broadly across Rensselaer in situations where it fits with the academic objectives and resource availability. Although a faculty process team had called for a complete conversion of introductory courses to the studio model, that has not been accomplished.

---

[6]Brad Lister: http://www.ciue.rpi.edu/interactive.htm.

As we examined this option more carefully, it did not make sense to make it a mandatory goal. We now have many advanced-level courses that are taught in the studio style and even a few graduate courses. We expect that mixture to continue to be in place indefinitely. There is no need or desire to convert all courses.

The studio model has also been adopted outside of Rensselaer, although each course differs, as the model is adapted to local circumstances and culture. The ability to adapt is one strength of the studio classroom. It is not a prescriptive approach that requires rigid standards and specific activities. Rather, it is more a collection of philosophical goals and pedagogical practices that can be used to design an effective and efficient learning environment in which students are active, engaged, and collaborating with one another, as well as their professor.

Across these different universities that have adopted versions of the studio classroom, there are some commonalities:

- There is motivation within these universities to examine traditional courses and to identify new effective learning environments.
- A critical focus in all these change efforts concerned how students learn and how to facilitate learning.
- The nature of the changes was both fundamental and evolutionary, versus incremental and short-term. That is, the goal was not to improve a single lecture or create a better laboratory, but to fundamentally change the learning environment.
- Multidimensional effectiveness criteria were used that reflected both learning, attitudinal, and economic factors.

There seems to be no obstacle to use of the model in distance learning environments and our experience shows that such courses can be conducive to learning and friendly to student and faculty. In creating a distance studio classroom, we have focused on the key features of the studio such as active learning, high levels of interaction, integration between laboratory experiences, class discussion, homework, and presentations. The learning environment is the driver, not the technology per se.

The growth, diffusion, and recognition of the studio classroom has been an exciting experience both for the students and the designers of this educational environment. The effectiveness of the studio has been affected by many factors. I will close this chapter by noting two. First, the design of the studio environment facilitates how students learn basic courses such as physics, mathematics, chemistry, and so on. Second, a great deal of ideas, time, and energy have been devoted to the implementation and evolution of the studio concept. It is, then, both the inherent features of the studio that facilitate active learning and problem solving in a highly interactive setting and the implementation of the studio that make the model work. There will be many new variations on the studio theme and many other models growing from the same research and experience base. That is good news for the students and the faculty of the future. It will be a good place to learn and a good place to teach.

REFERENCES

Chronicle of Higher Education. (1997, May 23). Singapore Hires MIT to Audit its Engineering Schools.

Chronicle of Higher Education. (1998, October 16). NYU Starts For-Profit Unit to Sell On-Line Classes.

Chronicle of Higher Education. (1999a, November 19). MIT and University of Cambridge Announce $135 Million Joint Venture.

Chronicle of Higher Education. (1999b, October 15). Microsoft Will Give MIT $25 Million for Educational-Technology Research.

CNET News.com (1999, November 5). MIT, Cambridge Team Up.

Cummings, K., & Marx, J. (1999). Evaluating innovation in studio physics. *American Journal of Physics, Supplement, 67*(7), S38–S44.

Halloun, I. A., & Hestenes, D. (1985). The initial knowledge state of physics students. *American Journal of Physics, 53,* 1043–1055.

Holmes, M., & Porter, D. (1996, June). Student notebook computers in studio courses. *ED-MEDIA '96 Conference, AACE Proceedings.* Boston.

Laws, P. (1991). Calculus-based physics without lectures. *Physics Today, 44*(12), 24–31.

MacDonald, W. M., Redish, E. F., & Wilson, J. M. (1988). The MU.P.P.E.T. manifesto. *Computers in Physics, 2*(4), 23–30.

Mazur, E. (1997). Understanding or memorization: Are we teaching the right thing? *Proceedings of the Resnick Conference on the Introductory Course* (pp.113–123). New York: John Wiley.

Thornton, R. (1990). Learning motion concepts using real-time microcomputer-based laboratory tools. *American Journal of Physics, 58*(9), 858–867.

Thornton, R. K., & Sokoloff, D. R. (1998, April). Assessing student learning of Newton's laws. The force and motion conceptual evaluation and the evaluation of active learning laboratory and literature curricula. *American Journal of Physics, 66*(4), 338–352.

Tobias, S. (1990). They're not dumb, they're different. *Research Corporation Report.* Tuscon, AZ.

Treisman, P. U. (1990). *Teaching mathematics to a changing population.* Report of the Professional Development Program at the University of California, Berkeley.

Treisman, U., & Fullilove, R. E. (1990). Mathematics achievement among African American undergraduates at the University of California, Berkeley: An evaluation of the mathematics workshop program. *Journal of Negro Education, 59*(3), 463–478.

Wilson, J. M. (1980). Experimental simulation in the modern physics laboratory. *American Journal of Physics, 48,* 701–704.

Wilson, J. M. (1994). The CUPLE physics studio. *The Physics Teacher, 32,* 518–523.

Wilson, J. M. (in press). The technological revolution: Reflections on the proper role of technology in higher education. In P. G. Altach, P. Gumport & D. B. Johnstone (Eds.), *The enduring legacies: In defense of American higher education.* Baltimore, MD: Johns Hopkins University Press.

Wilson, J. M., & Jennings, W. (2000, January). Studio courses: How information technology is changing the way we teach, on campus and off. In S. Director & F. Ulaby (Eds.), *IEEE Proceedings Special Issue on Electrical and Computer Engineering Education, Proceedings of the IEEE.*

Wilson, J. M., & Redish, E. F. (1992a, March/April). The comprehensive unified physics learning environment: Part I, Background and system operation. *Computers in Physics, 6*(2), 202–209.

Wilson, J. M., & Redish, E. F. (1992b, May/June). The comprehensive unified physics learning environment: Part II, The basis for integrated studies. *Computers in Physics, 6*(3), 282–286.

Zemsky, R., & Massy, W. (1995). *Using information technology to enhance academic productivity.* Washington, DC: EDUCOM Report.

Chapter 11

Concluding Thoughts

Paul S. Goodman
Carnegie Mellon University

I n this collection of essays about the role of technology in education, the primary focus has been to raise issues and questions and provide some answers. The collection cannot be comprehensive. There are other topics to be discussed, and thousands of possible applications. But the contributors have focused upon areas of key concern where there is substantial knowledge and experience.

The focus has been on tertiary institutions, with acknowledgment of the tremendous diversity within this sector, both within and among countries. Readers need to focus on the critical issues and relate those to the context of their particular institutions. For example, the issue of maintaining adequate library resources in a university, given rising costs and the alternative of digital libraries, confronts universities throughout the world. Whereas the issue and alternatives are generalizable, how each institution deals with this issue and the various alternatives will depend on its context.

Although there are no common models or solutions, some themes, issues, and challenges are interwoven in the text. These are important to note because the authors come from different perspectives and each wrote independently of the others. In this closing chapter, I will highlight some of the themes and related challenges. Some difficult choices lie ahead for leaders of tertiary institutions.

One clear theme is that technology should be the servant and not the master. Throughout the book each author notes that technology must ser-

289

vice learning and education. That idea is clearly reinforced by Herb Simon's exploration of human learning processes in chapter 3, in which he highlights the need for understanding the learning process and the learning tasks prior to any focus on the technology. The point is also made in chapter 4 by José-Marie Griffiths and Alan McCord, who focus on infrastructure. Here one might expect to see the benefits of technology to be exalted. Instead, there is a major emphasis on thinking about technology from a sociopolitical perspective.

Technology is a greater force in our lives than it was 10 years ago, and this force is likely to accelerate. The increase is partly driven by the inherent value of technology. It is also driven by a set of powerful economic and institutional processes. It is difficult to be exposed to any of today's media without also being exposed to technology. Across the many forms of formal and informal communications that affect our lives, there is a constant message about the benefits of technology. There are people aggressively selling technology. The choices faced by the university administrators and designers of new learning environments are: first, to develop a vision and strategy about the role of new technological environments that fit the context of their institution, and second, to articulate at a strategic level what and how they want people to learn differently. At this point, technology is likely to be the servant, not the master.

Another of the book's major themes is integration. Almost all the chapters recognize the need to integrate multiple systems in order to build effective new learning environments. The idea of integration appears at both the macro and micro level. In the former, a clear theme is the need to think about total system changes. Changes in learning environments represent a coherent set of changes in human, organizational, and technical systems. If we want to move toward collaborative learning environments, for example, we need to craft a technology platform that fits the concomitant changes in human systems (students, professors, administrators) as well as organizational systems that support (via training or help desks) and legitimate (via norms and values) these learning environments.

A different example appears in chapter 5, on digital libraries, by Sara Lou Whildin, Susan Ware, and Gloriana St. Clair. In many ways, libraries are stand-alone institutions within larger universities. In the digital library environment, it is argued that the library, as a resource, needs to be tightly integrated in the learning process. The librarian should serve as a member of the team designing new learning environments. The move to digital libraries then implies that other changes in the roles of the professor and students, as well as the design of the curriculum process, are necessary to fully utilize the ability to access information anytime and anywhere.

What, then, is the challenge about integration in these macro examples? There is much evidence in the literature on change that most industrial organizations, which operate in a much more competitive environment than do universities, do not fully understand the integration concept. That is, there are many documented examples of failed change implementations caused by a lack of integration of human, organizational, and technological systems. The technology may be well designed, but there is no attempt to think about how the other complementary systems need to be redesigned to create an effective change. One reason that integration is hard is because the idea of congruent "sociotechnical" systems is fairly abstract. This concept, which is well accepted in the literature, does not give the university administrator many clear guidelines about how to redesign social and technical systems. There are no checklists mapping exactly how to do this. Another reason why this integration will be hard for universities is that it requires changes in multiple systems and universities are characterized by high levels of inertia. On an optimistic note, there are more examples of organizations learning how to do these complicated multiple-system changes. A number of the chapters (e.g., 2, 4, 5, and 6) provide some guidance on this issue. The application chapters represent different and specific models of multiple-system changes in a university environment.

Another version of the integration theme occurs at the micro level. Here we are examining a specific learning environment. There are at least three questions: What do we want people to learn? How do people learn? What are the appropriate learning environments? The point of intersection among these three questions is critical. Do the learning environments facilitate the learning processes that help us reach the learning objective? The challenge in building an integrated learning system is that it is both necessary and hard to do. The concept of congruency or integration is fairly abstract, and there are no general guidelines.

In an earlier example (chap. 6), I posed the task of learning how to work effectively in virtual team environments. Some aspects of that learning focused on explicit knowledge about the mechanisms of how the team was going to function. Other knowledge was more tacit and focused on interacting effectively in virtual environments. The challenge is to build a learning environment that is congruent with different learning objectives (in this case, different types of knowledge) and the processes to create this knowledge.

Another problem is there are some pervasive beliefs in our current culture of education. For example, it is difficult to go to a meeting or conference today about new educational paradigms without hearing about active learning or collaborative learning. Now, there clearly is theoretical and empirical evidence about these two forms of learning and why they may be better than the lecture mode of delivering education. But if these concepts are understood only at a very general level, they will not be a good guide for designing integrated learning environments. If you believe that active practice is important for learning, you need to think about creating active practice opportunities, about what behaviors, and how these relate to your learning objectives. Deep thinking about the integration of what we want people to learn, how people learn these behaviors, and the appropriate learning environment is a necessary and difficult challenge for designers of new forms of learning.

The theme of change also permeates the book. Chapter 1 sets the stage by detailing past and future changes in technology. Chapter 2 dramatically captures the changes in the educational marketplace—changes in the profiles of competitors, changes in the demand and profile of customers, and changing economics.

At a much more micro level the dynamic aspects of change are captured in our applications. These applications are designed and introduced with different goals in mind. Their content and customers are different. But once these changes are introduced into the educational environment, other forces drive their continual redesign. A careful reading of the evolution of the FAST technology (chap. 8) or the Tutors (chap. 9) shows continual forces for redesign. There are no steady states. Changes in the environment (e.g., Internet) or learning from within drives a continuous redesign process. One gets a sense that the redesign process accelerates over time rather than remaining constant.

This theme of dynamic changes generates a number of possible challenges. First is the issue of survival. A clear argument made in chapters 1 and 2, which is hinted at throughout the other chapters, is that many tertiary institutions will not survive the current period of change. New competitors that may be more agile and able to provide flexible instruction at a lower cost represent a real threat. New forms of technology give competitors opportunities to access once protected marketplaces. These market changes are real and significant. Many tertiary institutions may not be capable of reacting. Their inability to change has been discussed throughout some of the chapters. Universities do not have good sensing mechanisms to assess the environment changes and build common understanding across the stakeholders about potential threats. Also, universities are characterized by high levels of inertia. The inability to assess the environment and experiment probably will increase the ratio of universities that cannot survive.

Although significant environmental and market changes are occurring, there also is an opportunity to innovate. Instead of focusing on the inevitable death or survival of institutions, it is a time to redesign them. A critical challenge for senior university administrators is their ability to "unfreeze" the existing system and mobilize energy for experimentation and fundamental redesign. Chapter 2 does an excellent job in enumerating some bench marking examples of redesign. Similarly, if you think carefully about chapter 10, you immediately see that the studio is not simply a way to teach physics differently. The chapter really is about a gradual, fundamental redesign of learning environments in a major university. For me, the change in the university itself is as important as the change in the individual learning environments.

Another challenge is whether there will be sufficient energy to sustain change. In the two learning environments mentioned in chapters 8 and 9, there is a continuous commitment to redesign these learning environments over relatively short periods of time. In many cases, including FAST (chap. 8), the decision to redesign is driven by external forces. The point is that this is very different from writing a textbook that at some later time might be revised. Once you initiate these new environments, there are continuous forces for redesign. The question is whether educational designers will have the commitment and energy for continuous redesign. An important role for university administrators is to better understand this continuous need for redesign and create support for the efforts.

Another problem is whether the survivors will design new educational environments without thinking hard about the unique features of our present environment. That is, will the focus on change dismiss some of the unique benefits we experience today? I could also generate many examples, but I will choose one from the chapter on digital libraries (chap. 5). Libraries, as we know them, are really wonderful institutions. Whether we visit the early Carnegie Libraries in Pittsburgh, Harvard's Widener Library, or other distinguished libraries around the world, we have to be struck both by their physical beauty as well as their enormous collections. But perhaps more important is being within the presence of a library. When we used to visit a library to access a book, what captured most of us was the opportunity to browse—to sample books, skim them, and perhaps check out an unexpected find. Whereas many of us now access books online, and clearly there are many search engines, the opportunity to personally browse was a creative and an unusual experience that can only come about from being there. As many of these forces (technological, economic, and demographic) drive us to new TEL environments, will they be able to capture any of the unique, innovative, and creative aspects of our present educational environments? If not, how can we formulate strategies that acknowledge and facilitate the benefits inherent in these different contexts for learning?

The last theme to be mentioned concerns assessment. I think of assessment of learning environments in the broadest way. The reference is not to course evaluations. Rather, educators want to understand the impact of these new learning environments on the major stakeholders (e.g., students, professors, support personnel). We also want to understand their impact in terms of learning, social, and economic indicators. Some of the applications, as described in the chapter on tutors and the studio, provide guides for thinking about assessment. Care is given not only to whether grades change, but also to the impact on the human, social, and organizational life of the universities. Also, there is a clear focus on the economics of implementing these new environments.

After visiting universities on three different continents, I find that little attention is given to broad-based assessment. That is, changes are going on, but there are few attempts to use scientific methods to assess learning, social, and economic results. Part of the problem is a lack of people who are well trained in broad-based assessment methodologies. Another problem is the failure to allocate resources to both train and support these positions. The consequence is there is no opportunity to gain feedback and redesign these learning environments over time, which is a necessary and sufficient condition for their survival.

Where there is a problem, there usually is an opportunity. This book has focused on one mission of the university—education. One of the other missions is in research. In this evolution or revolution of new technology-enhanced learning environments, there are a host of timely research questions. These range from more psychologically oriented research on learning process and outcomes to the economics of running universities. There is also a broader range of issues concerning intellectual property, copyrights, privacy, computer security, and telecommunication policy, all of which can be approached at a national or cross-national level.

Research and education are disconnected in many universities. This book suggests possible points of connection between the two realms. Perhaps one of the unintended yet bountiful benefits of this movement toward new technology-enhanced learning environments is the creation of new opportunities to bridge the research and educational mission of universities.

Author Index

A

Anderson, J. R., 64, 68, 74, 235, 237, 242, 244, 245, 249, 262, 263
Angelo, T. A., 131, 150
Argyris, C., 155, 177
Ault, R., 172, 174, 175, 177

B

Bates, A. W., 52, 58
Beamish, R., 145, 150
Beatty, C. A., 157, 177
Bednarz, N., 249, 262
Beer, M., 155, 177
Beyer, H., 253, 262
Bikson, T. K., 157, 177
Bjork, R. A., 63, 74
Bloom, B. S., 235, 262
Boylan, M. G., 157, 179
Bransford, J. D., 261, 262
Brown, A. L., 261, 262
Brown, J. S., 162, 168, 178, 235, 236, 263
Brownston, L., 237, 262
Bruer, J. T., 261, 262
Bunge, C. A., 131, 132, 150

C

Cairncross, F., 39, 58
Carbo, T., 129, 150
Chabay, R., 160, 178
Chartier, R., 26, 58
Chickering, A. W., 130, 134, 150

Childers, M., 172, 174, 175, 177
Cocking, R. R., 261, 262
Cohen, P. A., 235, 262
Collis, D., 44, 58
Conrad, F. G., 237, 242, 262
Cooper, R. B., 157, 178
Corbett, A. T., 64, 74, 235, 237, 242, 245, 262
Cummings, K., 280, 287
Cummings, T. G., 155, 178

D

Daniel, J. S., 32, 58
Dean, J. W., 173, 178
Dodin, B. M., 42, 59
Drucker, P. F., 44, 45, 59
Druckman, D., 63, 74
Duguid, P., 162, 168, 178
Dwyer, C., 175, 179

E

Earl, M. J., 48, 59
Ehrmann, S. C., 130, 133, 134, 150
Eisenstat, R. A., 155, 177
Elimam, A. A., 42, 59
Ettlie, J. E., 157, 169, 173, 178
Eveland, J. D., 157, 179

F

Farrell, R., 237, 262
Ferguson, C. D., 131, 132, 150

295

Subject Index

299